Praise for *Leverage Leadership 2.0*

"Paul Bambrick-Santoyo has his boots on the ground. This gifted teacher, school leader, and leader of leaders does the work every day in his highly successful Uncommon Schools. *Leverage Leadership 2.0* affirms his rare ability see what works in school leadership—and to share those best practices with others. This book is as crucial for superintendents as it is for principals, teacher leaders, and policymakers. A must-read!"

—**Kim Marshall**, consultant, principal coach, and
author of *Rethinking Teacher Supervision
and Evaluation* and the Marshall Memo

"In the fight to eradicate the achievement gap, *Leverage Leadership 2.0* is the complete arsenal. Culled from thousands of hours of observing extraordinary leaders obtaining exceptional results, this book identifies the seven key levers of school and student success. But it doesn't stop there. The real gems here are the detailed systems and strategies that any leader can apply to transform his or her schools and replicate the staggering success of the Uncommon Schools. Don't just read *Leverage Leadership 2.0*, implement it—now! The state of our schools demands it."

—**Elizabeth Topoluk**, director, Friends of Education

"*Leverage Leadership 2.0* is a stand-out among the million books principals have cluttering their shelves on leadership and student achievement. This one won't collect dust! Bambrick-Santoyo provides an unequivocal blueprint on implementing effective change that will bolster student achievement in an actionable way."

—**Nakia Haskins**, principal, Brooklyn Brownstone School

"As a school leadership coach, I often see leaders struggle with making meaning of complex systems, harnessing the power of data in all its forms, and navigating lead team dynamics. In *Leverage Leadership 2.0*, Paul distills the essentials of school leadership, beginning with what leaders are doing well in schools right now, naming what and how they do it, and empowering readers to make change in their own schools or districts tomorrow. It can't get any simpler than that!"

—**Denise M. de la Rosa**,
senior director of leader development, IDEA Public Schools

"*Leverage Leadership 2.0* is the 'how' behind my 'why': excellent education for all. Bambrick-Santoyo distills leadership moves until they are replicable and repeatable— read this book and learn from one of the best!"

—**Tera Carr**, principal,
Hamilton Elementary School, Tulsa Public Schools

"This is it! *Leverage Leadership 2.0* is a masterful example of what key actions—or 'levers'— leaders can take to bring about change in schools and improve student achievement. Working in an urban school, I needed to understand what great leaders do in order to bring about significant change. *Leverage Leadership 2.0* provides that answer: a detailed plan on what matters most—the quality of your instructional leadership!"

—**Ginger Conroy**, principal, Denver Center for International
Studies at Ford Denver Public Schools

"Most books on school leadership tell you what to do. Bambrick-Santoyo goes further: he not only tells you what to do, but more important he shows you how to do it. *Leverage Leadership 2.0* provides school leaders comprehensive steps and clear models to create positive school change for all students—every school, every classroom, every day."

—**Mary Ann Stinson**, principal,
Truesdell Education Campus, District of Columbia Schools

"*Leverage Leadership 2.0* provides a clear blueprint to navigating the complex waters of school leadership to create dramatic gains in student achievement."

—**Erica Jordan-Thomas**, principal,
Ranson Middle School, Charlotte-Mecklenburg Schools

"*Leverage Leadership 2.0* is the playbook that prioritizes the work for every school leader who strives to maximize outcomes for all kids. If you want to move from 1.0 to 2.0 in your capacity to lead, *Leverage Leadership* is your guide."

—**Eneida Padro**, principal,
Roberts Elementary School, Dallas Independent School District

LEVERAGE LEADERSHIP 2.0

A Practical Guide to Building Exceptional Schools

Paul Bambrick-Santoyo

Foreword by Doug Lemov

Uncommon Schools | Change History.

JB JOSSEY-BASS™
A Wiley Brand

Published by Jossey-Bass

A Wiley Brand

One Montgomery Street, Suite 1000, San Francisco, CA 94104-4594—www.josseybass.com

Jossey-Bass books and products are available through most bookstores. To contact Jossey-Bass directly call our Customer Care Department within the U.S. at 800-956-7739, outside the U.S. at 317-572-3986, or fax 317-572-4002.

Wiley also publishes its books in a variety of electronic formats and by print-on-demand. Some material included with standard print versions of this book may not be included in e-books or in print-on-demand. If this book refers to media such as a CD or DVD that is not included in the version you purchased, you may download this material at http://booksupport.wiley.com. For more information about Wiley products, visit www.wiley.com.

Library of Congress Cataloging-in-Publication Data has been applied for.

ISBN 978-1-119-49659-5 (pbk); ISBN 978-1-119-49662-5 (ePDF); ISBN 978-1-119-49660-1(epub)

Cover image: © Veer
Cover design: Wiley

Printed in the United States of America
FIRST EDITION
PB Printing   10 9 8 7 6 5 4 3 2 1

Contents

For children everywhere—that we can build you schools of excellence that allow you to fly.

DVD Video Content

Here is an overview of the video clips for your quick reference.

Introduction

Clip	Technique	Description	Page
1	See It, Name It, Do It—Weekly Data Meeting	**"What is the conceptual understanding that [your students] would need?"** Laura Garza works with her fifth-grade math teachers during a weekly data meeting to determine the highest leverage conceptual understanding for a reteach lesson, planning side-by-side with her team before they practice.	12

Data-Driven Instruction (Chapter 1)

Clip	Technique	Description	Page
2	See It, Name It (Gap)—Weekly Data Meeting	**"What are the key misconceptions demonstrated in this student work?"** Mary Ann Stinson and her teachers use student work to identify the highest-leverage gap that needs to be retaught.	26, 63
3	Think-Aloud—Set Listening Task (Teaching Clip)	**"I want you to write down what I'm doing."** Art Worrell prepares his students to take notes during the think-aloud.	52
4	Think-Aloud—Model the Thinking (Teaching Clip)	**"When I think about the Era of Good Feelings, right away I'm thinking about nationalism."** Art Worrell walks his students through the thought process he uses to read a history text effectively, modeling annotation skills and providing the rationale for them step-by-step.	53

Clip	Technique	Description	Page
12	**Do It (Practice)—Weekly Data Meeting**	**"Now we are going to take this practice live."** Denarius Frazier gives specific feedback while his teacher practices the reteach lesson.	66
13	**Do It (Follow Up)— Weekly Data Meeting**	**"I am going to come in on Friday at 9 a.m."** Mary Ann Stinson asks her teachers to list all the action items at the end of the weekly data meeting and to schedule the follow-up.	67
14	**Do It (Follow Up)— Weekly Data Meeting**	**"We can spiral this task . . ."** Denarius Frazier works with his teacher to identify multiple opportunities for assessing the identified reteach skill, and they establish a comprehensive timeline for next steps.	67

Observation and Feedback (Chapter 3)

Clip	Technique	Description	Page
15	**Do It (Practice)— Feedback Meeting**	**"What are you looking for?"** Ashley Anderson has Ijeoma "take it live" and practice the aggressive monitoring plan that they developed together during their feedback meeting.	128, 161
16	**See It (Model, Gap)— Feedback Meeting**	**"What is the biggest gap between your practice and what you just saw Mr. Frazier do?"** Ashley Anderson begins her feedback meeting by prompting Ijeoma to analyze a model for aggressive monitoring and to apply that model when identifying a gap in her own teaching of geometry.	156
17	**Name It—Feedback Meeting**	**"What is your action step this week?"** Ashley Anderson asks Ijeoma to name her teaching action step and write it down.	158
18	**Do It (Plan)—Feedback Meeting**	**". . . and we will spar with what we both got."** Ashley Anderson and Ijeoma apply the teaching action step by planning side by side, comparing their plans, and then revising the plan based on key takeaways.	160

Clip	Technique	Description	Page
19	Real-Time Feedback	**"When I put my hand over [the student's head], stop, make eye contact, and give a What to Do direction."** Nikki Bridges gives whispered and nonverbal feedback to Jackson while students work independently.	164

Professional Development (Chapter 4)

Clip	Technique	Description	Page
20	Do It (Practice)—Leading PD	**"Teacher 1, please stand and begin practice."** Kelly Dowling gives clear directions before the role play and facilitates practice during PD.	182, 201
21	See It and Name It—Leading PD	**"The quality of your prework dictates the quality of your students' class work."** Kelly Dowling leads PD using an exemplar annotated handout to identify what makes aggressive monitoring effective.	197
22	Do It (Plan)—Leading PD	**"Who can share a piece of feedback they just got from their partner?"** Jesse Corburn asks a groups of teachers to write exemplar responses to prework questions during PD.	200
23	Do It (Plan)—Leading PD	**"Spar with your table about the highest leverage gap to close."** While leading a PD with Uncommon instructional leaders, Denarius Frazier asks coaches to plan before practice with their partners and then spar with a larger group at their table.	200
24	Do It (Practice)—Leading PD	**"One minute for the final round of feedback."** Denarius Frazier gives feedback during practice to partners and the whole group throughout several rounds of role play.	201

Clip	Technique	Description	Page
25	**Reflect—Leading PD**	**". . . Let's take a moment now of reflection."** Juliana Worrell prompts the group to write and reflect at a strategic point during the Guided Reading PD.	203
26	**See It—Practice Clinic**	**"I'm actually doing this next period."** Syrena Burnam leads a practice clinic with a group of teachers around What to Do directions.	210

Student Culture (Chapter 5)

Clip	Technique	Description	Page
27	**See It (Model)—Morning Routines**	**"Our Character Counts word of the week is 'equality.'"** Students at Laura Garza's school in Dallas, Texas start their morning with a warm welcome and a nourishing breakfast.	222, 226
28	**See It (Model)— Academic Discourse (Teaching Clip)**	**"What is going to happen when he lets the pendulum go?"** Emelia Pelliccio launches her AP Physics class and guides student discourse toward a key conceptual understanding.	225
29	**Do It—Roll Out to Staff**	**"Handshake, high-five, or hug?"** Tera Carr begins her student culture rollout by presenting the model to her staff.	238
30	**Do It—Roll Out to Staff**	**"[A system] exists because it is going to help us function as a team."** Eric Diamon reviews the written morning routine and then asks a teacher, Julia Goldenheim, to demonstrate the morning routine for the staff.	239
31	**Do It—Rehearsal**	**"Two minutes of uninterrupted practice."** Tera Carr asks her staff to practice the student culture routine she modeled at the start of the day.	240
32	**See It—Student Culture Reset**	**"Our gap is in the following: we lack precise What to Do [directions]."** Nikki Bridges prompts a group of teachers to see the gap in student culture after the first few days of school.	247

DVD Additional Materials

Here is quick overview of additional materials available on the DVD.

Resource	Description
PD Sessions for Observation and Feedback, Leading PD, and Student Culture	All the materials needed to lead a professional development session for instructional leaders on three of the levers—Observation and Feedback, Leading PD, and Student Culture: • Session agenda with presenter's notes • PowerPoint presentation • Handouts (including one-pagers)
Data-Driven Instruction—key implementation resources	Key resources to support the implementation of data-driven instruction (DDI), including: • Data-Driven Instruction and Assessment Rubric • Weekly Data Meeting one-pager • Assessment Results Template • Teacher Analysis and Action Plan Template • Interim assessment calendars for elementary, middle, and high school • Data-Driven Instruction Monthly Map
Planning—key implementation resources	Key handouts to support the implementation of unit and lesson planning, including: • Planning Meeting one-pager • Sample lesson and curriculum plans

Resource	Description
Get Better Faster Scope and Sequence and Coach's Guide	Print-friendly version of the scope and sequence of action steps for teachers that appears in Chapter 3, Observation and Feedback, as well as the coach's guide to coaching teachers to perfect those action steps.
Observation and Feedback—key implementation resources	Key handouts to support the implementation of observation and feedback, including: • Giving Effective Feedback one-pager • Observation Tracker
Professional Development—key implementation resources	Key handouts to support the implementation of PD, including: • Professional Development one-pager • Professional Development Delivery Rubric
Student Culture—key implementation resources	Key handouts to support the implementation of student culture, including: • Student Culture Rubric • Minute-by-minute exemplars for whole-school and in-class routines • Rollout exemplars for whole-school and in-class routines • The Classroom You Want one-pager • 30-Day Playbook—HS Sample
Finding the Time—key implementation resources	Key handouts to help leaders find the time for what matters most, including: • Sample leader weekly schedules for elementary, middle and high school • How to Create a Monthly Map one-pager • Monthly Map Template • Monthly map samples for data-driven instruction and student culture

Foreword

When *Leverage Leadership* was first published six years ago, the Urban Institute had recently set out to answer a question that had immense ramifications for education and educators. The question had nothing to do with curriculum or governance or instructional methods. It wasn't about the strategic use of data, a topic about which the author of this book, Paul Bambrick-Santoyo, has written the quintessential volume and which, he shows, can cause a sea change in the effectiveness of day-to-day instruction. The study had nothing to do with accountability or human capital management. In short, the study was silent on the issues we most commonly believe—with some justification—drive excellence in schools.

Still, the study yielded critical insight about the things that stand in the way of excellence for a typical school and its leadership team, even if the study's focus seemed a bit pedestrian. The question it set out to answer was how principals spend their time. To do so, it followed sixty-five principals in Miami's public schools as they worked, keeping track of what they did and for how long. The study found that on average, principals spent more than 27 percent of their time on administrative tasks—managing schedules, discipline issues, and compliance. They spent 20 percent of their time on organizational tasks such as hiring, responding to teacher concerns, or checking to see if there was money in the budget for projector bulbs or travel to workshops. These two types of tasks, administrative and organizational, were the largest sources of time allocation.

On the other end of the spectrum, principals spent, on average, less than 6 percent of their time on what the study called "day-to-day instruction": observing classrooms, coaching teachers to make them better, leading or planning professional training for teachers, using data to drive instruction, and evaluating teachers. It turned out that day-to-day instruction—what teachers did in the classroom with their students and how—

wasn't really the focus of most school's leadership. The most important work in the building—the most important work in our society, you could argue—went unmanaged 94 percent of the time in the face of a thousand other tasks and distractions.

These numbers are dispiriting for a variety of reasons, not least of which is that the tasks described in the "day-to-day instruction" category include, as Paul Bambrick-Santoyo explains in this book, the tasks that essentially determine student achievement levels. The 6 percent of leadership spent on the five tasks amounts to just thirty-six minutes in a ten-hour day spent on all of them combined, or just over seven minutes per day on each the tasks. That's about seven minutes a day observing classrooms. Seven minutes a day coaching teachers to make them better. Seven minutes a day developing and leading training for teachers. Seven minutes a day using data to drive instruction. Seven minutes a day evaluating teachers.

You almost don't have to read the rest of the study to know what comes of those kinds of numbers: lower student achievement and the death spiral of a rising number of distractions that only increase as achievement declines. The precious minutes spent on key tasks are even fewer and farther between. You can hear the echo of those principals, their shoes striding down the hallway from one low-value task to another. (You can download the complete report from https://www.urban.org/research/publication/principal-time-use-and-school-effectiveness.)

Sadly, for the most part, this remains just as true today as it was when this study was first released. I suspect the principals probably know the truth—that they are not spending their time doing and getting better at the tasks that would bring about excellence. In many cases, they may even choose not to do them because, in the end, they do not have time to do them well or perhaps because they have not seen a model of excellent implementation. And this is especially disappointing, because the people who run schools are almost all driven, hard working, committed, and passionate. Given the right tools and protected from distractions, they are capable of running outstanding schools.

An organization or a society ought to be able to remove incentives (or requirements) to spend time on secondary tasks, provide a clear sense of *how* to do the most important tasks well, and provide tools to ensure their ease and efficiency. That's what organizations *should* do for their people, but in fact they are too often looking in the wrong direction—looking for the next new idea rather than studying how to do the core tasks, fighting a philosophical battle when it's the tasks that pop up from below and the systems that manage them that make the champions of school leadership successful.

But what happens when that changes? For answers, look at what has happened in the six years since the book in your hands was originally published. In the cities of Newark, Camden, Boston, New York City, Rochester, and Troy, Paul Bambrick-Santoyo and the school leaders who work alongside him have continued the success of Uncommon Schools: a growing network of elementary, middle, and high schools attended by students almost entirely of poverty and facing every difficulty you might imagine, yet that consistently put students on the path to college—reliable, even predictable excellence in the face of the sort of everyday adversity that keeps so many potentially strong leaders from performing their best. The schools have quietly gone about this work for more than twenty years now, changing lives and providing the proof that making schools great can be systematically accomplished.

Yet the impact doesn't stop there. In a variety of cities you'll see represented in these pages—from Denver to Dallas to Memphis and beyond—more and more leaders are achieving similar results in equally challenging circumstances. We are witnessing the growth of a new generation of principals who are proving that unprecedented levels of success are not only possible but replicable. These successes, *Leverage Leadership 2.0* reveals, are the result of two things above all. The first is a relentlessness about spending time on the most important things and on as little else as humanly possible. The second, far harder, is bringing an engineer's obsession to finding the way to do those things as well as humanly possible. These are simple tools—focus on the right things, intentionally study how to do them well—but their simplicity should not suggest that they are easy. Insights are hard won and implementation is harder. The steps from "I get it" to "I can do it" to "I know people in the organization will reliably do it" are gigantic. Paul has spent years refining both the keys to success and the systems that help people use them. Over time he has chosen to focus on making each idea a little bit better every day, turning his insights into a management system that—like the flywheel in Jim Collins's legendary book *Good to Great*—keeps an organization (and a leader) getting better and better as a matter of habit.

Now, in this second edition of *Leverage Leadership,* Paul makes the workings of that system and each of its pieces available to all—honed and sharpened by the work in thousands of schools across the country and the globe. It is of course not as sexy as a brand-new pedagogy or shiny technological machine, but in the end it is far more powerful. If you are one of those educators who understands the power of doing the most important things not only well but better over time, of holding fast to what works instead of chasing temporary "revolutions," then this book will serve as a touchstone, a guide to which you will return over and over again for guidance, insight, and strategy that can help you and the educators with whom you work to achieve the greatest possible success—to build outstanding educational organizations and to make the greatest possible difference in the lives of your students.

Doug Lemov

Doug Lemov is a managing director of Uncommon Schools and the author of *Teach Like a Champion, Teach Like a Champion 2.0, the Teach Like a Champion Field Guide, Practice Perfect,* and *Reading Reconsidered.*

Acknowledgments

When *Leverage Leadership* was first published in 2012, most of my work was born on-site in working directly with school leaders in my own schools. Fast-forward to today, and we've now had the chance to work with more than twenty thousand school leaders worldwide. And through the Leverage Leadership Institute, I've gotten to work closely with some of the highest-achieving principals and principal managers from across the country. Mary Ann Stinson, Wade Bell, Ashley Anderson, Kelly Dowling, Laura Garza, Adriana Gonzalez, Antonio Burt, Eric Diamon, and many more cited in this text—they are the real heroes of this book, as they do the work every day. *Thank you* to each and every one of you: you inspire me and many others, and you give us a pathway to success for children for generations to come.

Just like running a school, writing a book is not possible without a tremendous support team. First and foremost, Alyssa Ross is my writing soul mate. She has assisted me once again as a writer extraordinaire—gathering ideas, shaping the drafts, and putting a touch of imagination into each round of edits. For seven years she has made my writing projects come alive. Without her, this project could never have been completed, and the writing would not have been nearly as effective.

The original laboratory for this book was my work with leaders across the Uncommon Schools network. I am indebted to Brett Peiser, mentor and colleague and expert on organizational culture. I have worked alongside Julie Jackson for over fifteen years, and she continues to be the most inspirational and talented leader I have ever met—and a dear friend. Everyone else at Uncommon has played a role: Mike Mann, Jesse Corburn, Tildi Sharp, Serena Savarirayan, Juliana Worrell, Maya Roth, J. T. Leiard, Kelly Dowling, Doug Lemov, and so many more.

The second learning hotspot has been the Leverage Leadership Institute and the Relay National Principals Academy. I'm so lucky to have worked with Kathleen Sullivan, Lindsay Kruse, Jesse Rector, Ben Klompus, Norman Atkins, and a legion of supporters.

Leaders on the front line are the easiest to see, as they are the face of the school. But as is mentioned in the chapter Finding the Time, you cannot focus on instructional leadership without someone doing the "dirty work"—everything operational and strategic. That has been no exception in my own work: Sam Messer, Jacque Rauschuber, and Michael Ambriz have silently and effectively managed all key operational issues in my work, allowing me to focus on growing schools instructionally and culturally. They will rarely ever get the praise they deserve, but their invisible work made this possible. They are accompanied by an extraordinary team that has codified all our best practices: David Deatherage, Amy Parsons, Althea Hoard, and Angelica Pastoriza.

The other silent partners in this work are even closer to my heart—my wife and children. Ana, Maria, and Nicolas were in elementary and middle school when my first book was published. They have blossomed along the way and turned into inspiring young adults. They've endured many an afternoon of me watching videos of leaders or pacing the house as I try to articulate an idea! My wife, Gaby, continues to be the rock—the steady presence of love and listening.

Thank you to each and every one of you. This book is a tribute to you all.

About the Author

Paul Bambrick-Santoyo is the chief schools officer for Uncommon Schools and the founder and dean of the Leverage Leadership Institute, creating proof points of excellence in urban schools nationwide. Author of *Driven by Data; Leverage Leadership; Great Habits, Great Readers*; and *Get Better Faster,* Bambrick-Santoyo has trained more than twenty thousand school leaders worldwide in instructional leadership, including multiple schools that have gone on to become the highest-gaining or highest-achieving schools in their districts, states, and/or countries. Prior to these roles, Bambrick-Santoyo cofounded the Relay National Principals Academy Fellowship and spent thirteen years leading North Star Academies in Newark, New Jersey. During his tenure at North Star, the schools grew from serving fewer than three hundred students to over three thousand while at the same time making dramatic gains in student achievement. North Star's results make them among the highest-achieving urban schools in the nation and winners of multiple recognitions, including the US Department of Education's National Blue Ribbon Award. Prior to his work at North Star, Bambrick-Santoyo worked for six years in a bilingual school in Mexico City, where he founded the International Baccalaureate program. He earned a BA in social justice from Duke University and his MEd in school administration through New Leaders from the City University of New York—Baruch College.

LEVERAGE LEADERSHIP 2.0

Introduction

Some people would say that Laura Garza has done the impossible. Indeed, in her first year as principal of Annie Webb Blanton Elementary School, there were those who warned her she was crazy to have dreams that big, considering that 84 percent of Blanton's students are economically disadvantaged, and over half are English language learners. More to the point, when Laura took leadership of Blanton in 2015, these children weren't learning what they needed to prepare for middle school, let alone high school and ultimately college: less than half of them were achieving at grade level for math and literacy.

Laura made it no secret that she was setting out to change those results—quickly. And she got pushback. "Some were so used to the way things were that they didn't see the need for change," she recalls. "Others saw the need, but didn't think it could be done."

Fast-forward to 2016. The results were in: student learning at Blanton had sky-rocketed. Now, 60 percent of Blanton's students were reading at grade level, and a triumphant 80 percent were at grade level for math. By 2016–17, Blanton's students were reaching even more impressive heights (see Figure I.1).[1]

It is not surprising that Laura was named Dallas Principal of the Year in 2017!

Figure I.1 Texas State Assessment (STAAR): Blanton Elementary School, Percentage at or above Proficiency

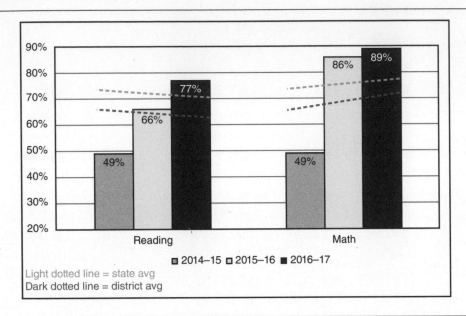

Light dotted line = state avg
Dark dotted line = district avg

  WATCH Clip 1: Garza—See It, Name It, Do It—Weekly Data Meeting

Numbers like these leave no question: Laura's mission of getting students who enter elementary school at a disadvantage to college may be ambitious, but it's far from impossible.

The obstacles facing Blanton—and so many schools like it across the globe—are so imposing that it might be tempting to dismiss Laura's success as a one-off wonder. But Laura is not a miracle worker. She is talented, driven, and incredibly hard working, but ultimately, she has led Blanton to success because of the choices she makes in how she uses her time: what she does, and how and when she does it.

How do we know? Because Laura's success is not an isolated phenomenon. Colleagues of hers within the Dallas Independent School District have achieved similarly outstanding results; Adriana Gonzalez at Lenore Kirk Hall Elementary School is one example.[2] (More about her in Chapter 6.) But beyond Dallas, at the time of this writing, more than twenty thousand leaders worldwide have implemented the practices that have made Laura successful, creating success stories from coast to coast and from Chile to South Africa. What did all of these leaders have in common? They knew how to spend their time and how to lead others to do the same.

A PARADIGM SHIFT: THE LEVERS OF LEADERSHIP

What makes education effective? The answer: great teaching. In the past decade, a host of studies has suggested that the decisive determinant of whether students will learn effectively is not school technology or building logistics or administrative funding but simply the presence or absence of great teaching. In recent years, a wide variety of scholars have recognized quality of instruction as a principal's or school leader's key responsibility.[3] Kim Marshall notes in *Rethinking Teacher Supervision and Evaluation* that "the quality of instruction is the single most important factor in student achievement."[4] Recently, Robert J. Marzano, Tony Frontier, and David Livingston have built on this work in their book *Effective Supervision: Supporting the Art and Science of Teaching.* They noted that "achievement in classes with highly skilled teachers is better than student achievement in classes with less skilled teachers."[5] How much better? Data suggests that low-socioeconomic-status schools that can offer students three consecutive years of strong teaching *close* the achievement gap, correcting for a host of external factors.[6] This is game-changing improvement.

Yet although it is easy to assert that great teaching creates great learning, it is much harder to encounter schools where all teachers are making this sort of learning happen. Why? The typical school leadership model has not been defined precisely enough to work for this purpose. Much of the current research has studied effective school leadership and identified the characteristics of effective schools.[7] Yet these are often the outputs of effective schools, not the actions leaders took to get there. At its best, the current leadership model encourages and develops a handful of great teachers, but it does not succeed in reaching further.

To envision what it takes to change this, consider the performance of an outstanding athletic team. The University of Connecticut's women's basketball team is the most successful program in the nation and in collegiate history: the team holds a record eleven NCAA Division 1 national championships as well as the two longest winning streaks of all time for any gender. When you watch them play, you can describe what this success looks like at game time: you might notice the superstars, but what is even more striking is how well *all* players work in unison. The offensive plays expose the gaps in the opponent's defense, the footwork is precise, the passing is phenomenal, and every player makes a maximal impact. But no one can replicate this success just by watching the game. The difference comes in what each player has in her mind of what she has to do. The point guard has to read the defense and determine where to break it down with either dribble penetration or an effective pass. The shooting guards have to rotate through their teammate's picks to isolate them for an open shot. And the forwards and centers must take up precise positions underneath the basket to receive a pass or get a crucial rebound. Each one knows the precise moment when she has to move or shoot or pass, based on thousands of drills done in practice. In essence, the team has a detailed step-by-step plan that is capable of adjusting to what happens in the moment.

What, then, is a school leader doing at each moment of a school day to make a great school run as effectively as a great basketball team? What are the "plays" that lead not just to somewhat effective learning but to phenomenal results? How does every member of a school's staff get on the same page about what needs to be done to win the championship? What do these leaders prioritize on a day-by-day, minute-by-minute schedule? And has anyone done all this in a replicable way, moving away from the "Superman" model of outstanding schools?

Answering these questions is what inspired me to write this book. Over the past fifteen years, I have had the privilege of working with thousands of school leaders across the country. During that time, I have observed firsthand the challenges facing school leaders. I have also witnessed how many have overcome those obstacles to make a difference in student learning. *Driven by Data* captured a number of those success stories. Yet *Driven by Data* focused only on one critical lever of leadership—data-driven instruction—and didn't try to put all the pieces together. This book sets out to show how a leader does it all.

To make this book come alive and to demonstrate its application to schools of all types, I have selected a small group of school leaders who have attained the same extraordinary results as Laura Garza. These leaders come from every type of school and every type of location: small and large, city and rural, district and charter, and everything in between. They hail from Dallas to DC to Denver to Memphis to New York City. They represent school leaders in the broadest sense of the word: they are in roles from principal to coach of principals. And they all meet two basic criteria:

Exceptional results that exceed expectations. By any metrics, the leaders achieved staggering academic successes. Their state test or AP results marked each leader's school as a top-performing school in its city or state. What makes this even more impressive is the population that these schools served. In all cases, the schools served populations that had large numbers of students receiving free and reduced lunch and that were mostly Black and Latino. But the point bears noting: the schools we found are not "good urban schools"; they are superlative schools outright.[8]

Replicable results. These leaders didn't succeed in some idiosyncratic way: they used replicable systems and structures that others can follow. The successes these leaders built were not the products of unique charisma; they came from strategies and systems that any leader can apply.

This book tries to answer another key question: Can this work for you? The question takes many forms:

- Can these solutions really work for my school?
- We serve a particularly challenging population and are a school traditionally labeled "failing"; will this turn my school around?
- I lead a big district; is this feasible for us?
- I work in a small rural school isolated from others—what about my school?

The answer to each of these questions is a resounding *yes*. Indeed, this book's goal is to show that the success these leaders enjoy does not stem from some magical quality but from a practical set of decisions that any leader, at any school, can apply. But don't take my word for it right away; in fact, given the number of impractical solutions and changes you've seen in the past, don't take my word for it at all. Instead, read about and listen to the leaders presented in this book. They are here not simply to *tell* their stories about leadership but to *show* how success is possible anywhere.

Over the course of the next chapters, you will hear the stories of Laura, Adriana, Jesse, Antonio, and many others. Each chapter in this book will highlight their success to teach us about leveraging leadership. Many of them have emulated these actions to replicate results or to turn around struggling schools. Examine their leadership up close, and patterns emerge that separate their practices from those of other school leaders I observed who were doing "well" but not achieving the same dramatic results. This comparison allowed me to identify the key levers of leadership that move a school from "mediocre," or even "good," to "great." The overwhelming conclusion was this: Each of them leveraged more out of each minute of the day. They carefully and intentionally chose the actions that would have the biggest impact on student learning—and they avoided those actions that wouldn't.[9] More specifically, they leveraged feedback and time for practice to transform teaching and learning. None of their practices were revolutionary in their own right: it was the combination of practices and the precision with which they were implemented that made the difference. The precision with which a leader uses his or her time for what matters most is what marks a paradigm shift.

So what really makes education effective? The answer: well-leveraged leadership that ensures great teaching to guarantee great learning.

> ### Core Idea
> So what really makes education effective? The answer:
> well-leveraged leadership that ensures great teaching to guarantee great learning.

Myths of Effective School Leadership

This paradigm has the potential to reshape any school in any context. To make this paradigm shift, however, leaders must avoid some of the common myths about effective leadership. Despite the growing body of work around the characteristics and actions of successful schools, certain myths or obstacles still persist:

Principals Are Administrators and Firefighters, Not Instructional Leaders

One of the largest obstacles blocking school leaders today is the sheer volume of noninstructional work. All too often, principals and other school leaders find themselves focused on a host of tasks far removed from directly improving instruction and learning: filling out compliance reports, attending noninstructional meetings, or managing facilities, just to name a few. This has led some to argue that principals should devote themselves to this work and shift instructional leadership to coaches whom they bring into the building. What I saw in exceptional school leaders, however, was an insistence on being instructional leaders. Even where they had coaches to support the development of teachers, they kept their actions and their eyes squarely on instruction.

Comprehensive Observations, Walkthroughs, and Teacher Evaluations Are Sufficient

Another growing wave of support in the leadership books is the push for comprehensive teacher evaluation rubrics, classroom observations, and building walkthroughs. All of these elements are important, but they occasionally forget their core purpose: to make teachers more effective. Every moment spent filling in a teacher evaluation rubric is a moment not used working with a teacher to improve. As we'll see in the upcoming chapters, exceptional school leaders are very intentional about how they use observations and walkthroughs, placing the utmost emphasis not on scoring but on giving the right feedback and follow-up to make sure teachers implement that feedback. (See more in Chapters 1–3.)

Change Is Slow—Teacher Development Takes Ten Years

There is a common belief in the education field that teacher development takes ten years and that any school change takes multiple years. From this perspective, only slow, gradual change—change based around the piecemeal introduction of various systems—is effective.[10] The leaders in this book dispel that myth quite dramatically. As high school principal Mike Mann says, "Our students cannot wait ten years for a teacher to become effective—that's their entire educational career." The leaders described here develop teachers in what matters most: making sure students learn. Whether or not these teachers would be labeled "master teachers" on a teacher evaluation rubric is beside the point; students learn at the levels they would in a master teacher's classroom. What are the keys? A detailed structure for teacher development that focuses on the highest-leverage teacher actions and that can adapt to the varying needs of teachers. We'll talk more about this in Chapter 4.

There Is a "Principal Personality"

Many believe that great school leaders have a "Principal Personality": extroverted, forceful, and charismatic. Many of the "good" schools I observed had leaders who met this profile, but they struggled to replicate their successes. By contrast, the leaders who succeeded *and* replicated exhibited an extraordinary variety of personality types. With the (important) exception of a willingness to work hard, the leaders we studied shared few personal traits. The one common trait—if it can be called that—was an incredibly self-critical eye and a "good-to-great" mentality. Each of them was far more likely to tell me the five things wrong in his or her school that had to be improved than the twenty things he or she was doing extraordinarily well. These leaders are far more motivated by self-improvement than simply by the results themselves. Outside of this trait, there is no one Principal Personality.

Culture Comes Before Instruction . . . or Instruction Before Culture

One of the great debates of school leadership is what should take priority: student instruction or student culture. In the culture camp, some argue that without order, joy, and respect, academic success is impossible. In their eyes, the game plan should be to "delay" instruction until culture is "right." On the other side, some argue that instruction creates culture, and that as teachers create engaging and rigorous lessons, student conduct and attitudes will naturally improve. Both views are badly flawed. If instruction is strong but culture is weak, a school's success is crippled: newer teachers face serious discipline challenges, students experience radical inconsistency between classes, and core values cannot be taught. Yet at schools that decide to "wait" on improving instruction, the end result is often order without rigor, a "false positive" that looks like education but is anything but. The truth is that both instruction and culture are vital, and both must be led simultaneously. Without this, neither can succeed.

The Seven Levers

Dispelling these myths, the leaders highlighted in this book followed a core set of principles that allowed for consistent, transformational, and replicable growth. These principles were truly levers: with the intentional focus on these areas, leaders leveraged much more learning from the same time investment. Fundamentally, each of these levers answers the core question of school leadership: What should an effective leader do?

The Seven Levers

Executing Quality Instruction and Culture

Instructional Levers

1. **Data-driven instruction.** Define the road map for rigor and adapt teaching to meet students' needs.
2. **Instructional planning.** Plan backwards to guarantee strong lessons.
3. **Observation and feedback.** Coach teachers to improve the learning.
4. **Professional development.** Strengthen culture and instruction with hands-on training that sticks.

Cultural Levers

1. **Student culture.** Create a strong culture where learning can thrive.
2. **Staff culture.** Build and support the right team.
3. **Managing school leadership teams.** Train instructional leaders to expand your impact across the school.

The levers tell you what to do, but we need a "light switch" to show you how.

Turning on the Light: See It, Name It, Do It

There's a well-loved proverb in literary circles to the effect that a writer works in the dark, until a reader comes along and turns on the light. That was certainly true of this book. When we published *Leverage Leadership* in 2012, we described each of the seven levers distinctly with their own language. However, as more and more leaders read *Leverage Leadership* and implemented the practices it advocates, a unifying framework began to illuminate what it really takes to implement each of these levers. It can best be encapsulated in my experience learning to cook cod.

When I was growing up, I never liked fish. Fast-forward years later to my first year living in Mexico City: my father-in-law, Miguel, prepared a delicious cod dish called Bacalao a la Mexicana. I was hooked! But I had no idea how to prepare it. I watched Miguel cook it once and wrote down the ingredients and instructions, but when I got around to cooking it myself, I couldn't remember the details. So I watched him again, this time noting the subtleties and writing them down: strain the diced tomatoes before adding to the mix, skim the water off the top, and continue cooking until only oil is bubbling along the edges of the pot. I asked Miguel to watch me, and he let me cook, just adding subtle tips. Sure enough, I was successful (although not quite as good as Miguel himself).

My experience in the kitchen mirrors what we saw when observing instructional leadership. Each lever boils down to a core process in three parts: see a model of success, name it in concrete steps, and do what it takes to make it real. See it. Name it. Do it.

Core Idea

The fastest way to develop a skill? See it. Name it. Do it.
Repeat until you've mastered it.

Think about how that played out for me in the kitchen. If I had not seen Miguel prepare the meal (see the model), I wouldn't have captured the subtleties that made his preparation magical—and far better than my own (see my gap). Then I needed to write down those steps (name it), and finally I needed to do it myself (do it).

This clearly doesn't apply just to cooking. We recognize this need in other professions as well. We'd never ask an aspiring doctor to perform an operation before seeing one in action, or a firefighter to rush to the scene of an emergency without having rehearsed the steps of getting there quickly and prepared. *Leverage Leadership 2.0* simply brings those same principles to education. See It, Name It, and Do It are the three essential steps to implementing any one of the seven levers of school leadership: *seeing* a model of excellence in clear detail (and the gap between that model and our own practice); *naming* the qualifying characteristics that make that model effective (so that others can name it as well); and *doing* those actions repeatedly—first behind the scenes in extensive practice sessions and then daily in the classroom.

Leverage Leadership 2.0 is built on the premise that we need a guide to lock down the same certainty of success in our schools that we can find on high-quality teams in any other profession. Our students deserve no less.

A "PRACTICAL GUIDE": WHAT YOU'LL FIND IN THE BOOK

In the pages that follow, we will offer a concrete, step-by-step guide to creating exceptional schools. The first seven chapters are devoted to each of the seven levers, differentiating between those that drive instruction (Chapters 1–4: Data-Driven Instruction, Planning, Observation and Feedback, and Professional Development) and those that build school culture (Chapters 5–7: Student Culture, Staff Culture, and Managing School Leadership Teams). These are followed by Part 3, Making It Happen, devoted to how to put this all together (Chapter 8 for school-based leaders—Finding the Time). In Appendix A we give you a sneak peek at our new companion guide, *A Principal Manager's Guide to Leverage Leadership* (perfect for superintendents, leadership training programs, and anyone who supports principals); Appendix B is a preview of the extensive professional development materials available on the DVD that accompanies this book for you roll out with your staff.

A Word on . . . What's New Here?

Key Differences Between *Leverage Leadership* and *Leverage Leadership 2.0*

Readers who are familiar with the Leverage Leadership model may be curious to know exactly how this text differs from the earlier version of *Leverage Leadership* published in 2012. Although the seven levers themselves remain the same, we've rewritten nearly 80 percent of the text in *Leverage Leadership 2.0*! Here are the key changes:

A unifying framework. See It, Name It, and Do It are three simple steps that summarize how to implement any one of the seven levers. This means that what we've formerly described as the six steps to effective feedback (in Observation and Feedback) and the Living the Learning framework (for leading professional development) have all been streamlined into the same process: See It, Name It, Do It. Our hope is that this makes the process of implementing each of the levers easier both to remember and to put into practice.

Globally field-tested. Since the publication of *Leverage Leadership*, more than twenty thousand school leaders have been trained in aspects of the seven levers. Following up with these leaders has given us far greater insight into what parts of *Leverage Leadership* worked well and were feasible for leaders to implement as they were written—and which ones needed fine-tuning. Those insights are reflected in *Leverage Leadership 2.0.*

New professional development materials. All of the PD materials on the DVD accompanying this book have been completely refreshed to capture the latest lessons learned through the training of such a vast array of school leaders. The See It, Name It, Do It framework is completely embedded into each training, and the trainings also include more targeted and effective opportunities for practice.

A more diverse, national array of leaders. With the sheer number of leaders who have made the seven levers their own in the past five years, we are able to highlight an even broader set of the most successful. These leaders have lifted the levers across the country in every context: bilingual schools, turnaround schools, and in district and charter schools alike. What all these leaders have in common is that they were able to use their time to transform their students' lives. The diversity of their experiences with the Leverage Leadership model enriches this book, showing how any school can use these steps to become not just a "good urban school" or a "good turnaround school" but a superlative school by *any* measure.

How does all of this play out in the text? We use the See It, Name It, Do It philosophy to drive the structure of the book

See It: Videos and Testimonials

Because seeing it is the first step to doing it, we've included a variety of tools throughout this text to help you See It as you read it.

Videos

In the DVD that accompanies this text, we've included a selection of video clips of top-tier leaders in action, working directly with their teachers. These videos are not staged, nor are they videos of principals' interactions with their strongest teachers. These videos show teacher–leader interactions with all types of teachers: struggling teachers, new teachers, and everyone in between.

In this sense, we bring these schools to you: every chapter is accompanied by high-quality video of the lever it presents, broken down to portray both the components of success and how it looks as a whole. Seeing exactly what the leaders in this book do, and how they do it, will make it possible to replicate their actions in a way that reading alone never could.

 WATCH Clip 1: Garza—See It, Name It, Do It—Weekly Data Meeting

---

Throughout the book, this symbol indicates that a given video clip on the DVD is crucial to the work and to the reading itself. Although it is possible to use this book without watching the accompanying video, we doubt it will be as effective. Watching exemplars of great leadership in practice will provide insights that words will not. These are also at the foundation of the training materials on the DVD that accompanies this book—more on that presently!

Findings from the Field

At its heart, *Leverage Leadership 2.0* is a field guide. It was not created in an ivory tower but in the practical laboratory of the school. Because of this, everything here is rooted in what real school leaders have implemented. Every school is different, and every leader faces different constraints. For some, the challenge will be taking struggling schools into productive places of learning. For others, the challenge will be driving a good school to finally attain excellent results. For others, the challenge will be applying these principles to a three-thousand-student high school or a two-hundred-student rural K–8 school. Recognizing this incredible variety, we've highlighted the practices of the most diverse leaders yet, from different geographies and with different student demographics and school types. We've asked a wide variety of additional school leaders to write about their experiences, describing how high-leverage school leadership has improved their own practices and their students' learning. You'll find them interspersed throughout the text as well as in boxes with the words "Findings from the Field" in the title, focusing on the strategies that leaders have taken even when given limited resources and facing great challenges.

When tough choices must be made, these success stories will help you make them.

Name It: Core Ideas and One-Pagers

The power of a common language to describe best practices is impossible to overstate. Here's how this book serves to provide one, naming the most important actions that lead to the results we need.

Core Ideas

Throughout the text, Core Idea boxes will pull out the most important key ideas from each section.

Core Idea

Effective instruction is not about whether we taught it.
It's about whether the students learned it.

The goal of each core idea is to make the complex ideas in this book as simple and as memorable as possible. If you take nothing else away from this reading, take these—and share them with your colleagues at your school!

One-Pagers

We have routinely received feedback that the concise, brief guides to specific skills are among the most useful tools in the book to aid in implementing best practices across your school. These "one-pagers" aren't invented from thin air. Catchy and precise, they simply name the key words and actions we observed in thousands of hours of video clips of the most effective leaders. They consolidate onto a single sheet (or two) the most important information to remember about any topic. Here's an example of part of the one-pager that sums up the process for weekly data meetings.

Weekly Data Meeting	
Leading Teacher Teams to Analyze Student Daily Work	

See It 13–18 min	See Past Success, See the Exemplar, and See and Analyze the Gap

	See Past Success (1 min):
	
	• "Last week we planned to reteach __, and we went from ___ % proficient to ___%. Nice job!"
	
	• "What actions did you take to reach this goal?"
	
	See the Exemplar (8 min):
	
	• Narrow the focus: "Today, I want to dive into [specific standard] and the following assessment item."
	
	• Interpret the standard(s):
	  o "Take 1 min: in your own words, what should a student know or be able to do to show mastery?"
	
	• Unpack the teacher's written exemplar:
	  o "Take 1–2 min to review the exemplar: What were the keys to an ideal answer?"
	  o "How does this [part of the exemplar] align with the standard?"
	
	• Analyze the student exemplar:
	  o "Take 1 min: How does your student exemplar compare to the teacher exemplar? Is there a gap?"
	  o "Do students have different paths/evidence to demonstrate mastery of the standard?"
	  o "Does the student exemplar offer something that your exemplar does not?"
	
	See the Gap (5 min):
	
	• Move to the sample of unmastered student work (look only at representative sample):

	See Past Success, See the Exemplar, and See and Analyze the Gap
	o "Take 2 min: What are the gaps between the rest of our student work and the exemplar?" o "Look back at our chart of the standard and exemplar: What are key misconceptions?"

One-pagers like this one appear throughout this book. Print them out and use them as a daily guide in your work—and distribute them among your staff after PD on each of these subjects so that they can do the same!

Do It: Materials to Make It Happen

It's one thing to have a guide; it is another to be able to roll this out. *Leverage Leadership 2.0* includes all the same tools that the leaders in this book use to lift the levers in their schools. We've included actual workshop scripts so that you can roll out training yourself. And even as you read each chapter, we give you the space to plan when and how you'll put these ideas into action.

Here's an overview that shows how.

Action Planning

Each chapter ends with a set of questions designed for you to assess your current school, choose the resources that will be most helpful from the book, and plan your first action steps. This sort of self-evaluation and strategic work is what makes meaningful change possible.

Pulling the Lever

Action Planning Worksheet for OBSERVATION AND FEEDBACK

Self-Assessment

- How frequently are your teachers being observed? _____/year or _____/month
- What is the current teacher-to-leader ratio? _____ teachers per full-time instructional leader
- Review the action steps for principals for observation and feedback (previous box). What are the biggest gaps in your implementation that you want to close first?

(*Note:* the action steps are listed in priority order, so "think waterfall": start at the top and stop at the first major growth area.)

_____

_____

_____

_____

_____

_____

Planning for Action

- What tools from this book will you use to improve observation and feedback at your school? Check all that you will use (you can find all on the DVD):

  ☐ Get Better Faster Scope and Sequence of action steps

  ☐ Get Better Faster Coach's Guide

  ☐ Giving Effective Feedback one-pager

  ☐ Observation Tracker

  ☐ Real-Time Feedback one-pager

  ☐ Videos of observation and feedback meetings

  ☐ PD materials for observation and feedback

Leader Schedule and Calendars

Chapter 8 will give you the opportunity to put it all together to create your own schedule to show exactly how you can make change feasible even as it is transformational. Table I.1 shows an example of the sample schedules we'll provide to concretely demonstrate how you can make time for these changes yourself.

Professional Development Materials

The book doesn't stop when you get to the final page. The DVD that accompanies it is the go-to location for everything you need to turnkey this material to train instructional leaders in your school or district. These workshop materials have been honed over years of workshops and represent almost a full week of PD materials. Now you don't need to spend hours designing training for your leadership team: the materials are here at your disposal.

Table I.1 Making It Work: Where Observation and Feedback Fit in a Leader's Schedule

	Monday	Tuesday	Wednesday	Thursday	Friday
6:00 AM					
:30					
7:00 AM					
:30					
8:00 AM			Meet Steele		
:30			Meet Campbell		
9:00 AM	Observe Perez, Snyder, Steele				
:30					
10:00 AM					
:30					
11:00 AM					
:30					
12:00 PM	Observe Campbell, Chen, Daf				
:30		Meet Perez			Meet Scherer,
1:00 PM		Meet Snyder			Meet Westbrook,
:30			Meet Chen	Observe Scherer, Westbrook, Smith	Meet Smith
2:00 PM			Meet Daf		
:30					
3:00 PM					
:30					
4:00 PM					
:30					
5:00 PM					
:30					

■ Work Time   ■ School Culture   ■ Observations   ■ Meetings

WHO SHOULD USE THIS BOOK—AND HOW

This book is for school leaders, but who exactly are school leaders? On the most obvious level, principals engage in school leadership. Yet if instruction and culture are to be the core focus of effective school leaders, then the "circle of leadership" not only extends to principals but also reaches out in all directions: to instructional coaches, department chairs, lead teachers, teachers, and any other staff whose primary purpose is improving a school's instructional capacity. It also must extend up to the level of superintendents and district directors of curriculum, instruction, and assessment.

In this book, we will highlight the work of leaders at all of those levels, from those who work with just two or three teachers to leaders like Teresa Khirallah, who has coached a growing cohort of principals to excellence. We have taken an intentionally broad view of who can serve as an effective school leader—and what steps they can take to bring great teaching to the classroom. For the purposes of simplicity of the narrative, we will often refer to the principal as the leader in question, but the actions are intentionally designed for all leaders. Meanwhile, *The Principal Manager's Guide to Leverage Leadership,* a companion volume to this book, takes a deep dive into leading the leaders. Specifically intended for superintendents, principal managers, and principal coaching organizations, it provides guidance for anyone who wishes to replicate the strategies in this book across multiple campuses.

As we have noted, the methods we offer here have worked in some of the most challenging conditions in American education. The fact that our case studies are drawn from underserved urban areas is no accident; the schools and students who most need dramatic change are those who are currently least well served. Yet although our main setting is urban schools, the systems we propose here, when used well, can generate significant impact in any school.

How to Read This Book, for Principals

The order in which you implement this leadership model will depend on you—your needs and your school's level of progress. However, after studying the impact of each of these levers in schools across the country, we have discovered a common order of implementation that is often most effective. You'll need to adapt this to your school, but here are some global recommendations.

Step 1: Start with the Super-Levers—Data-Driven Instruction and Student Culture

Of the seven levers, two are the fundamental foundation of any school's success. We have dubbed these the "super-levers": robust data-driven instruction (Chapter 1) and student culture (Chapter 5) systems determine your school's *instructional capacity*—the upper bounds of how successfully your school can teach its students. Without such capacity, transformational growth is not possible. Our experience since *Leverage Leadership* was first published has only strengthened this conviction: in nearly every case we have studied where once-struggling schools experienced significant turnarounds or good schools became great, these levers were the game-changers. By contrast, schools that had not mastered data-driven instruction or student culture found it impossible to significantly boost student achievement, despite spending significant time on the other levers. **If in doubt, data and culture must take priority.** Before you determine whether your school has mastered these levers, read those chapters. They will help you determine your next steps even if you have already implemented these to a certain extent.

Step 2: Build the Observation and Feedback Cycle

Student culture and data change the game plan, and the observation and feedback cycle is the tool to develop teachers to execute that plan. Rather than infringe on the super-levers, the cycle simply enhances them. And when done well, it has a ripple effect on all other levers: strengthening planning and staff culture, and functioning as the tool for following up on professional development. As such, building and implementing the observation and feedback cycle has been the next most important step for most effective schools. It is also the habit that is hardest to establish for a leader who has not been observing frequently.

Step 3: Implement Remaining Levers as Much as Is Feasible in Year 1

Once leaders have solid data-driven instruction, strong student culture, and an observation and feedback cycle, the remaining levers can turn good schools into great ones. Whatever you cannot focus on in Year 1 can then become a project for your second year of leadership. It is worth repeating: all of these levers are doable simultaneously. We have given you multiple leaders' schedules to prove this. But you do not need to start with all levers simultaneously to enact effective change. (In fact, if you don't yet have a solid foundation, trying to launch all seven at once can easily hinder your success.) You know the needs of your school best to determine the speed of implementation beyond these first levers.

How to Read This Book, for Coaches and Other Instructional Leaders

If your role is that of a coach or instructional leader, here's how to tailor the tools in this book to meet your needs—and those of the individuals you coach.

Step 1: Start with Data-Driven Instruction and Observation and Feedback

Many coaches do not have a prominent role in leading school-wide student culture. If that is your situation, focus on the other two most important levers. Combined, the systems for data-driven instruction and observation and feedback go a long way in empowering coaches to train teachers more quickly and effectively.

Step 2: Build In Planning

After these two levers have been put in place, you may switch your focus to planning (Chapter 2), the next key driver of teacher development.

If Applicable: Add Professional Development

If you have been assigned to lead group training for peers or teachers, you will benefit from focusing on delivering effective professional development sessions (Chapter 4).

How to Read This Book, for Principal Managers and Superintendents

Finally, here's how to use this book to your advantage as a leader of principals.

Step 1: Start with the Top Three Levers—Data-Driven Instruction, Student Culture, and Observation and Feedback

If you have limited time and are not sure where to begin, start with the super-levers of data-driven instruction (Chapter 1) and student culture (Chapter 5) and add observation and feedback (Chapter 3).

Step 2: (If There's Time) Read the Rest of the Book

If you cannot read all of it, read Finding the Time (Chapter 8) before transitioning to the companion guide.

Step 3: Move to the Companion Guide Specifically Designed for You

In our conversations with principal managers and superintendents across the country, we heard that there is dearth of practical guidance written about how to be effective in leading multiple schools. *The Principal Manager's Guide to Leverage Leadership* is published intentionally as a companion to this book to fill that void. The guide offers a deeper dive into the critical role you play in driving school quality.

There you will find resources specifically designed for principal managers, including examples and testimonials from superintendents and principal managers from across the country.

THE PATH AHEAD

Over the course of the past fifteen years, I have observed firsthand the challenges facing school leaders, some specific to their unique regions, and others startlingly similar. But if all these leaders have taught me one thing, it's that no challenge is too great to be overcome. I have seen schools rise above endemic illiteracy, hunger, centuries-long legacies of systemic racism, and more; and I have seen them soar. There's as much commonality among the solutions to these crises as there is to the obstacles they fling in our way. All over the world, the seven levers of leadership give leaders the power to meet their students' needs.

This book is about the action steps behind those success stories. It's about the leaders who have built oases for learning even in the harshest of landscapes. It is important to recognize that these improvements demand hard work. But one thing we've noticed across the country is that most school leaders already work very hard. The power of these steps is that they help you work "smart"—they lock in the results you strive for and your students deserve. If we've learned anything from these transformational school leaders, it is this: work both hard and smart, and results will follow. Read on to find out how.

Part 1

Instruction

Chapter 1

Data-Driven Instruction

Peer-to-Peer: Thirty Minutes That Tell It All

One of the most remarkable places to observe at Truesdell Education Campus in Washington, DC, is not just the classroom but the conference room. At 11:15 on a Monday morning, the third-grade team has gathered during their prep period around the conference table, accompanied by principal Mary Ann Green Stinson. The walls are not covered with beautiful pictures but rather by multiple charts from previous meetings. You see charts describing what students need to know and do around fractions as well as how to write an effective argument after reading a passage. That is where the teachers' attention is now.

As one teacher is charting, the others are scanning the chart to identify the biggest gap in student learning. One by one, the teachers speak up, unassuming but confident. "I think they could benefit from more work on sentence expansion," says one teacher, Ms. Mack. "They're expressing ideas, but they're not extending them by using 'because.'"

Another teacher nods. "You can see in the second example, there's kind of a big run-on because they're not using the sentence expansion correctly," she says. "And also, the selection of evidence here is not necessarily text-dependent."

Mary Ann nods. "So thinking about some of those misconceptions, what do you think the one key misconception is that we should focus on for the reteach?" A third teacher, Ms. Isaac, speaks up. "I think, looking big-picture, it's twofold," she says. "Selection of text-dependent evidence, and then expanding that, explaining."

"Okay," Mary Ann agrees. From there, the group goes on to plan their reteach, developing a concrete action plan to address what their students still need the most support to learn.

 WATCH Clip 2: Stinson—See It, Name It (Gap)—Weekly Data Meeting

In 2010, Mary Ann Green Stinson was seeking a job as a principal in Washington, DC. She'd been inspired by her work in the classroom and as an assistant principal in Richmond, Virginia, and she was eager to be in a position where she could impact more children's lives. The only trouble was, the chancellor of DC Public Schools wasn't sure where to place Mary Ann.

"Just give me your toughest school," Mary Ann told the chancellor. Somewhat reluctantly, the chancellor agreed.

That's how Mary Ann began her career at Truesdell Education Campus. As she walked through the school prior to starting, she understood all too well why her supervisor had hesitated to place a first-year principal at this site. The conditions were, as she puts it now, "chaotic," making her concerned not only for students' education but also for their safety. Academics were suffering so deeply that 80 percent of students were reading below grade level, and some students were expressing their frustrations at school violently. Mary Ann came away from those early visits with a nonnegotiable mission: "to guarantee Truesdell was a safe place to teach and learn."

So Mary Ann dove into her new leadership role with two sharply pointed areas of focus: student culture and student learning. You'll read more about student culture in Chapter 5; for learning, Mary Ann asked herself two basic questions:

- How do we know whether students are learning?

- And when they're not, what do we do?

"We had to fix instruction," recalls Mary Ann. "With so many students falling behind, that was a tier 1 move." That meant that even with so many different demands on Mary Ann's time and energy to improve student culture, she also had to ensure that she was focusing on learning: "I had to transition from being a disciplinarian to being an instructional leader." That act of tuning into learning can be called data-driven instruction.

Over the course of the next few years, the impact of Mary Ann's work was stunning. Right away, she and her colleagues began seeing children move, slowly but surely, from below grade level to almost on grade level to unquestionably on target. Today, more Truesdell students than ever before are reading on grade level—and those numbers are still climbing (see Figure 1.1).

Figure 1.1 Washington, DC, Assessment: Truesdell Education Campus, Percentage at or Above Proficiency

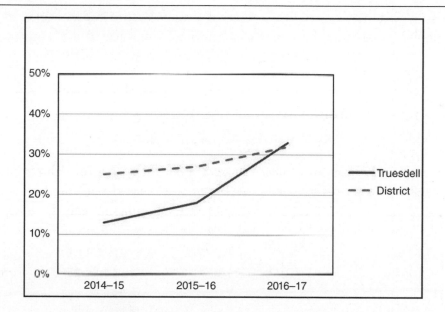

In just a few short years, Mary Ann completely altered the learning environment—and outcomes—of her school. But Mary Ann didn't get results like these by changing her students' economic situations (the vast majority of them are economically disadvantaged) or their racial backgrounds (96 percent are black or Latino).[1] She did it by embracing data-driven instruction.

Data is an increasingly contentious word in some educational circles. But true data-driven instruction isn't about limiting the content we teach or about reducing our students to numbers. To the contrary, data-driven instruction is about knowing precisely what our students need, and meeting them there every step of the way.

It's about shifting our daily focus from "Did we teach it?" to the much more pertinent "Did they learn it?"

Core Idea

Effective instruction isn't about whether we taught it.
It's about whether students learned it.

Implementing this simple principle fundamentally transforms schools. More important, it transforms *all* types of schools, from district schools to turnaround schools to charter schools, forging success stories all across the globe.

Over the past fifteen years, I have observed a vast variety of leaders worldwide who have implemented data-driven instruction effectively to get results. Leaders from Louisiana to Nevada and from Chile to South Africa have achieved results like the ones shown here.

Data-Driven Instruction in Action

Results from Across the Nation

Minnesota Achievement Results: Friends of Education Schools, Multiple Measurements Rating (MMR)

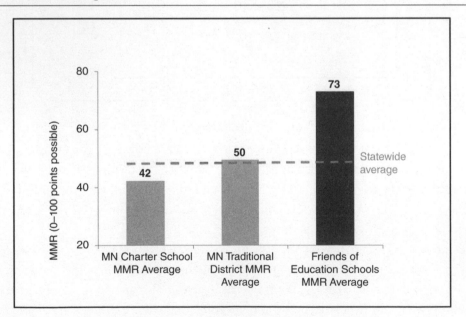

Louisiana and Nevada State Test Results: Jefferson Parish and Clark County, Percentage at or Above Proficiency

School	Math			Reading			Gains	
	Year 1	Year 2	Year 3	Year 1	Year 2	Year 3	Math	Reading
Jefferson Parish (LA)								
Gretna Park	36	51	67	47	41	62	+31	+15
Washington	56	59	72	37	78	74	+16	+37
Clark County (NV)								
Carson	62	69	76	45	66	76	+14	+21
Elizondo	44	62	75	38	53	60	+31	+22
Hancock	58	79	86	49	70	83	+30	+34

Oklahoma, Utah, Colorado, New Mexico, and Louisiana Results: Proficiency Gains Compared to State Gains, 2013–2016

School	Gains	
	Math	Reading
Westwood Elementary (Caddo Parish, LA)	+24	+31
Fair Park High School (Caddo Parish, LA)	+16	+26
Anadarko High School (Anadarko, OK)	+40	+0
Lincoln Elementary (Ogden, UT)	+27	+20
Manaugh Elementary (Cortez, CO)	+23	+16
Apache Elementary (Farmington, NM)	+37	+34
David Skeet Elementary (Gallup, NM)	+30	+31
Crownpoint Elementary (Gallup, NM)	+25	+30

In listening to these leaders' stories and observing their implementation, I am even more convinced than ever that data-driven instruction is the single most effective use of a school leader's time.[2] The thirty-minute weekly data meetings that Mary Ann has implemented are the highest-leverage, most game-changing thirty-minute conversations possible—conversations that lead to results.

If we teach but students don't learn, is it really teaching? Leaders like Mary Ann don't take that risk. As Mary Ann put it herself, they *guarantee* learning in their schools. To that end, throughout the year, they make sure they know when teaching in their schools is working. And when it isn't, they fix it.

Core Idea

The most effective teachers and leaders know when teaching is working.
And when it isn't, they fix it.

In this chapter, we'll take a closer look at the work of leaders like Mary Ann to determine exactly what powerful actions make this possible. You'll see that they fall into three phases of an ongoing cycle of teaching and learning:

1. **Assess:** set the road map for rigor

2. **Analyze:** identify the gaps in student understanding

3. **Act:** reteach key content to get students on track

The pages that follow will cover all of these in depth, as well as the systems you'll need in place to roll them all out. Without further ado, let's dive in.

ASSESSMENT: WHAT WILL STUDENTS LEARN?

We tend to think of assessment as the endpoint of learning, but in reality, it's where learning begins. Here's why.

Where Is the Bar for Rigor? Beginning from the Endpoint

Imagine a group of sixth-grade math teachers who are all charged with teaching their students the following standard:

Sixth-Grade Math Standard

Ratio and Rate Reasoning

- Use ratio and rate reasoning to solve real-world and mathematical problems.
  - Use ratio reasoning to convert measurement units.
  - Manipulate and transform units appropriately when multiplying or dividing quantities.

—CCSS.Math.Content.6RPA.3.D

These sixth-grade teachers are each given a curriculum and a math textbook that is aligned to this standard, and they go out to teach their students. At the end of the week, each one creates his or her own one-question assessment/Exit Ticket to see whether students have mastered the standard. As you look at their assessments here, consider this question: How does what students have to know and be able to do change from one of these assessment items to the next?

The Power of Assessment

Sixth-Grade Math Assessment Questions

1. Joe can mow a lawn in 2 hours. At this rate, how long will it take him to mow three lawns?

2. Joe can mow three lawns in 4 hours. At this rate, how long will it take him to mow one lawn?

3. If it Joe mows four lawns in 7 hours, then at that rate, how many lawns can he mow in 35 hours? At what rate were the lawns being mowed?

4. If it took 2 hours to mow three lawns, how much can be mowed in 20 minutes at that rate?

5. Joe has two 7-foot-long boards. He needs to cut pieces that are 15 inches long from the boards. What is the greatest number of 15-inch pieces he can cut from the two boards?

Stop and Jot

How does what students have to know and be able to do change from one of these assessment items to the next?

_____

_____

_____

_____

_____

_____

_____

_____

If you take a moment to solve each of these problems, you will quickly notice how different they are. Generally, each question ratchets up the rigor from the question before it. Whereas question 1 is a simple ratio, question 2 requires division of hours into minutes: ¾ into 45 minutes. Question 3 requires all of those skills as well as setting up the proper proportion. Question 4 adds on the conversion of units (hours to minutes) right at the beginning, and question 5 is in an entirely different orbit. Not only do you have to convert units (feet to inches), but you have to deal with remainders: if you cut the 7-foot board, you will have five pieces and 9 inches to spare. If you are not careful, you might think you can add the two 9-inch pieces together to form an additional 15-inch piece. Yet the answer is ten pieces, not eleven.

Now consider what would happen if these five teachers met to talk about their students' success on this standard. Teacher 1 might say that 90 percent of her students have mastered the standard, and Teacher 5 might respond, "Wow, that's amazing: only 40 percent of my students have mastered it." Even when they are using the same curriculum, the same textbook, and the same standard, they wouldn't be talking in the same language!

Why is this so important? Because it drives home a critical point about instruction: standards are meaningless until you determine how to assess them.

> ### Core Idea
> Standards are meaningless until you determine how to assess them.

The best-worded standard and most sophisticated curriculum don't tell you what students need to do; the question you ask them does. The assessment, then, sets the bar for rigor.[3]

This core principle has game-changing impact on how we think about instruction. Traditionally, we have told teachers to backwards-plan from standards. Plan out your lessons to help students master the standard; and after teaching, plan an assessment that you will use to measure it. This thinking process, however, is backwards. What this leads teachers to do is to design an assessment that matches how they taught, which may or may not guarantee the rigor as question 5 does. Essentially, we are allowing each teacher to define his or her own bar for rigor, which means every classroom will learn content at highly varying degrees of difficulty.

Now contemplate the reverse. Imagine if *before* you start planning the teaching, you design the end assessment. Then you ask yourself, "How do I have to teach this for my students to be able to master this level of assessment?" You have changed the order of instruction: you make assessment the starting point, not the end.

Core Idea

Assessments are the starting point for instruction, not the end.

Mary Ann's teachers understand this idea, and it changes the way they plan and execute their teaching. They work backwards from assessments that demand the level of rigor they need their students to be capable of achieving, and they plan what to teach from there. With assessment as their starting point, they travel a much more direct journey to get to the proper destination.

A Word on . . . Rigor, Multiple Choice, and Open-Ended Responses

One of the most common criticisms against data-driven analysis is that it reduces learning to "rote level" or "basic" skills, preventing students from engaging in "real" learning. Underneath that critique is a belief that the *type* of question matters more than the content. By this reasoning, some assessment types, such as multiple-choice questions, are inherently "unrigorous" and lacking in any value. Let's evaluate that claim by taking a look at the following question about Shakespeare's *Macbeth*:

Directions: In this scene, Macbeth is discussing a prophecy he received from the witches. Read the passage, then answer the questions that follow:

> **Macbeth:**
> They hailed him [Banquo] father to a line of kings
> Upon my head they placed a fruitless crown,
> And put a barren sceptre in my gripe,
> Thence to be wrench'd with an unlineal hand,
> No son of mine succeeding. If 't be so,
> For Banquo's issue have I filed my mind;
> For them the gracious Duncan have I murder'd

1. The description of Macbeth's "barren sceptre" contributes to the unity of the passage in which of the following ways?

   A. As a parallel between Macbeth's possible children and Banquo's possible children.

B. As a satirical comment on challenges Macbeth will face with infertility.

C. As a comparison between Macbeth's strong formal authority and his lack of popular influence.

D. As an ironic contrast between Macbeth's power and his inability to produce future kings.

Consider the skills required to answer this question correctly: students would need to be able to combine an understanding of vocabulary in context with the larger connotative and figurative meanings of the phrases. Even if students correctly identify the meaning of "barren sceptre," they may still select option B, unless they can discern that this phrase is not a work of satire, which leads to the correct answer of D. If a rigorous understanding of English is the goal, it's hard to imagine a better way to assess for it. And this is the sort of question that appears on Advanced Placement exams.

Now consider an alternative option: having students write an essay or short answer to the following prompt:

- Analyze the following passage of Shakespeare. How does it contribute to one of the central themes of Macbeth?

Without doubt, this is a quality prompt that could be used to assess students' analytical abilities. They have to generate their own argument and support it with evidence from the text.

In the end, both the multiple choice *and* open-ended questions add value, and they complement each other in very important ways. One (open-ended) requires you to generate your own thesis, and the other (multiple choice) asks you to choose between viable theses—with one being the best option. In today's world, we need both of those skills: the ability to discern between close options and to generate our own arguments. We also need them pragmatically: all our lives we will be asked to perform on multiple-choice assessments (SAT, LSAT, GMAT, USMLE, firefighter's exam, and so on) as well as with essays (college "blue book" exams, the Bar, written presentations, and the like). Anyone who claims that only multiple choice or only essays can exercise both abilities would be missing out on the opportunity to develop a child's intellect fully.

The key, then, is to make sure that our assessments include multiple types of questions, and that each of those questions is rigorous. For multiple-choice questions, the options and text difficulty determine the rigor.[4] For open-ended questions, it's not the prompt but the rubric that determines the rigor. Keep those principles in mind, and you can create effective, balanced assessments that prepare children to demonstrate mastery now and in the future.

Designing effective assessments doesn't just work at the elementary school level; it applies to all grades. The question is: How do you design assessments that meet the right level of rigor?

Where Is the Starting Line? Keys to Effective Assessments

Almost all schools strive to offer instructional "rigor." Authors from Dagget to DuFuor have offered definitions of rigor.[5] Barbara L. Blackburn has defined it as "creating an environment in which each student is expected to learn at high levels, and each is supported so he or she can learn at high levels, and each student demonstrates learning at high levels."[6] And as Del Stover underscored in a 2015 article for the *American School Board Journal,* creating the right assessments to give students the opportunity to demonstrate that high level of learning is an indispensable step to creating a rigorous environment.[7] But all of this just goes to raise the question: What does a rigorous assessment actually look like?

At Truesdell, and at schools that achieve similar results, leaders and teachers use the following criteria to design their assessments.

Common

If assessments define rigor, then they must be common across all classes and grade levels if we want to guarantee equal rigor in each classroom. "Common assessments are a nonnegotiable," Mary Ann notes. Without common assessments, we will have some teachers who push their students to the highest levels of learning and others who don't. This is not just true for elementary schools; it applies at every level. Mike Mann is the principal of the North Star Washington Park High School, one of the highest-achieving urban high schools in the country (more on him in Chapter 2, on planning).[8] Mike explains, "Measuring outcomes is only useful if you know what the target should be. If the target is different in each classroom, then we have no way to know how students are doing across the cohort relatively to each other. The students are stuck with varying degrees of rigor depending on which teacher they have. That's not fair to our students."

Transparent

If standards are meaningless until we define how to assess them, then teachers and leaders need to see an assessment *before* teaching in order to be able to teach to that degree of rigor. This flies in the face of conventional educational wisdom. Yet to conceal assessments from educators is something akin to asking a group of hikers to climb a mountain without telling them which peak they need to scale. Teachers need to see the destination to be able to navigate the route.

> ## Core Idea
>
> Concealing assessments is akin to asking a group of hikers to climb a mountain without telling them which peak they need to scale.
> Teachers need to see the destination to be able to navigate the route.

Interim

Great schools like Blanton Elementary schedule *interim* assessments to identify problems *while change is still possible.* Many educators have referred to year-end assessment analysis as equivalent to performing an autopsy. If you had a sick child, what would you do? You would seek medical help. No one would recommend waiting—you would be held liable for that child's future! Yet schools do just that with student achievement. Rather than identifying what's making a child's learning "sick" during the school year and finding the right medicine to attack the disease (that is, make it possible to learn more effectively), schools wait to analyze year-end assessment results after some of the students have already failed to learn. Rick DuFour stated it succinctly in 2004: "The difference between a formative and summative assessment has also been described as the difference between a physical and an autopsy. I prefer physicals to autopsies." The top-tier school leaders highlighted throughout this book give school-wide interim assessments four to six times a year, and never more than eight weeks apart. This distribution rate allows time for teachers to make changes, while not overwhelming students (and faculty) with "test fatigue."[9] In addition to those interim assessments, Mary Ann and other successful school leaders also develop systems to work with fellow leaders and teachers to review student work on a weekly basis—more on that later in this chapter.

Aligned

To make sure that interim assessments have sufficient rigor, they must be carefully aligned to the "end-goal" assessment of that class. Herein lies the critical question for any teacher or leader: What end goal will you aspire to for your students? Remember: it is not enough to say that we want "critical thinking" for our students or "problem solving." Too many schools have fallen into the trap of thinking they're making progress simply by espousing these words. Your assessment will define what you mean. There are a few levels of alignment:

- **State-test aligned.** I do not know of students who can fail their state test and be ready for college. That being said, there are many students who pass their state tests and are *still* not ready to attend or succeed at college. State tests, then, are a necessary but insufficient step toward college readiness. It is important to make sure students can meet this bar, and if that is in question, then part or most of the interim assessments should be aligned to the preliminary rigor of the state test.

- **College-ready aligned.** This is the ultimate goal. For high school, there are many assessments already well defined: Advanced Placement, International Baccalaureate, SAT. These can be complemented by performance assessments, such as a well-designed research paper that all students will be required to master. For elementary and middle schools, the task of being college ready is less well defined, but the leaders cited in this book aspired to above-grade-level proficiency for all their students. That takes the form of integrating algebra earlier into the math curriculum (and assessing accordingly) or setting higher targets for proficiency on leveled reading assessments. In each case, the leaders were not satisfied with state proficiency alone. One common pitfall of implementing data-driven instruction is that if schools do not have a single "north star" assessment they can use to align their rigor to college-ready standards, they err on the side of administering too many different assessments, few of which reflect a college-ready level of rigor. Thus another important step is to eliminate any assessments that *aren't* aligned to college-ready rigor, and to build all assessments and curriculum around a limited number that *are*.

Blazing a Trail: A High School Approach to "College-Ready Rigor" on Interim Assessments

In concrete terms, what does it mean to design an assessment with college-ready rigor? Although the specific steps may vary depending on the content area involved, there are several common features. For example, when Mike Mann's teachers at North Star Washington Park High School design their interim assessments, they start with existing high-rigor materials. One of Mike's English teachers, Beth Verrilli, shares: "It starts with taking every practice AP and SAT exam out there and looking at the types of passages they have: the lengths, whether fiction or nonfiction, if nonfiction then what type of nonfiction." Once the passages were identified, Beth then looked to the type of questions being asked and their level of challenge: literal comprehension, main idea, tone, and perspective.

Finally, Beth and the English Department adapted their curricula based on the level of challenge identified in order to be "college ready." "The early high school years serve as a bridge between the eighth-grade state test level of challenge and the more rigorous demands of college-ready assessments," Beth explained. "Because we know where our end goal is in year 4, it makes planning years 1 and 2 much easier."

- **Curriculum sequence aligned.** Once you have an assessment that establishes the appropriate level of rigor, then you need to make sure that those assessments are aligned to your curriculum. Namely, in the corresponding six to eight weeks prior to each assessment, does your curriculum teach the standards that will appear on that assessment? If not, teachers will rightfully protest that you're not testing what they're teaching—which defeats the whole purpose of interim assessments.

Cumulative

Interim assessments are not unit tests: they need to keep measuring all that has been learned throughout the year, not just the most recent unit. This is critical because of how difficult it is for children—and adults—to retain learning. Think about your own education. Many of you took classes like calculus in high school or college. If you had to take a final exam in that subject today, you likely would not do nearly as well as you did then (unless you continue to use that math). Why? If you don't use it, you lose it.

> ### Core Idea
>
> If you don't use it, you lose it.
> Reassess student material all year long to help students hold on to the learning.

If this is the case for us as adults, why do we expect third graders to learn about measurement in September and be able to show mastery in March if they are not asked to do any measurements in the months in between? Reassessing standards throughout the year makes retention possible. This principle is just as critical at the high school level. If students are preparing for an AP exam with vast amounts of content, they need to keep using that content to help them retain it.

A Word on . . . Data-Driven Instruction and Kindergarten

To those who think that data-driven instruction has nothing to do with kindergarten classrooms, you haven't talked to kindergarten teachers! Strong kindergarten teachers are the most data driven of any: they track students' performance on their letters, sounds, shapes, numbers, and so on. Although these teachers don't use traditional paper-and-pencil assessments, they are driving instruction with data every day. That is a huge reason why kindergarteners can make such gigantic leaps in learning. Respond to student needs, and learning improves. Kindergarten teachers can teach us this lesson as well as anyone!

Developing interim assessments that meet these high bars can be a challenge. Back in 2010 when *Driven by Data* was first published, many of the most successful schools simply created their own. The drawback, however, is that the whole-cloth creation of new assessments can be extraordinarily time consuming, especially if a school has not done it before. Thankfully, that is no longer the only pathway. A second possibility is for leaders to request interim assessments from schools that have already been successful in implementing data-driven instruction. For the most part, these schools will be happy to share their approach to testing, saving an incredible amount of time. If you do use another school's materials, it is still important to make sure that any "borrowed" assessment is well aligned. Each state has different benchmarks and year-end assessments, and each school and district has a separate sequence of teaching its standards. If you're taking tests from elsewhere, there's a good chance your curriculum won't line up chronologically. This will leave you with one of two options: change your curriculum sequence to match that of the interim assessment, or change your interim assessment to test standards in the same chronological order as your curriculum. Either way, you have still saved a ton of time in creating assessments.

Feasibility Tip: Coping Mechanisms for Imperfect Assessments

In many large school districts, principals and teachers may be required to use district-mandated assessments that don't meet all the criteria we've described. Fortunately, we've seen public schools nationwide work around these limitations in order to build effective data systems. Here are a few of the most common strategies used:

Common, interim: Are they not every six to eight weeks?

- Too far apart: place an additional interim assessment in the gap.

- Too many assessments too frequently: deprioritize some to focus only on those where deep analysis is possible and most valuable.

Transparent: Do teachers not see the interim assessments in advance?

- Give teachers the interim assessments to review at a faculty meeting.
- Give teachers a set of proxy questions from an item bank that are tightly aligned to the rigor of the interim assessment.

Aligned: Are they not aligned to your state's standards and the rigor of the questions?

- Add questions from item banks that are more aligned to the difficulty level of your year-end test.
- Give teachers sample items and have them design more.
- Borrow other schools' assessments.

Aligned: Are they not aligned to instructional sequence?

- Change sequence to match assessment (or vice versa).

Cumulative: Do they not spiral content throughout the year?

- Add spiraled content questions to the end of assessment.

The box "Data-Driven Instruction" summarizes the key criteria for effective assessments, both on a global level and specifically for interim and weekly data collection, respectively.

Data-Driven Instruction

Key Criteria for Effective Assessment

- **Common, interim**
  - At least quarterly
  - Common across all teachers of the same grade level
- **Transparent**
  - Teachers see the assessments in advance
  - The assessments define the road map for teaching
- **Aligned**
  - To state test (format, content, and length)

- To instructional sequence (curriculum)
- To college-ready expectations
- **Cumulative**
  - Standards that appear on the first interim assessment appear again on subsequent interim assessments

---

A Word on . . . "Teaching to the Test"

One frequent objection to data-driven instruction is that a focus on assessment amounts to empty "teaching to the test." In this view, data forces teachers to choose between "real" teaching and irrelevant test preparation. If the assessments a school uses are not rigorous enough, or if they are not aligned to what students need to know, then this is a valid critique. However, when interim assessments are well constructed and college ready, they are an unparalleled resource in driving student learning. If you want students to be able to write a six- to eight-page paper stating an original argument, why wouldn't you teach to get them to do so effectively? In the same way, if students will need to solve a quadratic equation embedded with an area problem on the SAT, shouldn't we prepare our students to succeed?

More pragmatically, in modern America the ability to do well on assessments is an unavoidable reality when it comes to gaining admission to the college of students' choice and in almost every major profession—from firefighters to doctors. One can argue that society *ought* to work differently, but as educators, we must prepare students to succeed in the real world around them.

In any case, the message is clear: students who are not prepared for high-quality end-goal assessments have not learned what they need.

In the end, data-driven instruction is not about teaching to the test; it is about testing the teaching. That makes all the difference.

ANALYSIS: WHAT AND WHY DIDN'T THEY LEARN?

Shane Battier's career stat line as an NBA basketball player is rather pedestrian: over fourteen years from 2001 to 2014, he averaged per game only 8.6 points, four rebounds, two assists, one steal, and one block.[10] Of course, just getting to the NBA is extraordinary, but against that level of competition, nothing in these statistics suggests preternatural talent. Yet he was one of the most sought-after defensive specialists, and he constantly guarded the most talented players of his era (Kobe Bryant and LeBron James, among others). The superstars routinely had subpar performances against him, but no one could figure out why. He wasn't fast, nor did he have quick reaction time, and he didn't force many turnovers. In fact, his opponents were so convinced that Battier was just "some chump" that they repeatedly attributed his defensive prowess to an "off night" on their end—even though they repeatedly had those off nights when he was the defender, and statistics proved it.

So why did Battier have such defensive success that he was dubbed by Michael Lewis the "No-Stats All-Star"?[11]

Because Battier's gift wasn't about his physical abilities: it lay in his ability to see. He could look at data about his opponents' past performances and see a clear path to the outcome his team needed. For instance, Battier knew that Kobe Bryant's ability to score points for his team dropped dramatically when Bryant shot from the left instead of the right, so he would force Bryant into that zone. Bryant would still make the shots at times; Battier was just lowering his odds. But over time, that added up to fewer points scored. In short, Battier looked at the right data, and deeply enough, to change the result—to change it so profoundly, in fact, that he made Bryant's team score *worse* than if Bryant had never been on the court that day.

What Battier did is part of a data analytics craze that has swept through every major sport in the world. Kevin Durant used the same approach to target his weakest shooting spots and increase his efficiency.[12] Swimmers and cyclists study their drag and form to shave milliseconds off of their times. All athletes follow tightly prescribed diets that maximize stamina, speed, muscle growth, and recovery. You no longer can win on just talent: data drives results.

Core Idea

You cannot win on talent alone. Data harnesses talent to drive results.

These same realizations have come into education. We know that good teaching has a positive impact itself, but there is never enough time in the school day to teach everything we would like. But therein lies the secret: if we want to have more time for teaching, we need to spend less time on what students already know, and more on what they need.

Core Idea

How do we make more time for learning?
Spend less time on what students already know and more on what they *need*.

Analysis of student work can buy us that time. In essence, you are learning to see what students need. What follows are the key strategies to make this sort of analysis possible.

Immediate Responsiveness

Mary Ann protects data analysis more diligently than any other action in her schedule. Why? Because data expires quickly. For every day that passes between the time of an assessment and the implementation of a new teaching plan, students are not learning what they actually need. Laura Garza, whom you met in the Introduction and will see again in Chapter 5, is of the same mind. "The rest of my calendar might need adjustment from week to week," says Laura, "but data analysis meetings—those are sacred times."

As a rule of thumb, this means reviewing student work as quickly and as efficiently as possible—within twenty-four hours or at maximum one week, depending on the length of the assessment. At the end of the chapter, we will address how to make a yearly calendar that incorporates time for analyzing results from interim assessments as well as more regular grade-level team data meetings.

User-Friendly Reports

Before you can analyze, you have to have the right data in hand. For starters, we are not talking about year-end data. At that point, the year is over, and there is nothing you can do to undo the learning or lack thereof. Great data analysis begins by looking at interim assessment results and then goes further into daily student work. To do so, you need clear and intuitive data reports.

The figure here shows a sample of what an effective data report might look like.

Literacy 5-3 Results

RESPEITO

Student Name	MULTIPLE CHOICE: TOTAL CORRECT	MULTIPLE CHOICE: % CORRECT	WRITING: AVG. SCORE (OUT OF 4)	1 Main Idea/Theme (RL.5.2)	2 Compare/contrast characters (RL.5.3)	3 Passage Structure (RL.5)	4 Figurative Language (RL.5.4)	5 Figurative Language (RL.5.4)	6 Narrative Point of View (RL.5.6)	7 Meaning of vocab/phrases in text (RL.5.)	8 Main Idea/Theme (RL.5.2)	9 Write--Compare stories same genre (RL)	10 Prepositions (L.5.1a)	11 Consistent tense (L.5.1d)	12 Perfect tenses (L.5.1b)	13 Too/to/two	14 Pronouns	15 Punctuation (L.5.2)	16 Main Idea/Theme (RL.5.2)	17 Meaning of vocab/phrases in text (RL.5.)	18 Main Ideas of a Passage (RL.5.2)
Ashanti	39	98%	92%					a				4									
Shelton	37	93%	83%									4									
Imani	27	68%	75%			c						3									
Lamar	32	80%	67%					d	d	a	d	2						c			
Mary	29	73%	67%				a	a	a	a	a	2					a				
Terrell	25	63%	50%		b	b	a					2									
Jessica	21	53%	58%				a	a	a		d	2	d	d	b		a	c			
Shannon	28	70%	50%			b			a			2		c	d					b	
Al-Quan	18	45%	50%	d	c	b					d	2	c							c	c
TOTAL CORRECT PER Q:	18			18	17	16	10	9	15	19	13	2.8	18	18	13	20	13	15	21	15	19
% CORRECT PER Q:	86%			86%	81%	76%	48%	43%	71%	90%	62%	62%	86%	86%	62%	95%	62%	71%	100%	71%	90%

Repeated 5-1 Standards: 73%

Standard	%
Main Idea/Theme--Lit (1,8,27):	76%
Main Idea/Theme--Info (16,18,38):	92%
Use evidence--Lit (3,6,29,31):	73%
Use evidence--Info (20, 39,42):	68%
Punctuation (15,24,32):	83%
Writing--persuasive (21):	48%

Repeated 5-2 Standards: 76%

Standard	%
Vocab/phrases in context--Lit (7):	90%
Vocab/phrases in context--Info (17,40):	55%
Characters: compare/contrast (2):	81%
Verb tenses (11,12,25,34):	71%
Other Grammar (13,26,33,36, 37):	83%
Writing from multiple texts (43):	67%

Respeito Performance 5-1 Standards: 60%

	MULT. CHOICE:	WRITING:
RESPEITO	73%	58%

Note the many remarkable characteristics of this table. First, everything for one group of students fits on one page. At a minimum, these reports show class performance at four levels:

1. **Question level:** how students performed on each question and what wrong answer choices they made. This is incredibly important; Beth Verrilli notes, "On a standard like main idea, it's not enough to know the overall percentage. I need to know what makes them struggle: Have they not mastered the skill of main idea in general, or was it the content of this passage that they were unprepared for, the challenge of new vocabulary, a challenging answer choice, or other factors?"

2. **Skill or standard level:** how students performed on each standard or skill.

3. **Student level:** how well each individual student performed.

4. **Global or whole-class level:** how well the class performed.

The template for a data report needs to be concise and easy to understand, enabling teachers to enter and interpret data with as small of a learning curve as possible. Although there are endless ways you could adapt data reports to summarize the results of different assessments, it is essential that the format you choose makes plugging in new data a simple matter and that the results are easy for others at your school to read and comprehend. If the data report is not intuitive, it will not be informative. And if it takes too long to fill out, you have less time to focus on actually analyzing it.

Back in 2010 when *Driven by Data* was first published, there were very few data reports that met these criteria; most were too cumbersome or provided too much data. Today there are a large number of online tools that process and display results like these. (Illuminate is one strong example.) But many of the schools getting strong results still use simple Excel spreadsheets. The key is not the sophistication of your tool but the simplicity of reading your data. Less is more.

Core Idea

The key to effective analysis is not the sophistication of your tool but the simplicity of reading your data. Less is more.

Deep Analysis—Teacher-Owned, Test-in-Hand

Once your data is in place, now you can do the actual analysis. Mary Ann, and leaders like her, start by figuring out where to focus.

Look for the Patterns

When Mary Ann dives into data analysis, her goal is to get every student to 100 percent mastery. This means that if 100 percent of a class is already answering a question correctly, she won't be looking into reteaching that content. Conversely, if a large portion of the class gets specific questions wrong, that material probably does need to be retaught; and within each set of incorrect answers, patterns in *where* students went wrong are extremely critical for Mary Ann to identify. Only then can she get students the instruction they need, instead of repeating what they already know.

To better understand how this works, let's apply the process to a multiple-choice assessment. Look at this data sample. Let's begin by analyzing the data at the standards level.

Standards-Level Analysis

	Sentence Completion	Main Idea	Extended Reasoning	Supporting Details	Vocabulary in Context
% Correct	73	55	76	60	75

It's apparent that main idea is a serious challenge for this group of students.

See the Gap

But when we analyze these assessment results at the question level, we find something unexpected:

Question-Level Analysis

Main Idea Question Number	10	19	29	32
% Correct	83	23	45	63

Zeroing in on specific questions related to main idea allows Mary Ann to see the most important gap in the students' learning. In this case, the students' problem is not with every aspect of main idea but only with certain types of main idea questions. To find out which part of this content is so difficult for students, let's turn to question 19, which only

23 percent of students answered correctly. The question concerns a short passage on the work of Edgar Allan Poe. Where did the class go wrong when they responded to it?

Single-Question-Level Analysis

1. The author's purpose in this passage is to [correct answer appears in **boldface**]:

    A. Detail the myths and inconsistencies surrounding the personal life of a renowned author

    B. Demonstrate that professional authors can succeed despite scathing criticism

    C. Call attention to the fact that literary critics have erred in their judgment of Poe's writing

    D. Argue that Poe's early negative publicity had continued repercussions throughout his writing career

    E. **Show that contradictions in Poe's life and work do not detract from his popularity**

Answer Choice	A	B	C	D	E
% of students who selected it	58	0	0	9	33

The data makes it clear that most students were drawn to answer choice A. Given the amount of time the passage in question spends discussing inconsistencies in Poe's work, this answer would seem plausible. Yet the final answer choice, answer E, is the only one to take into account the passage's substantial discussion of Poe's popularity and legacy, a key part of the text that answer choice A misses. In short, students are selecting a "narrow" answer that does not cover the whole passage. Question 29, which saw similarly low levels of student performance, revealed the same error pattern: when students were wrong, their answers did not encompass everything they had read. That's the gap in the learning.

Informed by this analysis, you can identify a few specific strategies that will be effective: prompting students to distinguish ideas that are too limited from those that are sufficiently broad, for instance; and requiring students to link a main idea they've identified back to each paragraph in a text. But just as important as the strategies you might now suggest to a teacher are the ones you'll know *not* to suggest. You wouldn't, for example, recommend repeated practice on discarding overly broad main ideas, because although developing too-broad main ideas is an error that English students often make, it's not the one these English students are making now. Again: focus on what students need, not on what they already know.

A Word on . . . Data Analysis for Open-Ended Questions

When it comes to data-driven instruction, open-ended questions present a unique set of challenges—and opportunities. Steve Chiger, an acclaimed former high school English teacher and the director of middle school–high school literacy for Uncommon Schools, shares that the beauty of analyzing student-generated responses is that doing so gives us the opportunity as educators to "geek out" together about the content we fell in love with.

Let's take a look at this open-ended response prompt designed by Steve.

Isaac, After Mount Moriah
Asleep on the roof when rain comes,
water collects in the dips of his collarbone.
Dirty haired boy, my rascal, my sacrifice. Never
an easy dream. I watch him wrestle my shadow, shut eyelids
trembling, one fist ready for me.
Leave him a blanket, leave him alone.
Night before, found him caked in dirt,
sleeping in a ditch, wet black stones for pillows.
What kind of father does he make me, this boy
I find tangled in the hair of willows, curled fetal
in the grove?
Once, I found him in a far field, the mountain's peak
like a blade above us both.

Saeed Jones

Prompt: How does Jones use language to characterize the relationship between Isaac and Abraham in "Isaac, After Mount Moriah"? Mention specific cases of figurative language the poem uses to make its point.

On paper, this looks like a very strong prompt. Yet recall from earlier that the rigor will only be determined by how we evaluate the responses. Although a rubric will help us somewhat, the best way to begin your analysis is with your own exemplar response. As I often state in PD on data-driven instruction, *you raise the bar when you spar with an exemplar.* Why? Because you don't limit yourself to what students were able to do but keep a clear focus on where you want them to go.

When you set out to script your own exemplar student responses to open-ended prompts, keep in mind the following tips:

- **Write at the level the medium- to high-achieving students in your class are capable of.** Ultimately, exemplar student responses come from your mid- to high-level students, so you'll set the right level of rigor by emulating them.

- **Don't worry about the exact wording or precise thesis of your response.** There could be many correct arguments to make about this poem, or any poem! The goal of an exemplar isn't to create a cookie-cutter answer that every student's response should match but to write a high-quality piece of literary analysis that would earn your students a 4 or 5 on the AP exam if they were to produce it themselves.

Crafting the exemplar changes the game for any subject—not only for open-ended literary analysis but also for written response questions in science or history and for problems that require showing your work in math. With an exemplar in hand, you will find that the analysis of student work becomes much easier: you look for the gaps (in thesis statements, evidence, transitional phrases, inferences, structure, and so on). In doing so, you will push the quality of the writing faster and more effectively.

A Word on . . . Special Needs Students and DDI

As we give workshops across the globe, one of the most frequently raised concerns is whether or not this actually works for special needs students.

I've had the chance to interact with and learn from the highest-achieving special education teachers, and to a person they tell me: data-driven instruction is at the heart of what they do. When you serve children with specific learning needs, you are identifying their personal gaps and designing teaching strategies to match. There is no other choice: if you aren't data driven, your children won't learn!

Natascha de la Torre, an incredibly successful SPED instructor at Vailsburg Elementary School in Newark, New Jersey, says data-driven instruction is one of the most important tools she uses to help special needs students meet learning goals. "You have to know where you want every student in your class to be, but also to understand each individual student's learning profile," Natascha says. "That means you need to identify a realistic place you might get that student to first. Being data driven lets you build a trajectory that will get them to that larger goal eventually. It might take some of my students longer to meet those goals, but we're not going to lower the bar."

Here are some of the tips special educators like Natascha have shared with me to pass on to you and your special education teachers.

First line of action: grab the low-hanging fruit.

Often the challenge of analyzing interim assessment data for a student with special needs can be that there are too many questions "in the red"—that is, where the student was not proficient. When that happens, start with the low-hanging fruit:

- Sort classroom data by students' scores: look for the questions that only the struggling students are getting wrong. These are likely the easiest access point, and other questions will likely be addressed by the general education teacher in the large-group setting. Natascha points out that this sorting process helps students of all learning abilities, because in addition to clarifying which standards need to be retaught specifically to special needs students, it also ends up underscoring the other standards that need to be retaught to *everyone*.

- From there, follow the same steps of analysis as for any other student:
    o What are all the steps the students need to take to answer these questions correctly?
    o Which of these steps need to be made more explicit to the students?
    o What sort of practice do the students need to master this standard—heavy repetition of computational skills? Following a multistep protocol?

Second line of action: provide in-class support during reteaching.

For special needs students who take classes with their general education peers, the best thing to do is support the general teacher during reteaching:

- What are the standards that will be reviewed or retaught for the whole class?

- Are the struggling students' misunderstandings on these standards different than those of the rest of the students?

- What additional support or steps will the struggling students need when these standards are being reviewed?

In short, as Natascha's colleague Michelle Rolfert puts it, "The only difference between the general education setting and the special education setting is the need to reassess more frequently and with differentiated assignments. The process is the same."

ACTION: TEACHING AND RETEACHING TO MASTERY

All the quality assessments and deep analysis are meaningless if we don't act. Until we teach differently, learning won't change. At the same time, action without proper analysis is meaningless: it's just spinning your wheels.

Core Idea

Assessments and analysis are meaningless if we don't act.
Yet action without analysis is meaningless: it's just spinning your wheels.

So what does effective reteaching—and teaching in general—look like to achieve mastery?

When I wrote *Driven by Data,* I was obsessed with trying to observe successful reteaching efforts in every school I visited. As I observed the highest-achieving teachers, I thought I would discover a multitude of different strategies for reteaching. Although I did, I also noticed that there was a pattern of effective reteaching, and that it could boiled down to two basic principles:

- Reteach the material in one of two ways: modeling or guided discourse

- Monitor student work—continually

Let's unpack these principles in detail.

Choosing How to Reteach

After observing thousands of teachers in action, we discovered that there are really two basic options for reteaching: modeling or guided discourse (with many variations within each). Modeling is called many things, such as the I Do or the think-aloud or even the mini lesson, but all of them focus on the teacher showing the students what to do. Alternatively, guided discourse—often called inquiry or class discussion or Show-Call—does the opposite. Its goal is to guide student discussion to get students to figure out the error themselves and coach each other to success.

Most teachers I've talked with have a strong opinion as to which is more effective. However, the best teachers use both methods, matching them to the needs of the students and the strengths of their teaching. Based on their guidance, the following is a quick summary of some of the pros and cons for each approach that can help you determine which method is the most appropriate in a given situation.

Modeling Versus Guided Discourse

Teaching Method	Pros	Cons
Modeling	<ul><li>Easier to plan.</li><li>If students don't have a model of success to refer to, they probably won't be able to replicate success.</li></ul>	<ul><li>Can be too procedural, as opposed to conceptual.</li><li>Dependent on students learning passively at first.</li></ul>

Teaching Method	Pros	Cons
	• Clarity: there are clear, bright lines around what students must do.	
Guided Discourse	• Stickier, because students learn more actively and do more of the thinking. • Easier to dig deeper on a conceptual level.	• Harder to plan, as it's dependent on excellent questions and ability to manage the discourse. • Dependent on some students being close enough to push remaining students the rest of the way. • Can result in only the most advanced students understanding.

In general, modeling is a better option for a newer teacher who is still working on classroom management, and also for reteaching when there's no exemplar answer in the classroom for students to turn to. If there is already an existing exemplar students can use to define what success looks like, guided discourse can often go deeper.

Let's dive into the details of how reteaching functions on the ground, beginning with the easier of the two: modeling.

Modeling

On the surface, modeling is simple: show the students what to do. Effective modeling, however, takes that simple idea and adds much more depth. Moreover, it can be effective not only for younger grades but for older students as well. Art Worrell from North Star Washington Park High School shows us what this looks like in his AP US History class.

WATCH Clip 3: Worrell—Think-Aloud—Set Listening Task (Teaching Clip)

WATCH Clip 4: Worrell—Think-Aloud—Model the Thinking (Teaching Clip)

Stop and Jot

What does Art do to model the thinking for his students?

_____

_____

_____

_____

_____

_____

_____

Art took a complex skill—unpacking the previous knowledge that can be ascertained from the prompt—and made it simple. But he also made sure the students were set up to maximally benefit from the model. Here are the keys.

Provide a clear listening or note-taking task. Art gives students a clear listening or note-taking task that fosters active listening to the model. Then he debriefs the model, asking:

- "What did I do in my model?"
- "What are the key things to remember when you are doing the same in your own work?"

Model the thinking, not just the procedure. What makes Art's model different than many is that he models the thinking it takes to solve the problem, not just a rote procedure. Narrow the focus of the model to highlight the thinking students are struggling with, and then demonstrate replicable thinking steps that students can follow. Students will then learn how to think, not just act. That will enable them to take on a much broader set of future problems rather than becoming procedural.

End with You Do. Of course, a model is only valuable if students then get the opportunity to apply it.

Guided Discourse

Guided discourse is often seen as the magic in the classroom, when students engage in rigorous dialogue that reaches deep, thoughtful conclusions. Yet there are many pitfalls to avoid. As one teacher shared with me, discourse can be like a squirrel—you never know quite where it is headed, and it can run up the wrong tree really quickly! So how you do get that squirrel of discourse running up the proper tree?

Andrew Schaefer shows us an example of how to do this. Andrew worked with Juliana Worrell at Alexander Street School in Newark, New Jersey, the site of the most successful school turnaround in Newark.[13] As Figure 1.2 shows, their results are truly groundbreaking (more on her top actions in *The Principal Manager's Guide to Leverage Leadership*).

In Clip 4, you'll see part of what made them so successful. Fifty percent of the class has gotten the wrong answer to question on a fraction of a whole. Watch what Andrew does to drive discussion.

WATCH Clip 5: Schaefer—Guided Discourse (Teaching Clip)

Figure 1.2 New Jersey State PARRC Test Results: Alexander Street School, Percentage at or Above Proficiency in Third and Fourth Grades

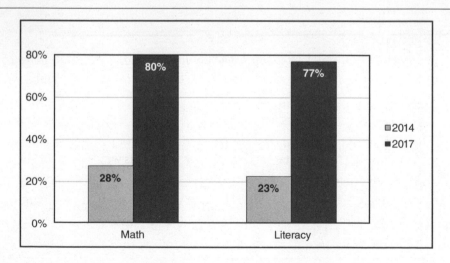

Have students write first, talk second. Before beginning discourse, Andrew has students complete a writing task. That enables him to monitor, collect data, and anticipate where the conversation will go. It also gives him the opportunity to determine which students have strong answers and which are struggling so that he can call on them at key moments during the discussion. Too often, teachers start with discussion; let 100 percent participate before you do so!

Use Show-Call. Andrew makes a very simple move at the beginning of the discourse that changes everything. Instead of talking, he simply displays two samples of student work. Think about the power of this action: he has reduced the amount of teacher talk taking place significantly, and he has shifted all of the thinking back to the students. Doug Lemov calls this Show-Call.[14] You can do this with exemplar student responses, incorrect responses, or, in this case, with both.

Start with a Turn and Talk, then poll the room. Rather than begin with large-group discussion, Andrew starts with a Turn and Talk. This action sounds simple, but it is often overlooked. Turn and Talks maximize the number of students who are sharing during discussion. They let everyone work their thinking out verbally with a peer before sharing in the large group. Andrew then takes it one step further by polling the room to see where students stand before starting the discussion. In this way, he has an immediate idea of where students are. This enables him to decide how to manage the conversation.

Employ strategic questioning. Once the class comes together for a large-group discussion, Andrew uses the data he collected from the writing task and classroom poll to call on students based on their learning need. In this case, everyone agreed with the right answer after the Turn and Talk, so Andrew can call on a student who initially had the wrong answer to check for understanding to make sure he or she knows why the right answer is correct. If most of the class was still struggling, he could call on someone who had the right answer initially to justify his or her response. Strategic questioning enables Andrew to reduce the likelihood of haphazard conversation and to get students grappling with the key learning challenge.

End with You Do. Just as with modeling, the learning that results from guided discourse doesn't get solidified until students have the opportunity to try it again on their own.

Monitoring Student Work—Continually

Active monitoring of student learning in the classroom is as important as the reteaching itself. Why? Because learning doesn't happen in a single moment—it happens over time.

When you are learning to master something, such as a piece of music on the piano, you first learn the basic chords and then add intonation and complexity to create a beautiful sound. That doesn't happen overnight. Neither does reteaching.

Denarius Frazier is a highly successful math teacher at Ashley Anderson's school, Uncommon Collegiate. (See more on Ashley and her success in Chapter 3.) He discovered early on that a single successful reteaching lesson didn't seal the deal for his students. "I needed to follow up for multiple days to see if they retained it," he recalls. "Only when they can utilize linear equations consistently in each upcoming unit do I know they have mastered it." Denarius stumbled on a key idea: reteaching is a relay, not a sprint.

Core Idea

Reteaching is a relay, not a sprint.

Any reteaching that ends on a single day won't have the same long-term success as reteaching to which a class returns multiple times: you might have won that leg, but not the race. Monitoring sets the teacher's focus on whether the students learned what the teacher taught—and learned it well enough to succeed consistently.

If you want to dive further into monitoring, we cover it quite extensively in *Get Better Faster* (see "Monitor Aggressively," pp. 205–220). Meanwhile, however, here are four core strategies that instructors like Denarius use to monitor learning day by day:

- **Monitor independent practice.** By circulating when students do independent work and reading their responses, Denarius can quickly see what they're able to do on their own.

- **Spiral content within lessons.** Denarius takes students back to previously covered material when they struggle, working to discover where their knowledge is breaking down—and to make sure they're remembering what he's already taught.

- **Observe small-group work.** What do students say to each other in pairs or small groups as compared to in a whole-class discussion? Denarius finds that the answers are incredibly revealing.

- **Adjust Exit Tickets, Do Nows, or homework.** When necessary, Denarius adjusts his assignments to his students both during and after class so that their work will show him what he needs to know about their learning.

Assess. Analyze. Act. Three basic actions that profoundly transform a school and the quality of student learning. Yet so many obstacles can get in the way of teachers and leaders remaining focused on this approach. What separates leaders like Mary Ann from the rest is the ability to implement the systems that lock in these actions. Let's take a look at what those are.

PUT IT ALL TOGETHER—LEAD DATA MEETINGS

What is the highest-leverage thirty minutes for a school leader? That is a loaded question, but let's give it some thought. Consider a principal who is committed to observing class instructions as often as possible. If the principal observed every teacher in his or her school for fifteen minutes a week, she would be among the most diligent school leaders in the country. Yet even at this breakneck pace, how much instruction would she actually see? Do the math:

- Typical teaching load: 5 classes/day, 50 minutes each
- Total minutes of instruction per week: 5 classes/day × 50 minutes × 5 days/week = 1,250 minutes
- One classroom observation per week: 15 minutes
- 15 minutes/1,200 minutes total instruction = 1.2% observation of instruction

As hard as it is to believe, she would see only 1 percent of the week's learning:

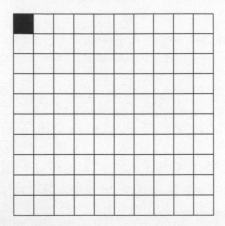

For all her attentiveness, this principal is watching her students through a peephole. Even if leaders are able to identify the most critical 1 percent with these observations, they would still need to make broad, vague conjectures about the standards learned the other 99 percent of the time.

Now consider a leader who has rolled out data-driven instruction. Reviewing interim assessments alone, that leader can gauge *six to eight full weeks of teaching*. No assessment can capture 100 percent of the learning in a class, but an effective assessment can certainly capture 80 percent of it. In one meeting, that leader has changed the percentage of instruction she observes from 1 percent to a game-changing 80 percent:

Observation Alone   Interim Assessment Analysis Meeting

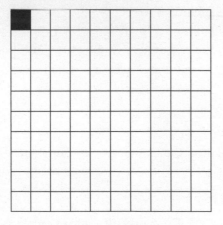

> ## Core Idea
>
> Data meetings shift the focus from observing 1 percent of the learning to 80 percent. That makes all the difference.

So what do effective data meetings look like? Mary Ann has made herself an expert in them. She follows a simple, replicable protocol that all of her grade-level teams use. We made mention of it in the Introduction: See It, Name It, Do It.

- **See It:** see the exemplar and the gap
- **Name It:** name the key gap in conceptual understanding for the students
- **Do It:** plan how to reteach the content with modeling or guided discourse, and build a follow-up plan

To see how these steps apply to a leader's work in practice, we'll follow Mary Ann's school through one of her data meetings. Read on to see what actions Mary Ann takes to make this meeting successful.

Prework

Muhammad Ali once said, "The fight is won or lost far away from witnesses—behind the lines, in the gym, and out there on the road, long before I dance under those lights." He won every championship before he even stepped foot in the ring.

Nowhere is this more the case than data analysis meetings. Mary Ann does not merely schedule data analysis meetings and sit back and hope they succeed; her actions prior to the meeting are what guarantee their impact. Follow her lead to set up effective meetings, be they interim assessment analysis meetings or weekly data meetings.

Analyze the Data *Before* the Meeting

Mary Ann doesn't simply hope for good analysis—she makes sure of it. She and her instructional leaders look at the student work in advance so that they can identify the patterns, pick out key questions where they can focus, and have a preliminary idea of the analysis and action plan. This will prepare them to step in to support the teachers whenever their analysis isn't deep enough or their action plan won't close the gap. To prime the pump for the meeting, do the following:

- Review or write the ideal interpretation of the standard being addressed.

- Identify the gap in student understanding.
- Plan the key part of an effective reteach plan to address that gap.

Have the Room and Materials Ready

One of the most striking things about highly effective data meetings is how smoothly they run. That is due in no small part to having the room set up with all the materials. Here is a quick go-to list that leaders like Mary Ann use to set up their meetings:

- Timer
- Copy of the standard and exemplar response
- Chart paper and/or whiteboard to take notes
- Upcoming lesson plans and any materials needed to plan a reteach lesson
- A sample of high, medium, and low student work—typical errors that are representative of the majority of the students (this will save hours of sorting student work during the meeting and let teachers focus on the analysis itself)

The importance of this preparation cannot be overstated: you are supercharging the meeting and stripping away time that would be lost in nonessential actions. In this way, you have thirty minutes of deep conversation, rather than just ten to fifteen; that makes a huge difference over time.

A Word on . . . Content Expertise

One of the most challenging aspects of preparing for data meetings—and participating in them—is having a level of content expertise that allows you to dive into the assessments to determine the errors. This can be a daunting task even for third-grade math, but it becomes even more challenging as you get into higher-level content. For a high school instructional leader, it is next to impossible to have enough content expertise to deeply analyze AP-level chemistry, English, history, calculus, Spanish, and more!

So what do leaders do when they have to coach outside of their own content expertise? They find other experts to help them.

Eric Diamon, whom you'll meet again in Chapter 8, has found this especially helpful when coaching his eighth-grade algebra teacher. Eric's background is in the humanities, and his knowledge of the content she teaches is limited. "I find that my work with her is where it's most challenging for me to be a value add to her work," Eric confesses. To support this teacher, Eric takes two steps: developing his own content expertise in math, and seeking out help from other educators. "I attend any math PDs I can, which has definitely been helpful," Eric says. He is on to something: to become a content expert, participate in as many data analysis meetings, planning meetings (see Chapter 2), and PD sessions as you can. Each time you engage in the content by looking at student work or planning a unit, by nature you gain more understanding. Little by little, you'll be on your way to supporting your teachers across all content areas.

Eric's other strategy is to work with another instructor who accompanies him on walkthroughs of STEM classrooms across his middle school campus. "That helps me develop my eyes for math," notes Eric. Support of this nature may come from a coach, department chair, strong teacher, or someone outside the school. Beyond this, you'll build your own content expertise simply by engaging in deep data analysis with your content experts again and again.

See It and Name It

With the preparation locked in, Mary Ann is ready to lead meetings of impact. Watch how quickly Mary Ann is able to dive into the work of the content itself. In this clip, she's working with her special needs student support team, and her assistant principal is also in attendance.

 WATCH Clip 6: Stinson—See It (Standard)—Weekly Data Meeting

Stop and Jot

What actions does Mary Ann take to start the data meeting successfully? Jot down what you noticed.

_____

_____

_____

_____

_____

_____

_____

See the Exemplar

The most tempting place to start a data meeting is looking for the gap in student work. Yet Mary Ann doesn't start there. Instead, she kicks off the meeting by celebrating the team's successes since the previous week. Then, she preselects a key question to focus on, and they dive in by reviewing the standard and the exemplar response. Why? Looking at the wrong answers first would be like starting a road trip before deciding where to go. You need the exemplar response to give you the pathway.

> ## Core Idea
>
> You don't know where to go if you haven't determined the destination.
> Use the exemplar to start with the end in mind.

The beauty of reviewing the standard and exemplar side by side is that the standard can give you academic language to describe the student thinking needed to answer the question.

What Mary Ann does in this meeting isn't rocket science, and she didn't become a master of on-the-spot thinking. Rather, she uses a set of prompts that are pretty applicable to nearly any assessment item at any grade level:

- "What does a student need to know and be able to do to master this standard?"

- "What were the keys to an exemplar answer?"

- "How does the exemplar response connect to the standard?"

- "How does your student exemplar compare to the teacher exemplar? What is the gap, or does it offer something yours does not?"

- "Do students have different evidence to demonstrate mastery of the standard?"

Step back and note the power of what Mary Ann has done. "Through the process of looking at the exemplar, my teachers got better at seeing what they needed to teach," Mary Ann shares. "That makes it easier to see the gaps. And they also are paying attention to strengths and not just weaknesses: kids came back with stronger and stronger responses every week."

For more evidence of the power of the exemplar in action, take a look at it in another context—math. Watch this video of Nikki Bridges, who at the time this video was filmed was the principal of Leadership Prep Ocean Hill in Brooklyn, New York.

WATCH Clip 7: Bridges—See It (Exemplar)—Weekly Data Meeting

Starting with the exemplar gives Nikki and her team of teachers clarity on what students have to be able to do to master the standard.

Core Idea

When you start from the exemplar, your analysis becomes exemplary.

See the Gap

With an unpacked exemplar in hand, Mary Ann and her teachers are now more equipped to get to the heart of the matter: What are the gaps between the exemplar student response and the student responses that don't reflect mastery? Rewatch Clip 2 from the beginning of the chapter to see how Mary Ann manages this.

 RE WATCH Clip 2: Stinson—See It, Name It (Gap)—Weekly Data Meeting

---

Stop and Jot

What actions does Mary Ann take to get her teachers to see the gap in student learning? Jot down what you noticed.

_____

_____

_____

_____

_____

_____

_____

_____

Here we see the power of unpacking the exemplar: the teachers can use it as a reference to identify the gaps in the rest of the student work. Seeing and naming the gap in this way makes the data meeting powerful. The teachers not only know what to target but also have done so in a collaborative environment that cultivates trust. In this context, discovering what needs to be retaught in a classroom isn't about pointing fingers at teaching "gone wrong." It's about seeing what students need with shared clarity, so that you can reach solutions together. (As you'll see in Chapter 6, looking at data as groups of teachers is a very effective building block for staff culture as well.) In Clip 8, Juliana Worrell accomplishes this just as Mary Ann did.

 WATCH Clip 8: Worrell—See It (Gap)—Weekly Data Meeting

Naming the exemplar and the gap seals the deal. Writing down the student error and the conceptual misunderstanding evident in that error locks in *what* went wrong, which will allow the teachers to quickly pivot to *how* to fix it.

> ### Core Idea
> You don't lock in the learning until you stamp it.
> Naming *what* went wrong makes it easier to plan *how* to fix it.

Do It

With a solid analysis, the teachers are ready to shift their focus to reteaching. Think this only works for younger grades? Not at all. High school principal Ashley Anderson of Uncommon Collegiate (more about Ashley in Chapter 3 on observation and feedback) finds the same value in data meetings like these. Watch in Clip 9 how her HS math instructional leader Denarius Frazier plans for action in his data meeting with a teacher whose students are working to master transformations (calculating the movement of objects in a plane). Then, take a look at Clip 10 to see how Mary Ann walks her team through the same process.

In both clips, you'll hear the leaders ask the teachers what they'll be looking for during different "laps." This refers to act of walking around the classroom to monitor student work. During each round—or lap—the teachers will check for key responses that will indicate that the students are understanding (e.g., in a math word problem, the first lap could be annotating the question, then setting up the proper equation, then solving correctly).

 WATCH Clip 9: Frazier—Do It (Plan)—Weekly Data Meeting
WATCH Clip 10: Stinson—Do It (Plan)—Weekly Data Meeting

Stop and Jot

What actions do Denarius and Mary Ann take to get their teachers to plan the reteach?

_____

_____

_____

_____

_____

_____

_____

Plan the Reteach

What Denarius and Mary Ann lead their teachers to do—plan the reteach—seems pretty standard. Yet most teams of teachers never get that far when analyzing student work. How Denarius and Mary Ann do so is what makes their leadership so effective. Giving the teacher time first to plan independently actually saves time: they have already articulated their ideas before they speak. But the real magic is having them "spar" with another reteach plan; this pushes them to excellence much faster. You need to perfect a reteach plan before you practice: if you don't, you'll just practice doing it wrong.

Core Idea

Perfect the plan before you practice.
If you don't, you'll just practice the wrong way to reteach.

Denarius and Mary Ann's teachers have the opportunity to improve their reteaching plans based on one another's. Bringing the focus to "what would you add" to your plan ensures that teachers focus on the most positive parts of the plan—the strongest elements of it. This way, they can combine their own strengths as school leaders. Both Mary Ann and Denarius use some key prompts that could be used in nearly any data meeting:

- "Should we use modeling or guided discourse?" "Why?"

- "Take ___ minutes and write your script. I will do the same so we can spar."

- "Let's compare our reteach plans. What do you notice? What can we pull from each to make the strongest plan?"

At this point, both Mary Ann's and Denarius's teachers are ready to put it all together. Watch how each leader does it.

 WATCH Clip 11: Stinson—Do It (Practice)—Weekly Data Meeting
WATCH Clip 12: Frazier—Do It (Practice)—Weekly Data Meeting

Stop and Jot

What actions do Mary Ann and Denarius take to facilitate effective practice? Jot down what you noticed.

_____

_____

_____

_____

_____

_____

_____

_____

Practice

Note how natural practice is for Mary Ann and Denarius and their teachers: as routine as any other part of the meeting. Rehearsing in this way may feel awkward at first, but when you develop it as an expectation with your teachers, it will quickly become more comfortable for them (and for you!). Build a culture of practice, and practice will happen—and it will change your school.

"Early on, sometimes my teachers would attempt a reteach, but really they'd just be teaching louder," Mary Ann recalls with a laugh. "So we'd have to go back and practice that, and we would have teachers role playing their reteach for each other." That strategy made all the difference. For Denarius, it is the same: practice makes perfect, and Denarius is even able to integrate student culture feedback within the reteaching practice to make it more likely to succeed.

Once you've practiced, it's time to lock in the actions your teachers have prepared to take. Watch how Denarius and Mary Ann both make sure the reteaching happens.

 WATCH Clip 13: Stinson—Do It (Follow Up)—Weekly Data Meeting
WATCH Clip 14: Frazier—Do It (Follow Up)—Weekly Data Meeting

Follow Up

At the end of the weekly data meeting, Mary Ann Stinson asks her teachers to list all the action items and to schedule the follow-up. Denarius Frazier works with his teacher to identify multiple opportunities for assessing the identified reteach skill, and they establish a comprehensive timeline for next steps.

Think of the power of what you just witnessed. In thirty minutes, Mary Ann's and Denarius's teaching teams deeply analyzed student work and came up with a concrete reteach plan for a challenging standard. Now multiply that impact by the regular meetings that her teachers have at every grade level across the entire year. These meetings not only impact the assessment items that they directly tackle, but also build the habits of mind for teachers to repeat this process every day with student learning in their classroom. By setting this foundation in place, Mary Ann has truly shifted the focus from the teaching to the learning, and she has raised expectations for everyone in school. Her results tell it all.

Core Idea

Teachers will rise to the level of our expectations:
If we expect them to practice, they will.

On the following pages, we've consolidated all the best practices of weekly data meetings into one precise, packed guide that you can use to lead data meetings yourself.

Weekly Data Meeting

Leading Teacher Teams to Analyze Student Daily Work

Prepare before the meeting	**Prepare**
	• **Materials ready:** identify student exemplar; teachers turn in student work, pull and categorize hi/med/lo student work (just a few of each), pull upcoming lesson plan(s) and pertinent prompting guides
	• **Prime the pump:** script the reteach plan and the gap in student understanding; unpack the standard
	• **Preview protocol with teachers:** assign roles, novice teachers speak first, veteran teachers add on and clarify, leader provides additional clarity at end, chart, preview the need for concision from more verbose team members, use of a timer, creation of note-taking template
See It 13–18 min	**See Past Success, See the Exemplar, and See and Analyze the Gap**
	See past success (1 min):
	• "Last week we planned to reteach ___, and we went from ___% proficient to ___%. Nice job!"
	• "What actions did you take to reach this goal?"
	See the exemplar (8 min):
	• Narrow the focus: "Today, I want to dive into [specific standard] and the following assessment item."

See It 13–18 min	See Past Success, See the Exemplar, and See and Analyze the Gap
	• Interpret the standard(s):
	○ "Take 1 min: in your own words, what should a student know or be able to do to show mastery?"
	• Unpack the teacher's written exemplar:
	○ "Take 1–2 min to review the exemplar: What were the keys to an ideal answer?"
	○ "How does this [part of the exemplar] align with the standard?"
	• Analyze the student exemplar:
	○ "Take 1 min: How does your student exemplar compare to the teacher exemplar? Is there a gap?"
	○ "Do students have different paths/evidence to demonstrate mastery of the standard?"
	○ "Does the student exemplar offer something that your exemplar does not?"
	See the gap (5 min):
	• Move to the sample of unmastered student work (look only at representative sample):
	○ "Take 2 min: What are the gaps between the rest of our student work and the exemplar?"
	○ "Look back at our chart of the standard and exemplar: What are key misconceptions?"
Name It 2 min	**State the Error and Conceptual Misunderstanding**
	Punch it—Stamp the error and conceptual understanding:
	• "So our key area to reteach is . . .":
	○ Describe the conceptual understanding
	○ (If needed) Describe the procedural gap (e.g., memorize multiplication tables) and/or missing habits (e.g., annotating text, showing work)
	• Write down and/or chart the highest-leverage action students will take to close the gap

Do It (Rest of the meeting)	Plan the Reteach, Practice, and Follow Up
	Plan the reteach (8–10 min):
	• Select the reteach structure:
	○ "Should we use modeling or guided discourse?" "Why?"
	• Select the task and ID exemplar response:
	○ Select materials: task, text, student work to show-call, what to chart.
	○ "What is the ideal answer we want to see that will show we've closed the gap?"
	○ (If needed—follow-up question): "What is the 'why' that students should be able to articulate?"
	• Plan the reteach:
	○ "Take ___ min and write your script. I will do the same so we can spar."
	■ **If a model:** write the think-aloud and questions
	■ **If guided discourse:** select student work for Show-Call, write prompts
	○ "Let's compare our reteach plans. What do you notice? What can we pull from each to make the strongest plan?" (Revise the plan)
	• Plan the independent practice:
	○ "What will you monitor to see if they are doing this correctly? What laps will you name?"
	Practice the gap (remaining time):
	• "Let's practice."
	○ **If a model:** practice modeling the thinking, precision of language, and change in tone/cadence
	○ **If guided discourse:** practice Show-Call, prompting students, and stamping the understanding
	○ **If monitoring:** practice the laps, annotations, prompts when students are stuck, or stop the show
	• (If a struggle) "I'm going to model the teaching for you first. [Teach.] What do you notice?"

Do It (Rest of the meeting)	Plan the Reteach, Practice, and Follow Up
	• Repeat until the practice is successful. Check for understanding (CFU): "What made this more effective?"
	• Lock it in: "How did our practice meet or enhance what we planned for the reteach?"

Follow up (last 2 min):

- Set the follow-up plan: when to teach, when to reassess, when to revisit this data
  - Observe implementation within 24 hours; teacher sends reassessment data to leader
- Spiral:
  - ID multiple moments when teacher can continue to assess and track mastery: Do Now questions, homework, modified independent practice
- Move to the lowest-scoring work:
  - "What students do we need to pull for tutoring? What do we need to remediate?"
  - "How can we adjust our monitoring plan to meet the needs of these students?"

Findings from the Field

Stephen Chiger

I came to data-driven instruction as an unashamed skeptic. "This sounds like another round of teaching to the test," I sniffed, as I begrudgingly shuffled in to a professional development workshop that would wind up changing the course of my professional life.

I'd been teaching in an urban high school for four years, and my idealism, while not extinguished, had begun to seriously sag under the weight of some questions that most teachers in underresourced communities face. How could I teach well when my students came to me at so many disparate levels? If my students' primary school education had been inadequate, was it too late to change anything by the time they were in high school? And even if I could run my class effectively, were the systemic expectations so low—and the drag of poverty so high—that my efforts comprised little more than blowing against the wind?

Suffice it to say, something happened during the course of that PD that altered how I saw education. I read the case studies of schools who had turned around student achievement. I analyzed student data and saw the kinds of insights it provided about learning. I thought of my students—of Zakiyyah, of Dawanna, of Porsalin and Paul and Gwen. Didn't I owe it to them to push myself and my school?

After hearing a segment on using assessments to improve literacy, I called the facilitator over.

"This sounds great," I said. "But this isn't how my department teaches English. We teach poems, we teach stories, we teach the five-paragraph essay."

"Well," the facilitator said, "it's not about which poem or story you teach; it's about how you teach it, assess it, and reteach it. That's what you need to rethink."

I still remember what I was thinking in that moment. First, I thought that this was an incredibly intimidating and outrageous thing to say. Second, I thought that it was exactly right. If we designed tests to measure student literacy, and if we set the rigor of those tests to match what we knew would be true college preparation, we could keep our curriculum focused on the material that really mattered—not just the idiosyncratic whims of the moment. We could, with the backbone of a data-driven program in place, transplant a refreshed academic vision, one to which all of us would be aligned.

A data-driven program wouldn't be teaching to the test; we'd be teaching to the *kids*. More specially, we'd be teaching to their needs because we'd know—precisely—what they were.

Now an instructional leader myself, I try to pay forward the wisdom I learned that day and from many inspiring leaders since. I prepare for data meetings with attentiveness and zeal. I analyze my teachers' data with the same alacrity I want them to apply. And I try to meet people wherever they are—whether new or experienced, struggling or masterful—so that together we can find the right answers for our students, by analyzing one question at a time.

MAKING IT WORK: HOW IT FITS INTO A LEADER'S SCHEDULE

All the data meetings that we just watched were highly impressive. However, such meetings won't have value if they happen only once a year. The second key system to making data-driven instruction work is a calendar that locks all of it in.

Yearly Calendar—Data-Driven Instruction

To make data-driven instruction work, it has to be the prominent lever in your yearly calendar. That entails first scheduling all key tasks related to it, and then building the rest of your calendar. "Data-Driven Instruction Monthly Map" is a sample template that is built on the experience thousands of schools, laying out all the prework and implementation work that will set you up to succeed. Feel free to take and adjust it to the needs of your own school.

Data-Driven Instruction Monthly Map

Key Tasks for the Year

Note: 1 represents the first week of the month, 2 is the second week of the month, and so on.

Month	Task
June	☐ 1 – Develop interim assessment calendar (IAs, analysis, reteach, PD) ☐ 1 – (If needed) Acquire/revise/develop interim assessments
July (summer tasks)	☐ 1 – (If new leader) Grade school using the DDI implementation rubric to ID where the school stands and where you need to be before the school year begins ☐ 1 – (If needed) Change curriculum scope and sequences to match interim assessments that will be used (or vice versa) ☐ 1 – ID who will help you complete the assessment/curriculum adjustment process to be ready for launch by the beginning of the school year
August	☐ 3 – Present DDI PD session to new teachers (use materials from *Get Better Faster* and *Driven by Data*) ☐ 4 – First week of school
September	☐ 2 – Have the first round of interim assessments (or the closest proxy) finalized

	☐ 2 – First interim assessments (or the closest proxy) have already been seen by the teachers (transparency) so that they can plan for mastery
	☐ 4 – Develop plan to determine how test scoring and analysis will be completed
October	☐ 1 – Have teachers predict performance on interim assessment 1 • Mark each question: "confident" (sure that the students will get it right), "not sure," and "no way" (students will definitely get it wrong)
	☐ 2 – Interim assessment 1
	☐ 2 – Deliver PD to school's instructional leaders in DDI analysis and leading analysis meetings (use *Get Better Faster* and *Driven by Data* for PD agenda, materials, and resources)
	☐ 3 – Teacher Analysis and Action Plan Template are in place
	☐ 3 – Teachers complete Assessment Analysis Instructional Plans
	☐ 3 – Instructional leaders run test-in-hand analysis meetings with teachers • Compare performance to what the teacher predicted: highlight areas of discrepancy (i.e., teacher over-/underpredicted how well the students were going to do on certain test questions) • Follow one-pager: Weekly Data Meeting
	☐ 3 – Principal observes analysis meetings, giving feedback to instructional leaders about their facilitation
	☐ 4 – Staff PD: • Conduct results meeting to plan to reteach challenging standards • Have teachers add rigor to their lessons using the rigor action steps from the Get Better Faster Scope and Sequence
November	☐ 1 – Second assessment is in the hands of the teachers so that they can plan to teach for mastery

	☐ 2 – Review lesson plans: Is there evidence of implementation of Teacher Action Plans from the assessment analysis meeting? ☐ 2 – Observe classes: Is there evidence of implementation of Teacher Action Plans and changed teaching practices? ☐ 2 – Evaluate school on DDI implementation rubric ☐ 3 – Have teachers predict performance on second interim assessment • Mark each question: "confident" (sure that the students will get it right), "not sure," and "no way" (students will definitely get it wrong)
December	☐ 1 – Interim assessment 2 ☐ 2 – Teachers complete data entry, analysis, and action plan ☐ 2 – Principal leads, observes, or models analysis meetings for instructional leaders ☐ 2 – Teachers complete Assessment Analysis Instructional Plans ☐ 3 – Staff PD: conduct results meeting to plan to reteach challenging standards
January	☐ 1 – Third assessment is in the hands of the teachers to plan for mastery
February	☐ 1 – (If needed) Follow up PD for school leaders to improve analysis meetings ☐ 1 – Interim assessment 3 ☐ 2 – Teachers complete Assessment Analysis Instructional Plans ☐ 2 – Data analysis and analysis meetings ☐ 3 – Staff PD: conduct results meeting to plan to reteach challenging standards
March	☐ 4 – Interim assessment 4
April	☐ 1 – Teachers complete Assessment Analysis Instructional Plans

	☐ 1 – Interim assessment analysis meetings	
	☐ 2 – Staff PD: conduct results meeting to plan to reteach challenging standards	
May	☐ 1 – State tests	
	☐ 2 – State tests	
June	☐ 3 – Final performance tasks	
	☐ 4 – Last week of school	

Weekly Schedule—Week of Interim Assessments

With the yearly calendar in place, you can lock in effective interim assessments. This sample high school schedule includes what to do during the weeks of interim assessments. (You can find elementary and middle school samples on the DVD accompanying this book.)

Interim Assessment (IA) Week Schedule—Sample

IA Week	Monday	Tuesday	Wednesday	Thursday	Friday
Morning	Literacy IA*	Math IA	Science IA	History IA	Spanish and Art IAs
Prep periods/ afternoon	Literacy teachers grade IAs	Math/literacy teachers grade IAs	Everyone grades IAs	Faculty mtg: cancel—give time to fill out analysis templates and action plans	Half-day PD (or 2nd wk)** Either: results meetings by grade level or department Or: Ind. creation of action plans

Week post-IA	Monday	Tuesday	Wednesday	Thursday	Friday
Classes	Reteach	Reteach	Reteach	Reteach	Reteach
Prep periods	One-on-one analysis meetings: literacy	One-on-one analysis meetings: math/science			Half-day PD (or 1st wk)** See row above

* Literacy assessments come first because they normally involve the most amount of essay grading, which takes longer.
** Half-day PD sessions are scheduled for the week of the assessments or the week after. This allows for time to complete analysis and action plans and to offer targeted PD to meet the student learning needs.

Weekly Schedule—Rest of the Year

Mary Ann also locks in regular data meetings through the year as a part of the standing grade-level team meetings.

Scheduling Weekly Data Meetings

Regular Week	Monday	Tuesday	Wednesday	Thursday	Friday
Teachers	Prep period: grade-level weekly data meetings	Teach new standards and spiral	Reteach key standard	Teach new standards and spiral	Teach new standards and spiral
Leadership team	Attend weekly data meetings (one leader per meeting)	Leadership team mtg: ID patterns from meetings and what to observe	Observe reteaching	Observe reteaching	

TURNAROUND—DDI IS THE STRATEGY

As noted in our Introduction, building a strong, data-driven foundation is one of the super-levers for schools looking for dramatic transformation. What are the first steps a leader can take to put this into action in a school that is struggling?

In all the other chapters, you'll find coping mechanisms and shortcuts to work through a challenging situation. In this chapter, by contrast, data-driven instruction *is* the turnaround strategy. This is the lever that will jump-start student learning, right alongside student culture. Your task is quite direct: take the monthly action plan ("Data-Driven Instruction Monthly Map") and adjust it to meet your school's yearly calendar. You need to implement each one of the action steps listed, but you can do so at the time that works for you within the framework given here. The best additional advice leaders like Mary Ann offer is to remove as many other initiatives and projects as possible to keep yourself singularly focused on making this work. Too often we take on more than we can handle, and nowhere is this more the case than in turnaround situations. Keep it simple: use this chapter as your prominent guide.

In the DVD that accompanies this book, you have the highest-leverage handouts for use with data-driven instruction. Access a full menu of PD materials in *Driven by Data*. You do not need to reinvent the wheel here: the work has been done successfully by hundreds of schools across the country. You can simply follow their example.

CONCLUSION

Mary Ann was up front with her staff during her first year leading Truesdell Education Campus: this year was not going to be easy. She recalled the initial reaction: "It was this way or the highway, and some chose the highway."

But the teachers quickly learned that they had more than an ambitious, passionate leader in Mary Ann—they had an ally. And this ally had a plan. "My role as principal was clear in my mind instructionally," Mary Ann says. "Using data to lead was absolutely life-changing. I got to have deep conversations with my teachers about their work. The more we perfected the analysis cycle, the more I didn't need to be the one in the classroom to make sure the reteach went well."

The teachers didn't need to buy into Mary Ann's mission in some abstract way: they got to see how much more their students learned. As mentioned in *Driven by Data*, when properly implemented, data-driven instruction does not require teacher buy-in—it creates it. With Mary Ann at the helm, teachers used the time available to them in a way that turned around the educational experience of every child at Truesdell. They didn't do it by magic: they did it by finding out what their students needed, and giving it to them unfailingly. That's the power of data-driven instruction.

Action Steps for Principals

Data-Driven Instruction

LEVER	KEY ACTIONS IN SEQUENCE
	PLAN
DATA-DRIVEN INSTRUCTION	**Assessments and Curriculum—Align the Rigor** 1. **Lock in quality interim assessments:** • ID the end-goal assessment (state test, college entrance exam, college assessment) that exemplifies what successful students should know and be able to do. • ID essential content and rigor that students must master for success on end-goal assessment. • Acquire or develop effective interim assessments (IAs) that are aligned to end-goal assessments. • Develop a common IA calendar that identifies when IAs will take place, who and what will be assessed, and when IA data analysis meetings will take place. 2. **Lock in high-quality lesson plans and curriculum materials that align to the assessments:** • See "Action Steps for Principals: Planning" for details. **Data Meetings—Tools and Structures for Weekly Data/IA Meetings** 3. **Establish essential data meeting structures that result in evidence-based action planning:** • Create meeting schedule to conduct data meetings to analyze IA data (every 6 weeks) and to conduct weekly data meetings (WDMs). • Establish consistent protocols and prework expectations for effective analysis meetings (e.g., IA analysis meeting protocol, WDM analysis protocol). • Develop a system to regularly collect high, medium, and low samples of student work (e.g., Exit Tickets, spiral review) to use as evidence to ID trends in student learning. 4. **Create effective principal monitoring tools for all post-assessment action plans, including:**

LEVER	KEY ACTIONS IN SEQUENCE

PLAN

- Develop an action plan tracker that identifies teacher reteach goals, timeline, and focus area.
- Create systems to have access to assessments and/or DDI action plan when observing.
- Create observation schedules to observe teachers in reteaching implementation.

ROLL OUT

PD on Data-Driven Instruction (DDI)

5. **Roll out PD for data-driven instruction:**
   - Plan and roll out PD on DDI, the power of the question, and writing exemplars.
   - Develop and roll out exemplar IA analysis to set clear expectations for teacher analysis.
   - Create repeated opportunities during PD to practice analyzing student data/work and creating 6-week action plans (IAs) or targeted reteach plans (WDM).

EXECUTE

Analyze for Trends

6. **Conduct a deep analysis of the data to ID school-wide and teacher-specific trends:**
   - Find the overall trend.
     - o For IAs: ID school-wide patterns in the data: outlier teachers and students (low and high) and key standards that need focus.
     - o For WDMs: review the student work to select the highest-leverage standards or question to focus on for analysis.
   - ID the key conceptual understanding and error for a given standard or task.
     - o Determine what students should be able to do and say to demonstrate mastery of the standard or task.
     - o ID the key gap between the ideal response and student work: both the key procedural errors and conceptual misunderstandings.

(sidebar) DATA-DRIVEN INSTRUCTION

LEVER	KEY ACTIONS IN SEQUENCE
	EXECUTE

<table>
<tr><td rowspan="2" style="vertical-align: middle;">DATA-DRIVEN INSTRUCTION</td><td>

o Determine the highest-leverage action steps to take to close the gap.

Data Meetings—Lead Effective Weekly Data and IA Analysis Meetings with Teachers

7. **Prepare:**

- Narrow your focus: pick the assessment item and student work in advance that highlight key errors.

- Prepare the exemplar and write your meeting script to ensure an effective, efficient meeting.

8. **See It:**

- Start with the standard(s): unpack the key parts of the standard that align to the student error to ID the most essential conceptual understandings that students must master.

- Unpack the teacher and student exemplars (or rubrics) to ID how the work demonstrates mastery of the standard.

9. **Name It:**

- Punch it: succinctly restate the key procedural errors and conceptual misunderstandings, then have the teacher repeat them and write them down.

10. **Do It:**

- Perfect the plan before you practice.

  o Plan the structure of the reteach: modeling or guided discourse.

  o ID the steps, student materials, and students to monitor.

  o Predict the gap: anticipate likely errors in execution and practice that part of the meeting.

- Practice the gap.

  o ID the most essential elements of the reteach for the teacher to practice, especially the parts that will be hardest to master.

  o Prompt the teacher to "go live" and practice the prompts that will be used during the reteach.

</td></tr>
</table>

LEVER	KEY ACTIONS IN SEQUENCE

EXECUTE

- Build an effective follow-up plan.
  - o ID when to teach, when to reassess, and when to revisit this data.
  - o Embed the action plan into upcoming lessons and unit plans.
  - o ID when observations will take place to see the plan in action and how it will be assessed.

MONITOR AND FOLLOW UP

11. **Actively monitor implementation of action plans:**
    - Observe the reteach.
      - o Start from the exemplar teacher and observe same-subject teachers back-to-back.
      - o ID the gap between the exemplar teacher and other teachers.
      - o ID the gap between the original plan and execution and between student work and exemplar.
    - Observe weekly data meetings (WDMs) of other instructional leaders (live or via video).
      - o ID the patterns across meetings and the key areas of growth for the leader's facilitation.
    - Track implementation of 6-week action plans and student outcomes following reteach.
      - o Have teacher post lesson plans and/or 6-week action plans in the classroom to be able to observe both the plan and the execution to ID gaps.
    - Create system for teacher teams to collect student work between WDMs.

12. **Monitor student work in each class using a sequence:**
    - (A) pen-to-paper, (B) annotations/strategies, and (C) right answers

LEVER (sidebar): DATA-DRIVEN INSTRUCTION

Data-Driven Instruction and Assessment Implementation Rubric

The rubric is intended to be used to assess the present state of data-driven instruction and assessment in a school. The rubric specifically targets interim assessments and the key levers leading to increased student achievement.

4 = Exemplary implementation; 3 = Proficient implementation; 2 = Beginning implementation; 1 = No implementation

Data-Driven Culture	
1. **Highly active leadership team.** Facilitate teacher-leader data analysis meetings after each interim assessment and maintain focus on the process throughout the year.	/4
2. **Introductory professional development.** Teachers and leaders are effectively introduced to data-driven instruction—they understand how interim assessments define rigor, and experience the process of analyzing results and adapting instruction.	/4
3. **Implementation calendar.** Begin school year with a detailed calendar that includes time for assessment creation/adaptation, implementation, analysis, planning meetings, and reteaching (flexible enough to accommodate district changes/mandates).	/4
4. **Ongoing professional development.** PD calendar is aligned with data-driven instructional plan: includes modeling assessment analysis and action planning and is flexible to adapt to student learning needs.	/4
5. **Build by borrowing.** Identify and implement best practices from high-achieving teachers and schools: visit schools/classrooms, share and disseminate resources/strategies.	/4
Assessments	
1. **Common interim assessments** 4–6 times/year.	/4
2. **Transparent starting point.** Teachers see the assessments at the beginning of each cycle; assessments define the road map for teaching.	/4
3. **Aligned to state tests and college readiness.**	/4

4. **Aligned to instructional sequence** of clearly defined grade-level and content expectations.	/4
5. **Reassess** previously taught standards.	/4
Analysis	
1. **Immediate turnaround** of assessment results (ideally 48 hrs).	/4
2. **User-friendly, succinct data reports** include: item-level analysis, standards-level analysis, and bottom-line results.	/4
3. **Teacher-owned analysis** facilitated by effective leadership preparation.	/4
4. **Test-in-hand analysis** between teacher(s) and instructional leader.	/4
5. **Deep:** moves beyond *what* students got wrong and answers *why* they got it wrong.	/4
Action	
1. **Reteach.** Use guided discourse or modeling strategies to reteach difficult standards.	/4
2. **Six-week action plans.** Execute plans that include whole-class instruction, small groups, tutorials, and before- and after-school supports.	/4
3. **Ongoing assessment.** Check for understanding every day: aggressive monitoring of independent work, questioning, and in-class assessments to ensure student progress between interim assessments.	/4
4. **Follow up.** Instructional leaders review lesson and unit plans and give observation feedback driven by the action plan and student learning needs.	/4
5. **Engaged students** know the end goal, how they did, and what actions they are taking to improve.	/4
TOTAL:	**/100**

Stop Here

Take a moment and use the Data-Driven Instruction and Assessment Implementation Rubric to evaluate your school. Then follow the steps here:

If your school scored below 70 on the DDI rubric:

As mentioned in the Introduction, data-driven instruction is the super-lever without which none of the other instructional levers work effectively. **If you don't think your school is proficient on this DDI rubric (a score above 70), then this chapter should remain your primary focus for instruction. Then skip ahead to Chapter 5 to implement the other super-lever, Student Culture.** Although you can implement the other instructional levers as well, don't launch anything that will prohibit your ability to implement DDI and student culture proficiently. *Driven by Data* is a great additional resource, as it includes all the PD materials and tools you need to launch this effectively in your school.

If your school scored above 70 on the DDI rubric:

Option 1: skip to Observation and Feedback (Chapter 3) and then Student Culture (Chapter 5). After data-driven instruction and student culture, observation and feedback is the next most important lever and would be the next best to lock in place.

Option 2: read the chapters in order—Planning, Observation and Feedback, and Professional Development (Chapters 2–4) and then the Culture lever. Planning is a lever that ties completely to data-driven instruction, as it sets you up to have effective curriculum, unit, and lesson plans to teach more effectively. Observation and Feedback and Professional Development give you additional tools to make teachers better and can support your drive from good to great.[15]

Pulling the Lever

Action Planning Worksheet for DATA-DRIVEN INSTRUCTION

Self-Assessment

- Assess your school on the Data-Driven Instruction and Assessment Implementation Rubric. What is your score? ___/100

- What items on the rubric are your biggest areas for improvement?

_____

_____

_____

_____

_____

_____

Planning for Action

- What tools from this book will you use to develop data-driven instruction at your school? Check all that you will use (you can find all on the DVD):
  - ☐ Data-Driven Instruction and Assessment Implementation Rubric
  - ☐ Weekly Data Meeting one-pager
  - ☐ Assessment Results Template
  - ☐ Teacher Analysis and Action Plan Template
  - ☐ Reteaching one-pager
  - ☐ Action—Follow-Up Accountability Measures
  - ☐ Interim Assessment Calendars—elementary, middle, and high school
  - ☐ Data-Driven Instruction Monthly Map
    Note: Additional data-driven instruction PD materials can be found in *Driven by Data*.
- What are your next steps for launching data-driven instruction?

Action	Date

Chapter 2

Planning

One-on-One: Planning with a Purpose

It is midmorning at David Skeet Elementary School in Gallup, New Mexico, and the school is already abuzz with activity. Amid the classrooms, principal Wade Bell can be found seated next to a teacher looking at her plans for the upcoming unit.

"Let's look at the upcoming assessment," Wade begins. "Let's also look at next week's lesson. Which questions are assessing the content of this part of the unit? What do students need to know and be able to do to master those questions?"

Wade's teacher responds, and then Wade summarizes her key points: "So the key standard that you need to focus on in this lesson is identifying the main idea of the passage? And the key gap is identifying key lines that reveal the main idea?"

His teacher nods. "Great. Let's look at Monday's lesson. I see you've already planned the Exit Ticket. Does it align to our end assessment?" They both look at the assessment and Exit Ticket side by side, and they affirm the alignment.

"Now let's plan how we are going to teach this."

For the next twenty minutes, Wade and his teacher plan out the reading lesson, determining the best activity to propel the learning forward and the right strategic prompts when students struggle.

Planning is a leadership lever that can help in every sort of school, from the lowest performing to the highest. Let's take a look at one example of each.

In 2014, Wade Bell became the principal of David Skeet Elementary School in Gallup, New Mexico. For seven consecutive years, the school had ranked in the bottom 5th percentile of the state in student achievement (and in the bottom 1st percentile in 2014), and New Mexico had just changed to a significantly more difficult state assessment that would raise the bar even higher. The majority of students (95 percent) are Native American, with many of them living on a local Navajo reservation, and there were more than a few voices around the state which suggested that nothing better was possible. Wade, however, saw something different: he saw children with potential and a school that didn't match that. "There really weren't any structures in place for student culture or data-driven instruction. And that was just the beginning." Wade immediately locked in data-driven instruction with all the central tasks mentioned in Chapter 1 (creating interim assessments, data analysis days, reteach plans, and so on). Then he and his staff made key changes to student culture routines so that learning would have the right conditions to take root (more details on this in Chapter 5 on student culture).

In launching these changes and talking with the teachers, Wade noted that they weren't afraid of the hard work ahead. What alarmed them more was that there was no shared understanding around what made for quality instructional planning. They couldn't envision how they would ever reach the goals that were set. "There were really no lesson plans, no common planning, and they weren't being supported," remembers Wade. "That was what made them so afraid of the turnaround process."

So Wade took data-driven instruction and combined it with a focus on planning—unit planning and lesson planning. He made this a team effort, with groups of leaders and teachers developing plans that they adjusted in response to student needs over the course of the year.

The results? "While our district went down as a result of the higher bar set by the new state assessment, our school's achievement went up immediately," says Wade. "We went from being eighteenth or nineteenth in the district to competing with top schools." By the end of the year, they had jumped nearly two hundred places and 35 percentile points in their statewide ranking. In effect, they went from completely failing to nearly making honor roll in a single year (see Figure 2.1). And they didn't just do it for one year—they maintained those results for multiple years.

Planning doesn't just help schools up from the bottom; it also helps them soar to new heights. Take a look at the AP results from Mike Mann's North Star Washington Park

Figure 2.1 New Mexico PARCC Assessment: David Skeet Elementary School, Percentage at or Above Proficiency

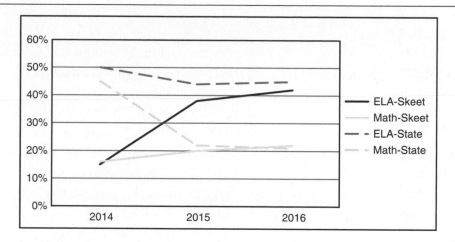

High School (Figure 2.2), which went from a pass rate of below 11 percent to one of more than 80 percent over the course of five years, results that continue to this day.

What was it about Wade's and Mike's approach to instructional planning that helped them make data-driven instruction a game-changer at David Skeet and North Star HS? They ensured that teachers teach the right material in the most effective way possible in the first place.

Data-driven instruction is about plotting the route to rigor, and effective lesson planning is about trying to get there on your first try.

Figure 2.2 Advanced Placement Results: North Star Washington Park High School, Percentage of AP Students with Scores of 3 or Higher

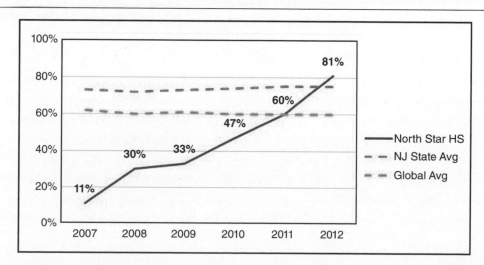

> ## Core Idea
> Data-driven instruction is about plotting the route to rigor.
> Planning is about getting there on the first try.

This chapter will show you how to leverage effective planning in the following ways:

- **Unit planning:** craft data-driven unit plans that are aligned to the level of rigor you wish your students to reach

- **Lesson planning:** build effective day-to-day lesson plans that will drive student learning

- **Coaching planning:** guide your teachers to master the skills that will make them outstanding lesson planners in their own right

- **Monitoring planning:** observe lessons in action to find out which parts of your plans are working—and which aren't

UNIT PLANNING

At its most basic level, planning is a natural extension of data-driven instruction: teach students what they need, not what they already know. Going deeper, planning is about linking together all of a student's learning to make it rigorous, memorable, and meaningful. What makes that so important? One 2016 study found that giving high-quality plans to weaker teachers had as high an impact as moving their students to the classroom of a teacher in the 80th percentile.[1] In other words, planning is an underutilized lever for driving higher achievement.

Let's unpack how to make planning more powerful. The key is to begin with assessment.

Plan Backwards from Assessment

It is impossible to talk about effective planning without starting from assessment. If standards are meaningless until we define how to assess them (a core idea from Chapter 1), then assessments are the starting point for instructional planning.

Too often, however, curriculum planning does not heed this guidance. In fact, many educational structures are set up directly in conflict with this premise: in many states and districts, curriculum planners often work totally separately from assessment writers. This is the top pitfall of planning, and it can limit the effectiveness of a curriculum plan. Without clarity on the rigor of the assessment, every teacher interprets the curriculum to different levels of rigor, creating vast disparities in children's experience with the content.

This resonates with Wade. "When I was preparing to be a teacher, I was never taught to think this way. And later as new principals we were told to look at data, but we didn't really know what to do with it. But as soon as I understood the connection between assessment and planning, everything clicked. Build your assessment with the standard in hand, then plan what you need to teach to get there. It finally made sense."

This is why Wade always has his teachers start from the assessments: they are the sunlight that can break through the clouds of imperfect curriculum.

Core Idea

Lock in your assessments first:
they are the sunlight that can break through the clouds of imperfect curriculum.

Stop and Jot

What are the key gaps right now in the alignment between your own school's curriculum and your assessments? What actions can you take to close those gaps?

_____

_____

_____

_____

_____

_____

_____

_____

Once you have locked in your assessments, you can then plan out all the teaching needed to prepare students to master them.

Teach Both Content and Skill

For decades, educators have debated about what is more important for students: knowledge or skill. On one side, you have E. D. Hirsch and the idea of "core knowledge" that is fundamental to advancing your understanding.[2] This has been furthered by the work of researchers such as Marilyn Jager Adams, who proved that on tests like the SAT, text complexity matters more in students' reading comprehension results than what skills the students are asked to use on those texts. (Thus, equipping students with the knowledge to understand increasingly more complex texts is more important than working on a skill such as inference.)[3] On the other side, you have those who champion critical thinking and the skills needed to solve the complex problems in our society, such as Diane Halpern and Robert Ennis.[4] As a real-world example, doctors can memorize thousands of details about every type of illness or disease, but if they cannot pull all of that together when treating an actual patient in front of them to achieve a proper diagnosis, they will not be an effective doctor. So what are we to do?

School leaders like Wade have figured out, as is often the case in education, that the truth is in the combination: you need both content *and* skill to achieve mastery.

Core Idea

You need both content and skill to reach mastery:
analysis without knowledge is not only superficial but also inaccurate.

Although this idea seems simple on the surface, how to implement it varies depending on the content you are teaching. In observing and learning from college professors and the most effective K–12 educators across the country, we've come up with a simple table (see the box "Both Content and Skill") to describe the key differences in the needs of some of the core content areas. As you read this table, think about how your school does in the implementation of both of these areas.

Both Content and Skill

Key Needs in Core Subjects

Subject	Keys to Content	Keys to Skill/Analysis
Math	**Mathematical fluency:** build proficiency at	**Application:** solve complex word problems

Subject	Keys to Content	Keys to Skill/Analysis
	solving efficiently in order to free up mental space for application (e.g., addition, multiplication tables, isolating variables in linear equations)	that integrate various standards into one problem, as would happen in both abstract math and the real world (e.g., find the value of x for a rectangle that has an area of 6 square feet with sides of length $2x - 1$ and x)
English	**Background knowledge/schema:** create and utilize background knowledge and vocabulary to be able to access increasingly complex texts	**Reading for meaning and analysis:** learn key reading and writing skills to be able to unpack meaning of any text and analyze it critically
Science	**Terms = concept:** understand and properly use scientific terms with precision; their use represents understanding	**Generating and applying own understanding:** use scientific method and knowledge of terms to generate additional understanding and analyze new scenarios
History	**Context of yesterday, not today:** internalize key knowledge of each historical era of study: key dates, events, trends, movements, and so on	**Historical thinking:** apply the knowledge of yesterday to evaluate and analyze historical sources
Foreign Language	**Vocabulary and grammar:** learn key vocabulary words and grammar and conjugation structures	**Interpretive/communicative:** understand the spoken and written word and communicate in speech and writing

Think about the power of this material to help educators on both sides of the spectrum. For example, a math teacher might be excellent in implementing inquiry-based lessons that focus on conceptual understanding of the math, but she might not give her students enough independent practice to nail down mathematical fluency. For future math, that fluency will be essential; without it, students won't have the mental space to learn the new concept. Or think of your history teacher. He might be excellent at more traditional instruction of history and get his students to internalize large amounts of key knowledge from a particular era. Yet those students might not be able to analyze Abraham Lincoln's Gettysburg Address if they don't practice historical thinking skills to unpack the deeper meaning.

In general, your unit has to match the needs of your subject, or it won't meet the needs of your students.

Core Idea

Your unit has to match the needs of your subject,
or it won't meet the needs of your students.

Stop and Jot

When you think of all the core subjects and teachers in your school, where do you have a lack of balance between content and skills?

_____

_____

_____

_____

_____

_____

_____

_____

Make It Memorable—and Meaningful

How many times has someone taught you something, and a few months later you cannot remember how to do it? How often have you attended a presentation and no matter how entertaining it was, a few weeks later you couldn't recall much of what you learned?

This is our experience generally, because our brain struggles to retain isolated pieces of information. If it happens to us as adults, it is easy to imagine that the same thing happens to children. Multiply this phenomenon by children's often having to learn five or six different subjects on a given day from different teachers—no wonder why retention is so difficult!

So what do Wade and educators like him do about this? Make curriculum memorable—and meaningful.

Grant Wiggins and Jay McTighe have been at the forefront of this effort with their work on "understanding by design" (also the title of their book).[5] Two of the key components of their approach tackle head on the problem of being memorable and meaningful: enduring understandings (key understanding students will have at the end of a unit) and essential questions (key relevant questions that students will answer). Enduring understandings and essential questions can make learning memorable in multiple ways:

Give students the "why": enable students to understand why they are learning this material and how it helps them understand the world

Make the experience sticky: increase students' motivation for learning by using essential questions that pique their interest

Make the learning sticky: increase retention by consolidating all the learning into overarching enduring understandings that make it easier to hold on to discrete skills and pieces of information

The last point—making learning sticky—warrants greater emphasis. According to top neuroscientists in the field of information retention, we cannot remember what we learn unless we can link it to other knowledge we remember.[6] This is easier to do in math—where subsequent lessons regularly require use of the learning that occurred previously (you cannot solve a linear equation if you don't know how to add or subtract positive and negative integers)—but it becomes much more valuable in a content-rich class like history or science. You can make the learning stick by sticking the content pieces together.

> ## Core Idea
>
> Make the learning stick by sticking the pieces of content together.

A Word on . . . Rigor and Relevance

In far too many instances, educators can feel as though they have to choose between maintaining high academic expectations and making content feel inspiring and relevant to the current world of our students.

Jal Mehta and Sarah Fine have been a part of a group of researchers who have begun to focus on questions of deeper learning,[7] and when Mehta has observed high schools, he has lamented how many schools think they are pushing for deeper learning with creative hands-on projects when really they end up lowering the bar.

This leads us to having AP courses that are rich in rigor—but only for the elite—and other classes that try to engage but don't demand depth or rigor of content. The highest-achieving schools that I have observed see this as a false dichotomy: you *can* have both rigor and relevance.

Let's take a few examples. Imagine the following task in a middle school science class: writing an essay based on the prompt, "If you were part of the cell, which part would you be and why?"

This is an admirable attempt to make the content sticky, but it doesn't get at any central understandings that will enhance the student's deeper understanding. The task could be strengthened simply by looking back at the assessment and the key enduring understanding and then converting the prompt to something stronger, such as: "What if our bodies were only one cell? What would happen?"

The latter question is provocative and interesting, but it also pushes students to deepen their understanding and connect what they've learned from the unit.

Keep this in mind when teachers are designing lesson activities as performance tasks, which are intended to be real-world applications of the content. These tasks are often woefully lacking in rigor.

Imagine the following task in history: "How would you feel if you were observing the Constitutional Convention? Write a creative story describing the scene and what you were feeling when observing."

With a little bit of additional creativity, that task can be made more rigorous: "You are an anti-Federalist at the Constitutional Convention, and you are charged with writing a rebuttal to the *Federalist Papers*. Prepare a speech that you will deliver to attack the weakness in these papers and advocate for stronger state rights."

The quality of both of these first depends on the quality of the rubric/exemplar that will be used to assess it. Both could demand that the student cite multiple sources as evidence. But the second one requires the additional work of writing a strong thesis rooted in the analysis of a key historical document. Even if both have a quality rubric, that will make the second task stronger.

Remember: rigor and relevance can ride together for incredibly strong results.

To see additional examples of effective unit plans across content areas and grade levels, look no further than the DVD, where we've included several plans that exemplify these core criteria.

Put It All Together

Plan backwards from assessment. Teach both content and skill. Make it memorable. The best way to understand how is to see what a data-driven unit plan could look like.

Let's take a look at this section of a unit plan from one of Mike Mann's teachers, Art Worrell (whom you saw modeling a think-aloud designed for AP US History in Chapter 1). As you review this unit plan, take note: How does it implement the three principles listed in this section?

Sample Unit Plan
AP US History

UNIT SUMMARY

The Revolution and New Republican Culture (1754–1800)

In this unit, students will recognize the long-term and far-reaching impacts of the American Revolutionary War while at the same time recognizing its limits. Students will examine topics such as the Proclamation of 1763, the Declaration of Independence, and the ratification of the Constitution.

ENDURING UNDERSTANDINGS

Students will know that . . .

1. Enlightenment thought and the Great Awakening promoted new ideas about the relationship between individuals and external authority, specifically government.

2. Social, economic, and political conflict can change the roles of citizens and existing structures of political systems.

3. Citizens can pursue change by many means. Knowledge of the roles of citizens and government enables individuals and groups who are in conflict to create change by working within or working against systems of government. In extreme circumstances, a new political system may be formed.

4. The effects of a political revolution can vary according to gender, race, class, region and other distinguishing features.

5. For more than 200 years the political system borne of the revolution has provided many means for change. The result has been a stable, yet flexible political system.

6. Republican government, like the one established after the American Revolution, often struggles to find the right balance between protecting the liberty of the people and establishing order.

ESSENTIAL QUESTION

> To what extent did the American Revolution fundamentally change American society? In your answer be sure to address the political, social, and economic effects of the Revolution in the period from 1775 to 1800.

ASSESSMENT SUMMARY

SUMMATIVE ASSESSMENTS		
Type of Assessment	Historical Thinking Skills	Task/Prompt
Interim Assessment	All	1. 55 stimulus/document-based MC questions 2. Document-based question essay 3. Three short answer questions
Document-Based Questions	All	1. Zinn's "Tyranny Is Tyranny" vs. traditional textbook 2. To what extent was 1763 a turning point in American History?

		3. Stamp Act (documents from British and colonists)
		4. John Locke's Second Treatise on Government and Declaration of Independence: What is the ideological basis for the American Revolution?
		5. Shay's Rebellion
		6. Preamble of the Constitution
		7. Federalist Papers
		8. Documents on Republican Motherhood and Early Abolition
		9. Virginia and Kentucky Resolutions, Alien and Sedition Acts
Essay and Guided Seminar	All	To what extent did the American Revolution fundamentally change American society? Just how revolutionary was the American Revolution? In your answer be sure to address the political, social, and economic effects of the Revolution in the period from 1775 to 1800.

STANDARDS

	Standard
3.1.I	The competition among the British, French, and American Indians for economic and political advantage in North America culminated in the Seven Years' War (the French and Indian War), in which Britain defeated France and allied American Indians.
3.1.II	The desire of many colonists to assert ideals of self-government in the face of renewed British imperial efforts led to a colonial independence movement and war with Britain.
3.2.I	The ideals that inspired the revolutionary cause reflected new beliefs about politics, religion, and society that had been developing over the course of the 18th century.

3.2.II	After declaring independence, American political leaders created new constitutions and declarations of rights that articulated the role of the state and federal governments while protecting individual liberties and limiting both centralized power and excessive popular influence.
3.2.III	New forms of national culture and political institutions developed in the United States alongside continued regional variations and differences over economic, political, social, and foreign policy issues.
3.3.I	In the decades after American independence, interactions among different groups resulted in competition for resources, shifting alliances, and cultural blending.
3.3.II	The continued presence of European powers in North America challenged the United States to find ways to safeguard its borders, maintain neutral trading rights, and promote its economic interests.

KNOWLEDGE AND SKILLS

KNOWLEDGE: Students will know . . .

Key Concept 3.1: British attempts to assert tighter control over its North American colonies and the colonial resolve to pursue self-government led to a colonial independence movement and the Revolutionary War.

Key Concept 3.2: The American Revolution's democratic and republican ideals inspired new experiments with different forms of government.

Key Concept 3.3: Migration within North America and competition over resources, boundaries, and trade intensified conflicts among peoples and nations.

SKILLS: Students will be able to . . .

Argumentation

E1—Articulate a defensible claim about the past in the form of a clear and compelling thesis that evaluates the relative importance of multiple factors and recognizes disparate, diverse, or contradictory evidence or perspectives.

E2—Develop and support a historical argument through a close analysis of relevant and diverse historical evidence, framing the argument and evidence around the application of a specific historical thinking skill (*e.g., comparison, causation, patterns of continuity and change over time, or periodization*).

Analyzing Evidence: Content and Sourcing

A1—Explain the relevance of the author's point of view, author's purpose, audience, format or medium, and/or historical context as well as the interaction among these features, to demonstrate understanding of the significance of a primary source.

A2—Evaluate the usefulness, reliability, and/or limitations of a primary source in answering particular historical questions.

Interpretation

B1—Analyze a historian's argument, explain how the argument has been supported through the analysis of relevant historical evidence, and evaluate the argument's effectiveness.

B2—Analyze diverse historical interpretations.

Comparison

C1—Compare diverse perspectives represented in primary and secondary sources in order to draw conclusions about one or more historical events.

C2—Compare different historical individuals, events, developments, and/or processes, analyzing both similarities and differences in order to draw historically valid conclusions. Comparisons can be made across different time periods, across different geographical locations, and between different historical events or developments within the same time period and/or geographical location.

Causation

D1—Explain long and/or short-term causes and/or effects of an historical event, development, or process.

Periodization

D5—Explain ways historical events and processes can be organized into discrete, different, and definable historical periods.

D6—Evaluate whether a particular event or date could or could not be a turning point between different, definable historical periods, when considered in terms of particular historical evidence.

Misconceptions

- The colonists were "right" in the sense that the British taxes were oppressive and unjust.

- Americans of all stripes took up arms out of patriotism.

Clarifications

- The tensions leading to the American Revolutionary War were far more complex. The divisions grew during the period of salutary neglect and were further solidified during the French and Indian War. The colonists' constant push for more land, which inevitably led to increased conflicts with Native Americans, forced the British government to exert tighter control over its colonies. This, in addition to the debt from the French and Indian War, the influence of Enlightenment thought, and the shared cultural experience of the Great Awakening ultimately led to the Revolution.

- As the war raged on, colonial governments had to resort to promises of land and ultimately conscription in order to continue the fight. Initially hesitant, New England states began to enlist African Americans, which was once prohibited. After 1777, the average Continental soldier was young, single, property-less, and poor. In some states, such as Pennsylvania, up to one in four soldiers was an impoverished recent immigrant. Patriotism aside, cash and land bounties offered an unprecedented chance for economic mobility for these men.

UNIT KEY VOCABULARY	
Enlightenment regulators	Battle of Saratoga
Sugar Act of 1765	Articles of Confederation
Stamp Act of 1765	Northwest Ordinance of 1787
Virtual representation	Shay's Rebellion
Quartering Act of 1765	Virginia Plan
Stamp Act Congress	New Jersey Plan
Sons of Liberty	Federalists
English Common Law	Antifederalists
Natural Rights	Federalist No. 10
Declaratory Act of 1766	Judiciary Act of 1789
Townshend Act of 1767	Bill of Rights
Nonimportation Movement	Proclamation of Neutrality
Committees of Correspondence	French Revolution
Tea Act of May 1773	Whiskey Rebellion
Coercive Acts (intolerable Acts)	Jay's Treaty
Continental Congress	XYZ Affair
Second Continental Congress	Naturalization, Alien and sedition Acts
Declaration of Independence	Virginia and Kentucky Resolutions

What follows is a week's worth of objectives that would move toward the goals of this unit.

Sample Unit Plan, Part 2: Five Days of the Unit Plan

Objective, Skills, and Resources

Monday	Tuesday	Week of: Q1, 8/28–9/1		
		Wednesday	Thursday	Friday
Proclamation of 1763 SWBAT explain the significance of the Proclamation of 1763 Skills: analyze documents, group evidence, and write thesis Resources: Howard Zinn, *A People's History of the United States*, "Tyranny Is Tyranny"; traditional textbook description	Proclamation of 1763 SWBAT explain why the year 1763 marked a turning point in US history Skills: analyze documents, group evidence, and write thesis Resources: primary source documents on the Proclamation of 1763	Causes of the Revolutionary War SWBAT analyze and summarize the causes of the American Revolutionary War Skills: causation, argumentation Resources: primary source documents on the Sugar and Stamp Acts and the Seven Years' War	Ideological Rationale for Colonial Resistance and Revolution SWBAT identify and explain the ideological rationale for colonial resistance and revolution Skills: central idea of a text, how structure of a text contributes to the meaning Resources: excerpts from John Locke's *Second Treatise on Government* and the Declaration of Independence.	Turning Points of the Revolution SWBAT understand the major events and turning points of the American Revolutionary War including the Battle of Saratoga Skills: argumentation, causation, comparison, contextualization Resources: n/a, content lecture

Note: SWBAT = students will be able to

The content of Art's unit plan is complex; such is the nature of what our students need to be able to do to be ready for college-level history work. Yet the key to a great unit plan is not its complexity but its ability to be broken down into simpler pieces: planned from assessment, teaches both content and skill, and made memorable.

LESSON PLANNING

Speaking of breaking down the unit plan into simpler pieces: once leaders like Wade and Art have solid curriculum units in place, they can shift their focus to dividing them up into daily lesson plans. Take a look at this exemplar lesson plan for World History from one of Art Worrell's colleagues Rachel Blakc. This plan is from a unit on the Enlightenment and the revolutions it sparked. Consider how it sets up a meaningful opportunity for students to practice.

Lesson 1.6—Enlightenment and Revolution

Haitian Revolution, Part 2

Objective

SWBAT analyze the causes of the Haitian Revolution and evaluate to what extent it should be considered an "Enlightenment revolution."

Do Now

Source: Jean-Baptiste du Tertre, "The Sugar Mill," Histoire generale des Antilles habitees par les Francais, 4 vols. (Paris: T. Lolly, 1667). This depiction of a sugar plantation in Saint Domingue emphasizes the grinding mill and refining vats. An overseer with a gun supervises the slave labor. By 1789, Saint Domingue excelled at sugar production, outpacing other French and British colonies.

1. Which of the following economic conditions was important in creating the need for the system portrayed in the engraving?
   A. Rising British demand for consumable goods like sugar and tea
   B. Enlightenment ideas about self-determination
   C. Increase in government profits from taxes on trade in the Indian Ocean
   D. The rise of joint-stock companies used by European rulers to control colonies

2. Which of the following conclusions about sugar production in the Americas is most directly supported by the engraving?
   A. Europeans were unaware of the labor systems used to produce cash crops.
   B. The production of sugar represented a sign of economic strength to Europeans.
   C. Europeans protested the use of coerced labor in the Americas.
   D. Sugar production in the Americas depended significantly on coerced labor.

Should the Haitian Revolution be considered an "Enlightenment revolution"?

_____

_____

Document 1

Source: The following account, gathered from local eyewitnesses, was taken to Paris and read to the French legislature on November 30, 1793, by envoys sent to seek assistance in quelling (putting down) the revolt. The account was immediately published and entered the propaganda war over slavery. An English translation, financed by the proslavery lobby, quickly went through four editions.

> In the night of August 22/23, twelve blacks reached the Noé plantation sugar factory in Acul, seized the apprentice refiner, and dragged him in front of the big house, where he expired [died] under their blows. His shouts caused the plantation attorney to come out, and he was laid low [killed] with two musket balls. The wretches proceeded to the quarters of the head refiner and murdered him in his bed. They struck with their machetes a young man lying ill in an adjoining room and left him for dead . . .

We learn of these facts from a sixteen-year-old youth who escaped from the cannibals' fury, wounded in two places. The sword was then exchanged for the torch; the canes [sugarcane] were set alight and, shortly afterwards, the buildings. It was the prearranged signal to announce the revolt, which then spread with the speed of lightning to the neighboring plantations. Everywhere whites were slaughtered indiscriminately, men and women, children and the elderly, all fell beneath the assassin's blade.

Document 2

Source: Toussaint L'Ouverture, excerpt from "Saint-Domingue Constitution," 1801

TITLE II – Of the Inhabitants
Article 3. There cannot exist slaves on this territory, servitude is therein forever abolished. All men are born, live and die free and French.
Article 4. All men, regardless of color, are eligible to all employment.
Article 5. There shall exist no distinction other than those based on virtue and talent, and other superiority afforded by law in the exercise of public function.

Document 3

Source: Proclamation of Haiti's Independence by the general in chief, Jean Jacques Dessalines, to the Haitian people in Gonaives, on January 1, 1804

Dear Citizens,
It is not enough to have expelled from your country the barbarians who have bloodied it for two centuries . . . it is necessary, by a last act of national authority, to assure forever an empire of liberty in this country our birth place; we must take away from this inhumane government, which held for so long our spirits in the most humiliating torpor [lethargy], all hope to re-subjugate us; we must at last live independent or die . . .
Let us swear to the entire universe, to posterity, to ourselves, to renounce forever to France, and to die rather than to live under its domination. To fight until the last crotchet [musical instrument] rest for the independence of our country!

Document 4

Source: "Revenge Taken by the Black Army for Cruelties Practiced on Them by the French," an 1805 engraving by J. Barlow depicting actions taken against the French in Saint Domingue's war for independence from France; from thelouvertureproject.org

Exit Ticket 1.6

Enlightenment and Revolution: Haitian Revolution, Part 2

Directions: Evaluate the causes of the Haitian Revolution. In your response, you must include:

- A – An analytical thesis statement that directly responds to the prompt (support-modify-refute)

- A – A topic sentence that states a subargument (ONE cause)

- N – Text evidence (from today's sources) and outside evidence

- E – Analysis explains how and why evidence supports your argument

- Z – Zoom out and tie back to your larger argument and the prompt

Tie evidence back to the prompt	Use more causation cue phrases
Analyze how and why	Add more specific, relevant evidence

Many elements of an exemplar lesson plan will shift from subject to subject, grade level to grade level, and so forth. Every lesson plan, however, has a few key elements that need to be in place to make them effective. Let's unpack these.

Data-Driven Objective and Exit Ticket

Take a look back at the objective and the Exit Ticket—a final task to end class—that were designed for Rachel's lesson. What makes them effective?

As you look at this example, one conclusion comes up right away: it is really difficult to assess the quality of an objective without seeing how we'll measure it. Just as we learned was the case with standards in data-driven instruction, lesson plans are meaningless unless we define how we will assess them.

Great objectives will vary from one content area and grade level to the next, but they will always share two important traits in common:

- **Data driven: aligned to the Exit Ticket and to the end-goal assessment.** Art makes sure that all the lesson objectives are aligned to what students need to be able to do at the end of the year, and to the Exit Ticket, which will describe what students should be able to do after that lesson. If these three components are aligned—objective, Exit Ticket, and end-goal assessment—learning accelerates.

- **Feasible.** A great objective must be accomplishable in one lesson. It's more efficient to go granular and meet objectives in bite-size pieces than to bite off more than students can chew.

Wade's experience at the elementary school level was identical to these high school examples. "Whenever I met with my teacher to plan a lesson, we always started by writing the assessment. At first that was time consuming, but as the weeks went by, it became easier and easier." If we start from assessment, we can clarify our objective and what we have to teach during the rest of the lesson to get there.

Adequate Time for Independent Practice

The best assessment in the world means little if students don't get the chance to practice the skills it tests. Too often, we hope that homework alone will suffice. But that leaves teachers little chance to identify the errors students make while learning and to help them along the way. That's why such a major component of Rachel's lesson on the Haitian Revolution is dedicated to a complex writing task. Art and his students will both learn more from the time the students spend writing their essays than from any other part of the lesson.

Want a quick rule of thumb? Make sure that at least ten minutes of every hour-long lesson is devoted to independent practice.

Modeling or Guided Discourse

The final piece of the planning addresses how to teach the new material. The heart of every lesson is how students learn something new. As we discussed in the chapter on data-driven instruction, most of that teaching can be put into one of two categories: modeling or guided discourse (see Chapter 1, Action: Teaching and Reteaching to Mastery). As a quick reminder, here are the keys to each one:

- Modeling:
  - Provide a clear listening or note-taking task.
  - Model the thinking, not just the procedure.
- Guided discourse:
  - Have students write first, talk second.
  - Use Show-Call.

- Start with a Turn and Talk, then poll the room.
- Employ strategic questioning.

What is striking for Wade is how easy this final piece becomes if you've done the first two. "If you know the Exit Ticket and the independent practice, you can anticipate where students will struggle, and then the decision of what to teach becomes clear."

Lesson Planning

Keys to an Effective Lesson Plan

1. Data-driven objective, aligned to the Exit Ticket, that is feasible for one lesson
2. Adequate time for independent practice aligned to the Exit Ticket (ideally at least ten minutes per lesson)
3. Modeling or guided discourse

Now you've had a chance to get a more intimate understanding of the unit and lesson plan forms. The next two sections of this chapter will show how leaders like Wade set up both of these structures in their schools: first through coaching around lesson planning, and then through monitoring.

COACHING FOR EFFECTIVE PLANNING

How do successful leaders like Wade coach for effective planning in their schools? Although there are many different means for that coaching—from working over the summer to planning as the year progresses, from working one-on-one with planners to working in teams—three familiar steps drive planning just as they did data-driven instruction: See It, Name It, Do It.

See It

Wade begins the process of coaching around unit planning by getting his teachers to see what he sees: a vision of what successful learning should look like.

- **See past success.** Praise the teacher specifically for past successes in curriculum planning, helping him build an understanding of what actions will make him successful.

- **See exemplar assessment.** To ground your coaching in what matters most for unit planning, start by looking with the teacher at the assessment you're both working to prepare students for during this unit. Have the teacher name the learning goals for this unit based on the assessment.

- **See exemplar curriculum unit plan.** Show the teacher what an exemplar unit plan looks like by examining one with him. Zero in on a part of the plan that relates to where the teacher is struggling to craft his own, and have him identify the characteristics that make it powerful.

- **See the gaps.** Work with the teacher to identify the gap that makes the unit plan he has drafted limited compared to the exemplar.

Name It

The next step is simple: have the teacher name the key to planning this unit effectively. "The teacher needs to know what will make this plan effective just as clearly as I do," says Wade. "Otherwise, the teacher may not be able to improve the plan—and they certainly won't be able to do so independently."

Do It

In the Do It phase of coaching around lesson planning, planning and practice become one. Have the teacher continue to work on developing the plan, and give him feedback along the way. If possible, repeat with an upcoming unit plan so that the teacher gets multiple opportunities for relevant practice!

Planning Meeting
Leading Face-to-Face Meetings to Guide Lesson Planning

Prepare before the meeting	Prepare
	• **Materials ready:** teacher lesson plans, curriculum and unit plans, six-week analysis and action plan (data-driven instruction), class materials and resources, student work, and feedback from previous lessons • **Prime the pump:** familiarize self with the standards for the upcoming lessons of that teacher
Map out the week 2–6 min	**Map Out the Week**
	[Proficient planners do this on their own.] **Map out the week jointly:** • "What are the key carryover standards/activities from previous week?" • "What school events will change the weekly routine?" • "Let's fill in the 'always' tasks (where to place the common routines each week—fluency work in a Math class, labs in a Science class, etc.)." **Set the content for each day:** • "What are the key lessons we need to include based on our 6-week data analysis plan and our curriculum/unit plan?" • "What objectives require more time given student misunderstanding on the last assessment? What units can be reduced to build in that time?" • "In order for students to be able to master [the unit goals], what lessons will we need to teach?"
See It and Name It 10–15 min	**Key Lessons—See the End Goal**
	Narrow your focus to key lessons: • "What are the key lessons of this week?" OR • "Let's look closely at _____ [the most challenging/important objective of the week]."

Taken from *Leverage Leadership 2.0: A Practical Guide to Building Exceptional Schools* by Paul Bambrick-Santoyo. Reproduced by permission of John Wiley & Sons, Inc. All video clips copyright © 2018 by Uncommon Schools, Inc.

Copyright © 2018 Paul Bambrick-Santoyo.

See It and Name It 10–15 min	Key Lessons—See the End Goal
	See the end goal (assessment): • "Let's look at the upcoming interim assessment questions or final tasks that are related to this objective. What are all the things students need to be able to do to master that assessment/task?" • "Of all of those things, what is the key skill here: what do you want students to be able to do by the end of this lesson?" • "If they got this right and you asked 'how do you know?' what would you want them to say?" **Name the exemplar (Exit Ticket or final work product):** • "Let's design the Exit Ticket first: how do you want to check to see if they have mastered the objective?" "Does it match the rigor of the interim assessment?" • "What will the exemplar response look like? Let's generate it." • "If they do well on the Exit Ticket/final product, will they have mastered your original objective? If not, what changes could we make to align it further to the objective?"
Do It (Rest of the meeting)	**Design Key Lesson Activities**

	Plan the core activities:
	
	 • "Let's plan the activity/task that will most help the students generate an exemplar response/master the Exit Ticket?"
	
	 • "What pedagogy will work most effectively for this lesson?" Options include:
	
	    o Guided Discourse (you do–we do–you do)
	
	    o Modeling (I do–we do–you do)
	
	    o Other
	
	 • "What will you monitor during independent practice? What prompts will you use?"
	
	 • "Where and how will you check for understanding during the lesson?"
	
	 • "What misunderstandings are likely to occur for the students?"
	
	    o "What adjustments can you make to the activities to help minimize the misunderstanding?"

Do It (Rest of the meeting)	Design Key Lesson Activities
	o "What scaffolded questions could you ask in the moment of misunderstanding?" **Practice (remaining time):** • Design the actual work products (worksheets, end products, rubrics) • Role play/practice implementing the plan **Follow up (last 2 min):** • (If applicable) ID next steps for completing lesson plans • (If applicable) Set timeline for completing lesson plans • "For next meeting, please bring: [choose—Exit Slips, independent work, video, quiz, or other major assessments]."

MONITORING PLANNING

Leaders are often surprised when I tell them the process I follow when I observe a class. When I step into a classroom, the first thing I do before observing the teacher or students is look at the lesson plan itself. Why?

Imagine that you walk in during the middle of a lesson cold, without having referred to the lesson plan beforehand. The teacher you're observing is using guided practice to teach her students how to add fractions with unlike denominators. Class engagement seems high, and each time the teacher pauses in her lecturing to let her students state what she should do next, a chorus of voices delivers the correct response. When the teacher gives her students a problem to solve on their own, you circulate throughout the room and see that most students who achieve at an average level or above are able to solve the problem successfully. After going over the problem, the teacher gives the students an Exit Ticket that offers them another opportunity to practice this same skill, and the class comes to a close.

On the surface of it, this seems like a successful lesson. The same could be true if you were to walk in on an animated class discussion analyzing a Shakespearean sonnet. Imagine that students are driving the conversation with thoughtful insights into the meaning and symbolism of various parts of the poem, and the teacher simply interjects with key questions along the way. It would seem like a masterful class!

In both cases, the instruction might be successful—but it might not. In order to see if the teaching craft worked, we have to step back and make sure: Are the students learning what they need? And how well can each student do that work independently?

Before I assess the second question, I always start with the first. I pull out the lesson plan for the day and review it for the following:

- What is the objective of this lesson? How will the end-goal assessment measure that objective?
- Does the Exit Ticket match the rigor of the end-goal assessment?
- Does the independent practice give students time to practice what they need?
- Does the modeling or guided discourse set up the students to be successful in their practice?

If I answer no to any of these questions, then the first problem lies in the lesson plan itself, not the execution. If I simply start observing the instruction, I might miss these critical factors. Then my observation will be about the teacher's craft but not about student learning.

This is not to say that what the teacher does in front of the students doesn't matter; it matters greatly. But it's irrelevant that the teacher is delivering instruction beautifully if that instruction doesn't align to the rigor that students need to succeed. If the lesson plan doesn't set the bar for rigor high enough, everything else that happens during the lesson is beside the point.[8]

Core Idea

Monitor the content of lessons before the craft of teaching.
If the content doesn't match the rigor of what students need,
the craft won't be enough to get them there.

To avoid that outcome, you'll need to recognize and name exactly what parts of a sequence of lessons need to be developed—or redeveloped—in order for that sequence of plans to succeed. The key lever for this is observation and feedback—more on these in the very next chapter. Leaders like Wade don't leave effective plans wallowing on the shelf; instead, they monitor to make sure they are being used and working well. Skipping the monitoring step of planning is like writing a recipe but never actually testing it to see how the food tastes!

The "Monitoring Planning" box shows how to zero in on the precise actions that will be necessary to make any series of lessons succeed.

Monitoring Planning

A Guide to Reviewing Lessons

Action	If Not . . .
1. **Look at the objective and the end-goal assessment:** Does the objective align to the rigor of the state or AP exam?	• Devise an assessment to test learning of this objective that would set the bar for rigor appropriately high (see Chapter 1). • With assessment in hand, move on to step 2.
2. **Look at the Exit Ticket:** Does it meet the bar for rigor set by the assessment for that objective?	• Revise the Exit Ticket, then continue to step 3.
3. **Look at the whole week's strand of lessons:** Do the other lessons in the sequence meet the bar for rigor?	• Complete this process for the whole week's strand of lessons.
4. **Look at the independent practice:** Does it prepare students to succeed on the Exit Ticket, and is there sufficient time?	• Revise the independent practice and/or the timing of it, and then continue to step 5.
5. **Finally, look at the strategies the teacher plans to use to teach the material:** Is the teaching strategy conducive to the students learning what they need to succeed on the independent practice?	• Revise the lesson accordingly.
6. **Now you can observe the teaching!**	• See Chapter 3, Observation and Feedback, for more guidance.

Getting to yes for each of these criteria is the most crucial way to support teachers in lesson planning.

TURNAROUND—WHAT TO DO FIRST

In a school in which teachers are not engaged in this depth of curriculum and lesson planning, leaders need to decide where to begin. The context of your school will dictate your choice.

For Schools Without Curriculum Planning Autonomy

The most common context for public schools is that you have a district curricular pacing guide that you must follow, but it doesn't actually address the depth of each lesson plan or the quality of the learning objectives. If this is your context, making sure the data-driven instruction model (Chapter 1) is in place is **always** the most effective step to accompany a pacing guide. Then your core focus is to find ways to give teachers feedback on how to set data-driven objectives and to align activities to those objectives. This is most easily accomplished during the weekly check-ins with teachers (more on that in Chapter 8!). Follow the guide to leading these meetings (embedded in this chapter), and you'll start to see the results. When leaders can carefully work with teachers on their plans, they will more consistently identify potential pitfalls and increase the quantity of effective teaching.

For Schools with Curriculum Planning Autonomy

Having curriculum planning autonomy gives leaders more options: plan their own (Wade's actions) or borrow from others. Wade decided to take it on himself, which involved a substantial amount of time before the school year began and during it. To ease the workload, the grade-level teams distributed the planning load: one third-grade teacher planned the math lessons for everyone, another the reading, and so on. They also made planning a natural extension of weekly data meetings and thus a core part of their regular team meetings—adding no additional time to the weekly schedule.

For other leaders, it might feel daunting to take this on in Year 1 of turnaround. In this case, it is best to see if you can acquire quality curriculum plans from another school and devote your efforts to supporting teachers in the daily lesson planning. If this is not possible, schools have also decided to simply map out the assessments and work products for each unit at the beginning of the year—creating a skeletal curriculum plan—and then dive into the weekly planning in subsequent years.

CONCLUSION

When Wade began the process of turning around David Skeet, he heard many naysayers: "I don't see a school that does 'good' with a population like this." He even heard it from the parents and students: many of them didn't think that high school graduation, let alone college, was a possibility in their future. Fast-forward to today: "You can walk around the school, and our kids will share with you that they're excited to go to high school and college," comments Wade. "Their conversations have changed now, because they have ideas."

Change didn't come from inspirational conversations: it came from changing the structures of instruction to accelerate learning. The power of data-driven planning is that it doesn't give just one teacher the tools to be successful. It builds a community that walks the most efficient possible path to success together. "You can build this yourself," advises Wade. "Our kids are waiting for it."

Action Steps for Principals

Planning

LEVER	KEY ACTIONS IN SEQUENCE
	PLAN

PLANNING	**Curriculum—Unit Plans Aligned to Assessment**
	
	1. **Design high-quality unit plans that align to the end-goal assessments:**
	    • Define success: ID exemplar unit plans and name the essential components—they are aligned to a college-ready end-goal assessment (see the Chapter 1, Data-Driven Instruction), teach both content and skill, and are memorable.
	    • Acquire or design unit plans that include all essential components.
	
	Lesson Plans
	
	2. **Plan effective lesson plans:**
	    • Define success: ID exemplar lesson plans and name the essential components—data-driven objective, aligned Exit Ticket, adequate time for practice, and effective guided discourse or modeling.

LEVER	KEY ACTIONS IN SEQUENCE
	PLAN
PLANNING	• Acquire or design lesson plans that include all essential components.
	Planning Tools and Structures
	3. **Establish essential unit and lesson planning structures that result in consistent lesson plan creation:**
	• Establish essential curriculum planning structures and templates for yearlong plans, unit plans, and weekly and daily lesson plans.
	• Establish effective protocols for creation of unit and lesson plans (when plans will be submitted, who will review them, etc.).
	EXECUTE
	Planning Meetings—Lead Effective Planning Meetings with Teachers
	4. **Prepare:**
	• Narrow your focus: pick the lesson or unit that requires the most focus.
	• Familiarize yourself with the standards, prepare the exemplar, and write your meeting script to ensure an effective meeting.
	5. **Map out the week:**
	• Set the core content for the week: key reteach standards to spiral, routine tasks (e.g., fluency work, labs, etc.).
	• Set the objectives for each day.
	6. **See It:**
	• Start with the assessment and standard(s): fully unpack the standard to ID the most essential conceptual understandings that students must master.
	• Write the teacher exemplars and rubric to name what work demonstrates mastery of the standard.
	7. **Name It:**
	• Punch it: succinctly state the key areas the teacher will work on mastering in this planning session.

LEVER	KEY ACTIONS IN SEQUENCE
	EXECUTE

	8. **Do It:**
	• Perfect the plan.
	  ○ Plan the overall structure of the unit or week.
	  ○ Plan the key lessons and student assessments or activities.
	  ○ Predict the gap: anticipate likely errors in execution and plan for those errors.
	  ○ ID when observations will take place to see the plans in action and to assess their success.

PLANNING	**MONITOR AND FOLLOW UP**

	Observe for Trends
	9. **Observe teaching to ID school-wide and teacher-specific trends:**
	• Create and use a rubric and set a schedule for review of lesson plan execution—embed as a part of your observation schedule (see Chapter 3, Observation and Feedback).
	• When observing, evaluate the quality and alignment of the key components of the plan.
	  ○ Objective aligned to the end-goal/interim assessment
	  ○ Exit Ticket aligned to the end-goal/interim assessment
	  ○ Sequence: lesson fits in a logical sequence of lessons that is building to student mastery
	  ○ Independent practice: adequate time for students to practice the new content and/or skill
	  ○ Modeling or guided discourse: effective instruction aligned to student learning needs
	• ID the pattern of error across a set of lesson plans, homework, or class materials to create a grade/school-wide goal/action step for improving rigor.

LEVER	KEY ACTIONS IN SEQUENCE
	MONITOR AND FOLLOW UP

Follow Up

10. **Follow up to achieve 90% implementation:**

- Conduct audits of lesson/unit plans and build plan for improvement.

- ID individual teachers who have not mastered or are not building effective lesson plans.

- Plan additional follow-up (modeling, focused planning, extra support).

PLANNING

Pulling the Lever

Action Planning Worksheet for PLANNING

Self-Assessment

- How frequently are your teachers getting feedback about their lesson and curriculum plans? _____/year or _____/month

- What percentage of your teachers' lesson and curriculum plans are well aligned with interim assessment data?_____%

- What percentage of the activities students do in class would you say are well aligned with lesson objectives and classroom assessments? _____%

- Review the "Action Steps for Principals" box. What are the top three action steps you could implement immediately to improve planning at your school?

_____

_____

_____

_____

_____

Planning for Action

- What tools from this book will you use to improve planning at your school? Check all that you will use (you can find all on the DVD):

  ☐ Planning Meeting one-pager

  ☐ Instructional Leadership Rubric

  ☐ Sample curriculum and lesson plans for elementary, middle, and high schools

- What are your next steps for improving lesson and curriculum planning?

Action	Date

Chapter 3

Observation and Feedback

One-on-One: Thirty Minutes That Move the Needle

It's early in the afternoon at Uncommon Collegiate High School (UCC), and the building pulses with the energy of hundreds of students. The sounds of learning emanate from each classroom—even from the one that is empty save for two adults.

Principal Ashley Anderson Martin is in the midst of her feedback meeting with her math teacher Ijeoma. Ijeoma is standing at the front of the room, and there are independent practice worksheets on every desk. She is about to practice the strategy she and Ashley have just gone over to improve Ijeoma's monitoring of independent practice.

"Okay, so talk me through it," Ashley says. "What are you looking for?"

"I'm doing four laps [walking around the classroom]," Ijeoma replies. "And during the first lap, I'm going to focus on them completing the square of trinomials."

"And how do students know that?" Ashley asks.

"I'm going to circle it if it's incorrect, highlight where they should be looking, and check if they should move on," says Ijeoma.

"And how are you collecting data?"

"With check marks on my exemplar," Ijeoma responds, confidently tapping the clipboard she's holding.

Ashley nods. "You ready?"

"Yeah," Ijeoma says, grinning. Ashley starts a timer, and Ijeoma dives into her teacher role. She uses the exact language she will use with her students to announce what she'll be looking for in their work, and then follows the same pathway she will during class to review their responses as they unfold. After a few attempts, she nails it.

"Perfect," affirms Ashley. "How did that feel?"

"Good," says Ijeoma. "I liked it a lot. I now know exactly where I'm looking. That was good!" Ashley beams, and the two sit down for a final debrief before their meeting draws to a close.

 WATCH Clip 15: Anderson—Do It (Practice)—Feedback Meeting

Of all the ways we can assess learning among high school students, Advanced Placement and International Baccalaureate exams may reflect the highest level of rigor. They are far more challenging than state exams because they're explicitly designed not only to prepare students for college but actually deliver that experience of rigor to them before they get there.

Ashley Anderson Martin knows the value of AP performance for opening the doors of college to her students. "Most of my students don't have parents who attended college, so they have no sense of what awaits them." Yet College Board research shows that students who take AP exams are more likely to graduate college on time, and the gains are largest for low-income students and students of color. This is a big reason why she has created an "AP for All" culture where all UCC students take at least two AP exams before they graduate, and most take many more. That's also why it was such a triumph for Ashley when 75 percent the Class of 2018 at UCC passed at least one AP exam. In doing so, they did far more than simply close the achievement gap: they doubled the performance of every state in the country and tripled the performance of 80 percent of them, as shown in Figure 3.1.

The outstanding results didn't stop there for Ashley: in spring 2017, every one of her seniors not only graduated from high school but also was accepted into a four-year college. The opportunity-rich future Ashley had set out to build for her students had already arrived.

To get results like these, Ashley could not simply hire strong teachers for the AP classes: she had to make sure every instructor at UCC was teaching students at a college-ready level. That's where observation and feedback comes in, as we saw in the opening vignette with Ijeoma.

Figure 3.1 Advanced Placement Performance Index, Percentage of All Students Who Pass an Exam: Uncommon Collegiate High School (UCC)

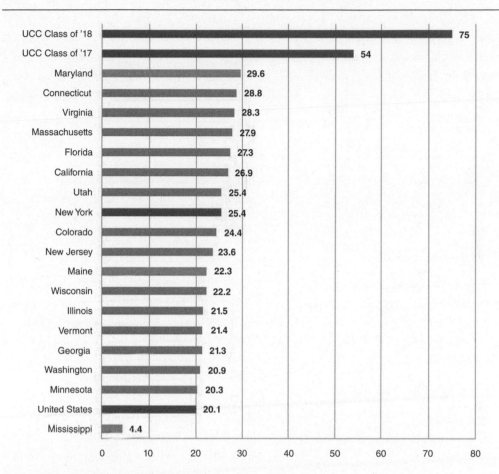

What made that feedback so powerful? The teacher didn't just hear sound advice: she practiced exactly what she needed to get better. Put another way, Ashley didn't use her observation to evaluate Ijeoma—she used it to develop her in the most effective way possible. By delivering coaching instead of evaluation, she made Ijeoma better at teaching, faster.[1]

Core Idea

The real purpose of observation and feedback is not to evaluate teachers but to develop them.

Walk the halls of the best schools in the world, and an indisputable pattern emerges: the difference between a good school and a great school is not seen in the strongest teachers; there are strong teachers in nearly every school. Instead, the gap can be found in the difference between the strongest teacher and the weakest one. If your strongest teacher is an island, then the rest are as well, stranded from the resources that could make them better. But if teachers across the campus learn and replicate what's working in the strongest teachers' classrooms, you've built bridges between those islands—and everyone's students will thrive.

Core Idea

If your strongest teacher is an island, the rest will be stranded as well. Coach every teacher, and you've built bridges between those islands— and then all students will thrive.

One of the most crucial questions any school leader faces, then, is: How can I close the gap that sets my best teachers apart from the crowd?

This chapter shows you how to bridge that gap in the same way Ashley did. We'll break the process down into these four key adjustments to the way you observe and coach:

- Observe more frequently and consistently.
- Identify the right action step for each teacher.
- Give teachers effective feedback.
- Monitor and follow up.

Keys to Observation and Feedback

- **Observe frequently and consistently.** Lock in frequent and regular observations.
- **Identify the key action step.** Identify the top areas for growth.
- **Give effective feedback.** Give direct face-to-face feedback that practices specific action steps for improvement.
- **Monitor and follow up.** Develop systems to monitor teacher development, and follow up accordingly.

OBSERVE MORE FREQUENTLY

Imagine you have a new passion—anything from weightlifting to playing bass guitar to dancing—and you are training every day to compete in a national competition. You are looking for the best coach to help you get better. Imagine that one of the coaches you find tells you, "I'll come watch you once or twice this year and then I'll send you written feedback." Unless you have no alternative, you would say no immediately.

If we would reject such periodic coaching for our passions, why do we accept intermittent coaching as the norm when it comes to teaching? Coaching is no less essential in teaching than in any other profession. As Robert J. Marzano, Tony Frontier, and David Livingston showed in their seminal text *Effective Supervision,* "Teachers need input from sources other than themselves."[2] Yet according to their survey of the largest K–12 systems in the United States, the median new teacher is observed only twice a year, with the median veteran teacher being observed only once every two years.[3] And although more frequent observation is on the rise in some circles, many of the most progressive educational initiatives in the country still require or recommend only two or three observations per teacher per year.[4]

Seeing a teacher once or twice a year simply isn't conducive to delivering coaching instead of evaluation. Just as a soccer coach would never coach a player by watching a few minutes of just two games out of the season, a coach of teachers needs a gaze that's sustained, not sporadic.

That's why leaders like Ashley adhere to a core commitment: fifteen-minute observations combined with fifteen- to thirty-minute feedback meetings—in the same week. Even if she accomplishes this only every other week, do the math: Ashley's teachers are getting as much feedback in one year as most do in *twenty.*

Core Idea

By receiving biweekly observations and feedback,
a teacher gets as much development in one year as most receive in twenty.

Getting to this frequency of observation is the first key to bridging the gap between your strongest teachers and your struggling ones. After all, you can't build a bridge to an island you can't see. (Even with this frequency, we acknowledge that these regular observations may still only allow you to see 1 percent of instruction compared to the 80 percent that data reveals, as Chapter 1 highlighted. Yet those observations can make the difference between illuminating the gaps in teachers' craft or leaving it all but entirely barred from view.)

The first question, then, is: How can a leader make the time to observe teachers weekly or biweekly? Part of the key, to be certain, is reallocating your time so that you spend less of it on work that doesn't impact student learning as meaningfully—something we'll show how to do in more detail in Chapter 8, Finding the Time. But you can also make regular observation and feedback more feasible simply by optimizing the efficiency of your observations. Two strategies for doing so are worth addressing here: sharing the work among multiple qualified leaders, and scheduling observations strategically.

Share the Work: Distribute Across Your Leadership Team

If you're thinking there's no way a single leader can possibly observe every teacher in a school every week, you're right (unless that school is extremely small). What a single leader *can* do, however, is observe up to twelve teachers per week, or twenty-four teachers every other week. And fortunately for students across the nation, most schools have a teacher-to-leader ratio that makes it possible to instate weekly or biweekly observations when you split them up among multiple leaders.

As a result of giving workshops all over the United States, we've found that about 90 percent of schools have a teacher-to-leader ratio of 24:1 or less, and an increasingly large number are getting to 12:1 ratios. We've also seen again and again that 12:1 is the golden ratio to make weekly observations sustainable.

Want to see if that would work at your school? Let's do the math.

Weekly Observation Feasibility Worksheet

Complete the following steps to determine whether you can feasibly observe **every teacher every week at your school.**

1. Add up all of the teachers at your school: _____ teachers

2. Add up all of the leaders at your school, including any assistant principals, coaches, deans, etc.: _____ leaders

3. Divide the number of teachers in your school by the number of leaders: _____ : _____ ratio of teachers to leaders

Results

- **If your ratio of teachers to leaders is 12:1 or less:** Congratulations! You have the resources you need to observe every teacher in your school once a week.

- **If your ratio is 24:1 or less:** Congratulations! You have the resources to observe every teacher in your school every other week.

  If you want to improve your ratio (you are greater than 24:1 or want to get to 12:1):

- **Count again:** Are you sure you've accounted for *every* adult in your school who could fulfill a leadership position?

- **Expand your leadership bench:** Consider ways you could maximize the expertise on your campus, such as by giving some teachers part-time instructional leadership roles. For example, a full-time teacher could coach one other teacher if you reduced a few other responsibilities, such as lunchroom duties.

The last bullet is important. Get creative about the ways you delegate the work of leadership on your campus if 12:1 initially appears out of reach. Take some time to reflect on this as we move forward, and return to this page when you begin building your schedule in Chapter 8.

Schedule Strategically

Observing teachers weekly is a significant time commitment, but you can limit the amount of time it demands by scheduling observations strategically. Here are five key tips.

Lock in Feedback Meetings

Schedule your weekly feedback meeting with each teacher *before* you plan when to observe her, and you'll have a built-in accountability tool for completing your observation—because you need to observe to know what action step to deliver during the feedback meeting. "Before I locked in feedback meetings, I wasn't really developing teachers to be great at what they do," reflects Mary Ann Stinson, whom you met in Chapter 1. "I have to see what they need to make sure they don't give up." Few things are as powerful motivators as knowing a teacher will be waiting in your office expecting that you'll have feedback for her!

Conduct Shorter Visits

In contrast to the traditional hour-long block, Ashley's observations only last roughly fifteen minutes per teacher. So long as leaders are strategic about what they are looking for, this shorter length of time is sufficient for thorough and direct feedback. Indeed, significantly longer observations are often inefficient, especially when they come at the expense of observing far fewer teachers.

Observe in Blocks

"Blocking" your observations—that is, observing multiple teachers back-to-back—reduces inefficiencies in traveling between rooms and transitioning between tasks. Scheduling three or four brief observations back-to-back is a good way to gain extra time. On multiple days per week, Ashley watches three teachers back-to-back, saving a great deal of time.

Adjust Your Schedule Week to Week

However finely tuned your schedule, there will be times when you need to make adjustments to keep it sustainable. Champions of frequent observation master the art of strategic flexibility, building directly into their schedules opportunities to adjust observations as needed. Laura Garza, for example, gives her teachers a weekly deadline—Wednesdays at 8 a.m.—to let her know what they're reteaching that week so that she can ensure that she observes the most crucial portion of instruction. Alternatively, Antonio Burt rotates his observations at his school's weekly leadership team meeting to focus on the key trends (more on this in Chapter 7 on managing school leadership teams). Depending on your school's biggest priorities and growth areas, any number of approaches like these may be fruitful. The key is having a locked-in time when you will make adjustments for the week—your leadership team meeting, Sunday evening, or Wednesday at eight. If you don't, you run the risk of simply not observing.

Combine the Feedback Meeting with Other Meetings

Rather than meeting only to discuss feedback, Ashley combines observation feedback with her other levers and agenda items for the teacher. In the first half of the year, that includes a discussion of the next week's plans (discussed at length in Chapter 2 on planning), but as a teacher becomes more proficient, Ashley more frequently combines the feedback meeting with the weekly data meeting (discussed in Chapter 1 on data-driven instruction). Here is the breakdown depending on the length of your check-in:

- 10–20 min: Observation and feedback (this chapter)
- 20–40 min: Planning (Chapter 2) or weekly data (Chapter 1)

Once you've locked in your meetings, you need to decide when to observe.

Make It Happen

Your first reaction might be to think that this is not all possible in a school leader's day. Let's show how by doing the math:

- Typical teacher-to-leader load (when all leaders are counted): 12 teachers per leader
- One classroom observation per week: 15 min
- Total minutes of observation per week: 12 teachers × 15 min = 180 min = 3 hr
- One feedback/planning meeting: 30 min
- Total minutes of feedback/planning meetings: 12 teachers × 30 min = 6 hr
- Total hours devoted to teacher observation and feedback: 9 hr
- Percentage of a leader's time (assuming 7 a.m.–4 p.m. school day): 20%

Table 3.1 shows how that looks in Ashley's schedule:

Table 3.1 Making It Work: Where Observation and Feedback Fit in a Leader's Schedule

	Monday	Tuesday	Wednesday	Thursday	Friday
6:00 AM					
:30					
7:00 AM					
:30					
8:00 AM			Meet Steele		
:30			Meet Campbell		
9:00 AM	Observe Perez, Snyder, Steele				
:30					
10:00 AM					
:30					
11:00 AM					
:30					
12:00 PM	Observe Campbell, Chen, Daf				
:30		Meet Perez			Meet Scherer
1:00 PM		Meet Snyder			Meet Westbrook
:30			Meet Chen		Meet Smith
2:00 PM			Meet Daf	Observe Scherer, Westbrook, Smith	
:30					
3:00 PM					
:30					
4:00 PM					
:30					
5:00 PM					
:30					

☐ Work Time ☐ School Culture ☐ Observations ☐ Meetings

As you can see, committing to observation and feedback does require a substantial time investment—but not an unreasonable one. You still have plenty of time for everything else. In Chapter 8 (Finding the Time), we'll dive even more deeply into additional strategies to keep noninstructional items from interfering with your ability to observe teachers.

Findings from the Field

Finish Your Prep Work in the Classroom

You won't be able to give all your teachers in-depth weekly coaching if it takes you too long to prepare for coaching meetings. How do great school leaders cut their prep time down to the bare minimum so that the kind of coaching we're about to roll out is sustainable?

To find out, we asked one. Serena Savarirayan was the founding principal of North Star Vailsburg Middle School in Newark, New Jersey, where students achieve at levels that far outpace the statewide averages in both math and the humanities. To make sure every one of her teachers got the weekly coaching they needed, she cut her feedback meeting prep time to an astonishing ten minutes. Here are her key tips for any leader who strives to do the same.

- **Prepare to give feedback while observing.** Whenever Serena goes to do an observation, she comes ready to also prepare her feedback. That means bringing her laptop with her (or pen and notepad), which allows her to plan her feedback meeting as she watches. Serena offers this rule of thumb: "I make a point not to leave the observation until at a minimum I've selected the action step. That lets me develop my action steps while the observation is freshest in my mind."

- **Have access to lesson plans.** Serena builds systems to have easy access to the teacher's lesson plans for the day and upcoming lessons. (Serena has teachers post them in their classroom; other leaders highlighted in the book receive them via email or hard copy or have them in a shared server where they can find them.)

- **Videotape while you observe.** "Whenever I observe, I make sure I have my iPhone so I can film the teacher if it is useful," Serena says. That way, Serena doesn't have to rely solely on her own memories of all the lessons she observes: she carries the most important evidence out of the classroom with her. When she does film, she marks the time stamps right in her feedback meeting script so that she doesn't have to rewatch the entire clip. "I can zero in immediately on the part that captured the area of growth for the teacher."

- **Think "best teacher."** "I'm always thinking: What would the best teacher I know do if she were teaching this lesson?" says Serena. Keeping an image of exemplar teaching in mind while she observes helps Serena select her action steps quickly.

As you start to build these actions into your daily coaching practice, don't be discouraged if it takes you longer (perhaps much longer!) than ten minutes the first time you plan a feedback meeting. Instead, rest assured that building these habits from the beginning will make you capable of incredibly quick planning in the long run.

Once you have developed a schedule like the one in Table 3.1, you are one step closer to making dramatic improvements in teacher development. The next step is to develop the know-how to identify what teachers need when you observe them.

IDENTIFY THE RIGHT ACTION STEP

Like many experienced educators, Ashley doesn't miss much when she observes a class. She immediately sees dozens of areas for improvement. We certainly have plenty of guidance on all the actions that get teachers better, from *Get Better Faster* to books like Doug Lemov's *Teach Like a Champion* and Jon Saphier's aptly named *The Skillful Teacher*. These books have already named the actions that define great teaching in rich taxonomies that cover everything from the proper posture to the best questioning strategies that make students think. For a diligent leader with access to these resources, the real problem is not identifying areas of growth so much as: "Where do I start?" In a book on teaching that is hundreds of pages long, where do we turn first to transform page into practice?

Characteristics of Effective Action Steps

Back in 2012, a team of educators I work with set out to answer a critical question: What do the most successful leaders do to develop their teachers most quickly—especially their newest ones? That began a multiyear on-site project to identify and codify those practices. One of the first big "aha" moments was when we looked at the type of feedback these leaders were giving their teachers. Here are some examples of the action steps they used in their feedback meetings.

Sample Action Steps from Top Leaders

- **Use economy of language.**
  - Give crisp instructions with as few words as possible (e.g., three-word directions).
  - Check for understanding on complex instructions.

- **Use universal prompts.** Push the thinking back on the students through universal prompts that could be used at any point:
    - Provide wait time after posing challenging questions.
    - Pre-call: let a student who needs more time know you're calling him or her next.
    - Roll back the answer: repeat the wrong answer back to the student (give student time to think and you time to build a plan).
    - Ask universal prompts to push the student to elaborate:
        - "Tell me more."
        - "What makes you think that?"
        - "How do you know?"
        - "Why is that important?"
- **Close the loop.** After correcting their error, go back to students who answered incorrectly to have them revise their answers.

Name It

Sample Action Steps from Top Leaders

What characteristics do these action steps have in common? Write your response here.

_____

_____

_____

_____

_____

_____

_____

You probably noted many characteristics in common, one of which was the size of them. In a way, they are the opposite of a several-hundred-page tome on teaching. They're not book-size but bite-size.

You might expect that the quickest way to develop a teacher would be to give him more feedback at once, but in fact, the opposite is true. Teachers grow most quickly when leaders narrow their focus to the highest-leverage feedback, and deliver that feedback in the form of the most specific, granular action steps possible. That's the power behind teacher actions like the ones Doug Lemov identifies in *Teach Like a Champion:* they are the smaller building blocks that form the foundation of great teaching.

In his excellent book *The Talent Code,* Daniel Coyle explains to great effect why this is the case. Traveling to talent hotbeds all over the world, he discovered that bite-size actions fueled the growth of excellence in nearly every field. At Moscow's Spartak Tennis Club, he found tennis players who spent hours upon hours correcting their racquet swing to the last movement before they practiced actually hitting tennis balls. At New York's Meadowmount School of Music, he found orchestras that practiced music at a snail's pace, getting each note exactly right in isolation before they tried hitting them at tempo.[5] Why does this work? Because if you master your grip on the racquet earlier, there's less to fix later. Building the right foundation from the start—down to the very last detail—builds deeper expertise faster in the long run. The smaller and more precise the action step, the quicker the growth.

Core Idea

The smaller and more precise the action step, the quicker the growth.
Be bite-size, not book-size.

So what makes a great action step? Here are three key criteria:

- **Highest leverage.** Will this help the teacher develop most quickly and effectively? Is it connected to a larger PD goal?

- **Measurable.** The action step is what the teacher can practice: it names the "what" (e.g., use economy of language) and the "how" (e.g., give crisp instructions with as few words as possible).

- **Bite-size.** If your teacher can't make the change in a week, the action step isn't small enough!

Keys to Great Action Steps

Great action steps are

- **Highest leverage.** Will this help the teacher to develop most quickly and effectively? Is it connected to a larger PD goal?
- **Measurable.** The action step is what the teacher can practice: it names the "what" and the "how."
- **Bite-size.** If your teacher can't make the change in a week, the action step isn't small enough!

Narrowing down action steps to what is highest leverage and measurable changes your whole mindset about feedback; it's the mental equivalent of shifting the zoom lens on your camera from macro to micro. But this mental exercise takes a lot of work—because you have to zoom in on the most important part! How can you develop the skill of writing bite-size action steps when you coach so many teachers—and have so little time?

To solve this dilemma, in 2012 we originally observed a cohort of eight leaders whose coaching results—especially with their newest teachers—were particularly extraordinary. We discovered that there was a commonality not only to size of the action steps these leaders were delivering to their teachers but also to the *order* in which those action steps were delivered. Great action steps go granular, but the greatest action steps build on each other logically. These leaders prioritize the most crucial skills of great teaching, carefully keeping their focus specific while addressing classroom management and the rigor of instruction in tandem.

Over the past ten years, we've gathered those action steps into one document, and we've tested it with thousands of leaders across the globe. The result? The Get Better Faster Scope and Sequence. This guide can save time for those leaders who strive to follow in their footsteps.

Read on to see the sequence! As you read, put a star next to any action step that stands out to you as something you could implement in your daily coaching practice—perhaps something you see your teachers stumble over often, or something that you haven't thought about since earlier in your career. Place two stars beside anything that strikes you as especially important to implement in your school right away. (If a step reminds you of a particular teacher you work with, consider putting that teacher's initials next to it.)

Get Better Faster Scope and Sequence

Top Action Steps Used by Instructional Leaders to Launch a Teacher's Development

Phase	Management Trajectory	Rigor Trajectory
Phase 1: Pre-teaching (Summer PD)	**Develop Essential Routines and Procedures**	**Write Lesson Plans**

	1. **Routines and Procedures 101:** Design and roll out
	
	• Plan and practice critical routines and procedures moment by moment:
	   ○ Explain what each routine means and what it will look like.
	   ○ Write out what teacher and students do at each step, and what will happen with students who don't follow the routine.
	
	• Plan and practice the rollout: how to introduce the routine for the first time:
	   ○ Plan the "I Do": how you will model the routine.
	   ○ Plan what you will do when students don't get it right.
	
	2. **Strong Voice:** Stand and speak with purpose
	
	• Square up and stand still: when giving instructions, stop moving and strike a formal pose.
	
	• Formal register: when giving instructions, use formal register, including tone and word choice.
		1. **Develop Effective Lesson Plans 101:** Build the foundation of an effective lesson rooted in what students need to learn
		
		• Write precise learning objectives that are
		   ○ Data driven (rooted in what students need to learn based on analysis of assessment results)
		   ○ Curriculum plan driven
		   ○ Able to be accomplished in one lesson
		
		• Deliver a basic "I Do" as a core part of the lesson.
		
		• Design an Exit Ticket (brief final mini-assessment) aligned to the objective.
		
		2. **Internalize Existing Lesson Plans:** Make existing lesson plans your own
		
		• Internalize and rehearse key parts of the lesson, including the "I Do" and all key instructions.
		
		• Build time stamps into the lesson plan and follow them.

Phase	Management Trajectory	Rigor Trajectory
Phase 1 (con't.)	*Note: Many other topics can be introduced during August training. What are listed above are the topics that should be addressed to reach proficiency. Other topics to introduce—even if teachers will not yet master them—could be:* *Least Invasive Intervention* *Narrate the Positive* *Build the Momentum* *Teacher Radar: know when when students are off task* *Do It Again: practice routines to perfection—have students do it again if it is not done correctly (and know when to stop Do It Again)*	

Phase 2 (Days 1–30)	**Roll Out and Monitor Routines**
	
	3. **What to Do**
	   • Economy of language: give crisp instructions with as few words as possible (e.g., 3-word directions). Check for understanding on complex instructions.
	4. **Routines and Procedures 201:** Revise and perfect them
	   • Revise any routine that needs more attention to detail or is inefficient, with particular emphasis on what students and teachers are doing at each moment.
	   • Do It Again: have students do the routine again if not done correctly the first time.
	   • Cut It Short: know when to stop the Do It Again.
		Independent Practice
		
		3. **Write the Exemplar:** Set the bar for excellence
		   • Script out the ideal written responses you want students to produce during independent practice.
		   • Align independent practice to the rigor of the upcoming interim assessment.
		4. **Independent Practice:** Set up daily routines that build opportunities for students to practice independently
		   • Write first, talk second: give students writing tasks to complete prior to class discussion so that every student answers independently before hearing his/her peers' contributions.

Phase	Management Trajectory	Rigor Trajectory

Phase 2 (con't.)	5. **Teacher Radar:** Know when students are off task
	
	• Deliberately scan the room for off-task behavior:
	
	   ○ Choose 3–4 "hot spots" (places where you have students who often get off task) to scan constantly
	
	   ○ Be Seen Looking: crane your neck to appear to be seeing all corners of the room.
	
	• Circulate the room with purpose (break the plane):
	
	   ○ Move among the desks and around the perimeter.
	
	   ○ Stand at the corners: identify 3 spots on the perimeter of the room to which you can circulate to stand and monitor student work.
	
	• Move away from the student who is speaking to monitor the whole room.
	
	6. **Whole-Class Reset**
	
	• Implement a planned whole-class reset to reestablish student behavioral expectations when a class routine has slowly weakened over previous classes.
	
	• Implement an "in-the-moment reset" when a class veers off task during the class period.
		• Implement a daily entry prompt (Do Now) to either introduce the day's objective or review material from the previous day.
		
		• Implement and review a longer independent practice and/or a daily Exit Ticket (brief final mini-assessment aligned to your objective) to see how many students mastered the concept.
		
		5. **Monitor Aggressively:** Check students' independent work to determine whether they're learning what you're teaching
		
		• Create and implement a monitoring pathway:
		
		   ○ Create a seating chart to monitor students most effectively.
		
		   ○ Monitor the fastest writers first, then the students who need more support.
		
		• Monitor the quality of student work:
		
		   ○ Check answers against your exemplar.
		
		   ○ Track correct and incorrect answers to class questions.
		
		• Pen in Hand: mark up student work as you circulate.
		
		   ○ Use a coding system to affirm correct answers.
		
		   ○ Cue students to revise answers, using minimal verbal intervention. (Name the

Phase	Management Trajectory	Rigor Trajectory
Phase 2 (con't.)	o Example: Stop teaching. Square up. Give a clear What to Do: "Pencils down. Eyes on me. Hands folded in 3-2-1. Thank you: that's what Harvard looks like." Pick up tone and energy again.	error, ask them to fix it, tell them you'll follow up.)

Phase 3 (Days 31–60)	**Engage Every Student**
	7. Build the Momentum
	• Give the students a simple challenge to complete a task:
	  o Example: "Now, I know you're only 4th graders, but I have a 5th-grade problem that I bet you could master!"
	• Speak faster, walk faster, vary your voice, and smile (sparkle)!
	8. Pacing: Create the illusion of speed so that students feel constantly engaged
	• Use a handheld timer to stick to the times stamps in the lesson and give students an audio cue that it's time to move on.
	• Increase rate of questioning: no more than 2 seconds between when a student responds and teacher picks back up instruction.
	• Use countdowns to work the clock ("Do that in 5, 4, 3, 2, 1").
	• Use call and response for key words.
	9. Engage All Students: Make sure all students participate
		Respond to Student Learning Needs
		6. Habits of Evidence
		• Teach students to annotate with purpose: summarize, analyze, find the best evidence, etc.
		• Teach and prompt students to cite key evidence in their responses.
		7. Check for Whole-Group Understanding: Gather evidence on whole-group learning
		• Poll the room to determine how students are answering a certain question.
		  o "How many chose letter A? B? C? D?"
		  o Students answer the question on whiteboards: "Hold up your whiteboards on the count of three . . . "
		• Target the error: focus class discussion on the questions where students most struggle to answer correctly.
		8. Reteaching 101—Model: Model for the students how to think/solve/write
		• Give students a clear listening/note-taking task that fosters active listening to the model, and then debrief the model:

Phase	Management Trajectory	Rigor Trajectory

Phase 3 (con't.)	• Make sure to call on all students.
	
	• Cold-call students.
	
	• Implement brief (15–30 second) Turn and Talks.
	
	• Intentionally alternate among multiple methods in class discussion: cold calling, choral response, all hands, and Turn and Talks.
	
	10. Narrate the Positive
	
	• Narrate what students do well, not what they do wrong.
	
	   o "I like how Javon has gotten straight to work on his writing assignment."
	
	   o "The second row is ready to go: their pencils are in the well, and their eyes are on me."
	
	• While narrating the positive and/or while scanning during a redirect, look at the student(s) who are off task.
	
	• Use language that reinforces students' getting smarter:
	
	   o Praise answers that are above and beyond, or strong effort.
	
	11. Individual Student Corrections
	
	• Anticipate student off-task behavior and rehearse the next two things you will do
		o "What did I do in my model?"
		
		   o "What are the key things to remember when you are doing the same in your own work?"
		
		• Model the thinking, not just a procedure:
		
		   o Narrow the focus to the thinking students are struggling with.
		
		   o Model replicable thinking steps that students can follow.
		
		   o Model how to activate one's own content knowledge and skills that have been learned in previous lessons.
		
		   o Vary the think-aloud in tone and cadence from the normal "teacher" voice to highlight the thinking skills.
		
		• We Do and You Do: give students opportunities to practice with your guidance.

Phase	Management Trajectory	Rigor Trajectory

Phase 3 (con't.)	when that behavior occurs. Redirect students using the least invasive intervention necessary:
	
	   ○ Proximity
	   ○ Eye contact
	   ○ Use a nonverbal
	   ○ Say student's name quickly
	   ○ Small consequence	

Phase 4 (Days 61–90)	**Set Routines for Discourse**
	
	12. **Engaged Small-Group Work:** Maximize the learning for every student during small-group work
	
	• Deliver explicit step-by-step instructions for group work:
	
	   ○ Make the group tasks visible/easily observable (e.g., a handout to fill in, notes to take, product to build, etc.).
	
	   ○ Create a role for every person (with each group no larger than the number of roles needed to accomplish the tasks at hand).
	
	   ○ Give timed instructions, with benchmarks for where the group should be after each time window.
	
	• Monitor the visual evidence of group progress:
		Lead Student Discourse 101
		
		9. **Reteaching 201—Guided Discourse:** Let students unpack their own errors and build a solution
		
		• Show-Call: post student work (either an exemplar or incorrect response) and ask students to identify why that answer is correct/incorrect.
		
		• Stamp the understanding:
		
		   ○ "What are the keys to remember when solving problems like these?" or "Can someone give me a rule?" (Students use their own words.)
		
		• Give them at-bats: give students opportunities to practice with your guidance.
		
		10. **Universal Prompts:** Push the thinking back on the students through universal prompts that could be used at any point

Phase	Management Trajectory	Rigor Trajectory
Phase 4 (con't.)	o Check in on each group every 5–10 minutes to monitor progress. • Verbally enforce individual and group accountability: o "You are five minutes behind; get on track." o "Brandon: focus."	• Provide wait time after posing challenging questions. • Pre-call: let a student who needs more time know you're calling on him/her next. • Roll back the answer: repeat the wrong answer back to the student. (Give the student time to think and you time to build a plan!) • Ask universal prompts to push the student to elaborate: o "Tell me more." o "What makes you think that?" o "How do you know?" o "Why is that important?" • Close the loop: after correcting their error, go back to students with wrong answers to have them revise their answers. 11. **Habits of Discussion:** Teach and model for students the habits that strengthen class conversation • Keep neutral/manage your tell: don't reveal the right/wrong answer through your reaction to the student response. • Agree and build off: "I agree with ___, and I'd like to add . . ." • Disagree respectfully: "While I agree with [this part of your argument], I disagree with ___. I would argue . . ."

Phase	Management Trajectory	Rigor Trajectory

Stretch It (Next Steps)	None!
	
	Once you get this far, you can focus entirely on rigor and deepening your content knowledge.
		Lead Student Discourse 201
		
		12. **Strategic Prompts:** Ask strategic questions to targeted students in response to student error
		
		• Prompt students to access previously learned knowledge:
		
		  o Point students to resources (notes, posted concepts and content, handouts).
		
		  o *"What do we know about____[content learned in previous classes]?"*
		
		  o Use a prompting guide (e.g., *Great Habits, Great Readers* Guided Reading Prompting Guide) to design questions.
		
		• Call on students based on their learning needs (data driven).
		
		  o Call on lower- and middle-achieving students to unpack the question.
		
		  o If they struggle, try a higher-achieving student.
		
		  o If they are easily unpacking, try a lower-achieving student.
		
		  o Create a sequence of students to call on based on the rigor of each prompt (e.g., first ask middle student, then low, then high, etc.).

Phase	Management Trajectory	Rigor Trajectory

Stretch It (con't.)		• Students prompting students: push students to use habits of discussion to critique or push one another's answers.
		  o Probe deeper: "[Peer], have you considered this point . . . ?"
		13. **Go Conceptual:** Get students to do the conceptual thinking
		• Ask students to verbalize a conceptual understanding of content, not just the answer to a specific question:
		  o "That's the procedure. Now tell me why that works."
		  o "Can you generalize that idea to apply to all problems like this one?"
		  o "Use the following terms [terms learned in previous classes] in restating your answer."
		• Upgrade vocabulary: ask students to use technical/academic language when answering questions:
		  o "That's the right idea generally. Now state it again using proper mathematical/historical/scientific language."
		  o "Correct. Now state it again using your Academic Word Wall as a resource."

Phase	Management Trajectory	Rigor Trajectory

Stretch It (con't.)		• Stretch it: ask particular students to answer a more difficult extension to a given question:
		
		  o "What would the answer be if I changed it to [change the problem to something more complex]?"
		
		  o "Is there an alternative way to solve this problem/do this task?"
		
		  o "What do you think is the strongest counterargument to yours, and how would you refute it?"

This guide doesn't pretend to cover *all* action steps that can be given to a teacher; it doesn't need to. Rather, it focuses on the sequence of actions that get teachers to a level of proficiency where they can fly to even greater heights—particularly in their content expertise. But if we can get all teachers in our schools to that level, we'll truly have built a land of excellence rather than isolated islands!

(The book *Get Better Faster* unpacks these action steps—and the coaching steps to train a teacher to perform each of them masterfully—in much greater detail. Look to that text for a month-by-month guide to coaching your teachers.)

Where Do I Start? Choosing an Action Step When Observing

Although having these action steps in hand is powerful, the next challenge is to identify which one to use when observing a teacher. What follows are a few case studies to give you some practice in doing so.

We've written two scenarios of what a coach might observe in a teacher's classroom. As you read them, keep the Get Better Faster Scope and Sequence handy. Which action step would you give these teachers if you observed them at work?

Observation and Feedback Case Study

Identify the Action Step

Scenario 1

As you walk into the middle school class, the students have just finished reading two passages, and they are getting ready to discuss them in small groups. The students seem to be pretty attentive as the teacher starts giving the instructions: "OK, class. Now you're going to discuss the articles and which you agree with. You should have a lot to talk about based the articles. If you need any help, you can consider the resources that you might have that could help you. Remember: make sure everyone gets a chance to talk. OK? You can begin."

The groups begin talking, and you notice that none of the groups are discussing whether or not they agree with the reading passages. The teacher floats around, and she also notices that students are getting off task. You hear her say the following to each group: "You should be talking about the two passages: Do you agree or disagree with each of them? Then you should use evidence from the passages." She also makes comments like "John, I need you to get back on task."

Based on this information, what action step would you give this teacher?

_____

_____

_____

_____

Scenario 2

As you walk into an elementary classroom, all the students have transitioned to the rug for a science lesson. "Today we are going to watch a video about plants. Before we do, I want each of you to grab a sticky note from up front and write down what you already know about plants. When you finish writing, just stick it up here on the whiteboard. Ready? Go!" The students all rise at once to reach the one pack of sticky notes at the front of the room. There is a fair amount of jostling, and some students complain about being elbowed or pushed. It takes a few minutes for each student to get a note, and by the time the last one gets one, many students have already finished writing. A few minutes later, everyone has put a sticky note up on the board and has quieted down.

The teacher reads aloud each of the notes: "A plant needs water, soil, and sunlight to grow." "A plant needs water and sun to grow." "Wow," says the teacher. "This is great: you already know a lot about plants! We're now going to watch a video about what plants need to grow. I'm going to pass out whiteboards, and I want you to write down what you learn from the video about what plants need to grow." The teacher then passes the whiteboards out, one at a time, and the students get a little restless waiting for their board. As soon as the teacher is finished, he starts the video. You see an image of a plant and hear the narrator saying: "Plants don't grow the same way we do. They use water and sunlight as their food, and that makes them grow."

Based on this information, what action step would you give this teacher?

_____

_____

_____

_____

Scenario 1 answer: Let's look closely at scenario 1. It appears that the class is pretty attentive at the start of the instructions; this suggests that the teacher has generally established her authority and that the students are engaged, given the right circumstances. So what breaks down? Is it their ability to do group work, or the teacher's ability to correct students who are off task, or something else? The key is to look for the root cause that started the problem. The problems begin when the teacher gives instructions: the students don't have clarity on what they should do. Any disorder or off-task behavior started at that point. So if we want to fix her class, the start pointing lies there:

- **What to Do:** give crisp instructions with as few words as possible (e.g., three-word directions). Check for understanding on complex instructions (Get Better Faster Scope and Sequence—Phase 2, Management, pt. 3)

Scenario 2 answer: More things are happening in scenario 2: the teacher implements a sloppy routine for writing on sticky notes, which slows down the class and creates some student conflicts. The teacher similarly loses some class time in his distribution of the whiteboards. We could also question just having the students watch a video. But where is the highest-leverage action? The most concerning part of this class is that students already knew the answers to the day's objective prior to even showing the video. In essence, they were not learning what they needed, but instead were spending time on something they already knew. Starting at the top of the Get Better Faster Scope and Sequence on the Rigor side, we find our highest-leverage action step:

- **Develop Effective Lesson Plans 101**—Write precise learning objectives that are data driven (rooted in what students need to learn based on analysis of assessment results)

Yes, we could make the routines more efficient (and we certainly will in upcoming sessions), and we could pick more valuable learning exercises. But if students aren't learning what they need, that will not matter. The class will look better on the surface, but actual learning won't make progress.

Kathleen Sullivan is the managing director of the Leverage Leadership Institute, and she spent multiple years as a principal manager. As she reflected on her use of the Get Better Faster Scope and Sequence, she used a simple mantra. "Think waterfall." Start at the top and work your way down until you hit the first major growth area this particular teacher needs.

Core Idea

When you choose an action step for a teacher, think waterfall. Start at the top of the Get Better Faster Scope and Sequence of skills for teachers, and stop when you hit the first major growth area.

"The Scope and Sequence is a lifeline in the choppy seas of a classroom with fifty things happening at once," Kathleen says. "Do I see evidence of this? Yes—move down to the next step. When you no longer see evidence of it, you are at your destination. It emboldens you as a coach to shut out the din of everything else in the class and focus on getting your teacher better one step at a time."

Findings from the Field

Spend Less Time on the "What" and More Time on the "How"

"When I started using the Scope and Sequence for action steps, my whole approach to teacher development changed. Before I felt like my feedback was a little like 'whack-a-mole': tackle a random problem over here only to have another one pop up over there. I felt pretty directionless. Now I have a clear starting point—has my teacher mastered Phase 1? Phase 2?—and a clear trajectory. This allows me to spend less time on 'what' my feedback should be and more time on 'how' to deliver that feedback and how to practice. In the process, I have seen my new teachers move so much faster than before."

—Patrick Pastore, principal, Rochester, NY

The two case study scenarios are just the beginning. Want to know the best way to practice? Go observe with another instructional leader. Starting with the Get Better Faster Scope and Sequence, walk into a classroom and decide independently what you think the action step should be. Then spar with each other's answers. The more you practice, the better you will get!

DELIVER EFFECTIVE FEEDBACK

Imagine you do everything we've already discussed in this chapter: you make sure every teacher in your school is being observed at least once a week, and you and your fellow leaders hone your skill at identifying the right bite-size action step at the right time. If you write that action step down on a form, leave it on the teacher's desk, and walk away until the following week, will your teachers succeed?

For the most part, no. Perhaps the most talented and motivated teachers will be able to translate written action steps into expert teaching, but most of us don't master skills from written feedback alone. Here are the top five errors to avoid when giving feedback.

The Top Five Errors to Avoid When Giving Feedback

Error 1: More is better.

- **Top-tier truth: Less is more.** Many leaders fall prey to the temptation to deliver feedback on every aspect of the lesson. Although that is a useful tool to demonstrate your instructional expertise, it won't change practice nearly as effectively. As we can learn from coaches in every field, bite-size feedback on just one or two areas delivers the most effective improvement.[6]

Error 2: Lengthy written evaluations drive change as effectively as anything.

- **Top-tier truth: Face-to-face makes the difference.** The reason why this error persists nationwide among school leaders is that there is a subset of teachers for whom lengthy written evaluations are effective (just as there is a small group of learners for whom lengthy lectures are most effective). This creates the dangerous conclusion that all teachers develop well from lengthy evaluations. In what other field do we permit this idea?

Error 3: Just tell them; they'll get it.

- **Top-tier truth: If they don't do the thinking, they won't internalize it.** In classroom instruction, highly effective teachers push the students to do the thinking. If teachers eclipse this thinking by providing conclusions or answers too quickly, students will disengage. Feedback is not any different: if teachers don't participate in the process of thinking about their teaching, they are less likely to internalize the feedback. This is metacognition applied to teacher development: having teachers think about their teaching improves their performance.

Error 4: State the concrete action step. Then the teacher will act.

- **Top-tier truth: Practice makes perfect.** If a surgeon simply tells a resident how to perform an operation, that resident will be less effective than if he or she practices with the surgeon's guidance. Teaching is the same: practicing implementation of the feedback *with the leader* is at the heart of speeding up the improvement cycle. It also allows teachers to make mistakes before they're in front of the students again.

Error 5: Teachers can implement feedback at any time.

- **Top-tier truth: Nail down the timing.** Having a concrete timeline in which feedback will be implemented serves two purposes: it makes sure everyone has clear expectations as to when this will be accomplished, and it will expose action steps that are not really able to be accomplished in a week.

What is the alternative to these errors? To lock in success for your school, you need to coach your teachers. And you can use the same See It, Name It, Do It structure that we presented in previous chapters. Here's how.

See It

Let's revisit the opening vignette and take a deeper dive into how Ashley coaches her teachers. In this clip, she is working with Ijeoma on what to do when students are in independent practice: Monitor Aggressively on the Get Better Faster Scope and Sequence. Let's watch it piece by piece to see her coaching. What does Ashley do to launch her feedback meeting?

 WATCH Clip 16: Anderson—See It (Model, Gap)—Feedback Meeting

---

Stop and Jot

How does Ashley launch her feedback meeting? What are all the steps she takes in coaching her teacher? Jot down what you noticed.

_____

_____

_____

_____

_____

_____

_____

_____

What Ashley does is quite powerful—and replicable. Let's break it down into steps that any of us could follow.

See the Success

Just as Laura did in the data meeting we looked at in Chapter 1, Ashley begins her work as a coach by getting Ijeoma to see, not what's wrong with her class, but what she's doing *right.* This sort of praise might seem obvious: you want to start off on a positive note and have someone feel good about what she is doing. But Ashley's actions go beyond that. Through specific praise and a simple follow-up question ("What was the impact of that on their practice?"), Ashley enables the teacher to see that the feedback she's received is working: she is getting better! When you set out to get teachers to see their success—especially when it's linked to previous meetings—you create a culture where feedback matters. You inherently help your teacher see the value of meeting with you.

See the Model

Then the magic of Ashley's work really takes off. She calls on Ijeoma to recall how something she's practiced before in PD feels when it's done well ("What are the keys to aggressive monitoring?"). Next, she shows a video that gives Ijeoma the chance to break down a master teacher's concrete actions around aggressive monitoring, asking her, "What is Mr. Frazier doing to ensure student papers look like his exemplar, and what impact does this have?" Through all these steps, Ashley does what words cannot do: she gets Ijeoma to *see* what excellence looks like.

Core Idea

If you want teachers to get it, get them to see it. To see it is to believe it.

There is so much power in this mantra, which is why See It permeates every chapter of this book! Without a clear model, there is no pathway to success. Moreover, if Ashley simply told Ijeoma what exemplar teaching looks like in so many words, Ijeoma wouldn't get as clear an image of what she needs to do—and she might not take Ashley's word for it. Show a model, however, and the teacher will see right away why the action is so powerful.

See the Gap

Once Ijeoma has seen the exemplar, Ashley gets her to identify the gap in her own teaching—and now it is easy to do so. She simply steers their conversation about what made Mr. Frazier so successful to the logical next question: "When you think back to your independent practice today, what is the biggest gap between what you did today and what you just saw Mr. Frazier do?" Ijeoma is able to articulate that gap right away. When you get a teacher it see it, her pathway becomes clear.

See It

Key Actions in Feedback Meetings

1. **See past success.** Name where the teacher has succeeded in implementing feedback.

2. **See the exemplar.** Narrow the focus and name the exemplar. If necessary, show the teacher a model.

3. **See the gap.** Ask the teacher: "What is the gap between what happened in the exemplar and what happened during your class today?"

Name It

Let's pick up Ashley's feedback meeting where we left off, once Ijeoma has identified the gap in her teaching.

 WATCH Clip 17: Anderson—Name It—Feedback Meeting

Stop and Jot

What does Ashley do to ensure that her teacher knows the action step? Jot down what you noticed.

_____

_____

_____

_____

_____

_____

_____

Ashley's first move was to have Ijeoma name the action step—just as in the case of seeing the action step, it's more powerful if Ijeoma can get there herself. But Ashley doesn't stop there: she then restates the action step in formal language. Why? This ensures that they have a common language of exactly what they are working on and can refer back to it throughout this meeting and beyond. Here are some prompts that accomplish this:

Prompt the teacher to name the action step:

- "Based on what we discussed today, what do you think your action step should be?"

Punch it: lock in the action step by stating it clearly and concisely in formal language, or "punching" it:

- Say, "So your action step today is _____":
  - *What* the teacher will work on (e.g., What to Do directions)
  - *How* the teacher will execute it (e.g., "1. Stand still, 2. Give a What to Do direction in less than five words, and 3. Scan for compliance.")
- Have the teacher restate the action step and then write it down.

Naming the action step seems basic and might feel unnecessary. Yet we don't lock it in until we name it clearly and concisely. You leave teachers with a single instruction that tells them both *what* to do and *how* to do it: an indispensable tool as they set out to put this new skill to use.

Core Idea

You don't lock in the learning until you punch it.
Transformative action steps name the *what* and the *how*.

A Word on . . . So What Happened to the "Six Steps of Feedback"?

For those readers of the first edition of *Leverage Leadership,* you will notice that we are no longer referring to the "six steps of feedback." What we discovered was that those six steps were too complex and didn't provide enough guidance to give effective feedback. Particularly, the "Probe" step led many meetings off track, as it was hard to determine what made effective questions. We also noticed that planning was more effective when done *before* the practice, because planning made the practice more relevant and perfected the practice.

What we present in this book is based on thousands of hours of additional work in observing and codifying effective feedback—and we hope it's simpler to follow! Here is a quick reference to how our guidance has evolved since *Leverage Leadership*:

	Leverage Leadership 2.0	Leverage Leadership
See It	• See the success • See the model • See the gap	1. Praise 2. Probe
Name It	Name the action step and punch it	1. Action step
Do It	• Perfect your plan • Practice • Follow up	1. Practice 2. Plan 3. Follow up

Do It

If the meeting ended there, most of your work would be for naught. What happens next is what converts an effective meeting to a transformative one:

 WATCH Clip 18: Anderson—Do It (Plan)—Feedback Meeting

Stop and Jot

How does Ashley ensure that her teacher will have a successful practice? Jot down what you noticed.

_____

_____

_____

Here Ashley brings to life the core principle of this entire book: for coaching to be effective, it needs to center around practice. Tennis players don't get better at swinging their racquets without doing it, and teachers won't get better at teaching without doing it, either. But if you want your practice to be successful, you have to plan it, and plan it well.

Core Idea

Perfect the plan before you practice. You cannot practice well unless you know what you're looking for.

Ashley takes many steps to make this planning as perfect as possible, and by doing so she sets up Ijeoma to experience success when she practices. First, she has Ijeoma plan on her own, asking her to consider: "What are the keys to an ideal answer?" Then Ashley completes the same process she's just asked Ijeoma to follow so that they can spar. "What are your key takeaways?" Ashley asks when they've compared notes. Informed by her leader's responses, Ijeoma can now revise her original plan to make it even stronger.

With planning squared away, Ashley and Ijeoma are ready to dive into the high-quality practice we saw them engage in at the beginning of this chapter. Take another look to see how they do it.

 REWATCH Clip 15: Anderson—Do It (Practice)—Feedback Meeting

Think about the power of what you saw in this meeting. Ashley and Ijeoma didn't just talk about teaching: they acted on it. And they didn't just practice—they practiced perfectly.

Core Idea

Practice doesn't make perfect. Perfect practice does.

To really understand the impact of this meeting, imagine what would have happened without getting Ijeoma to step up and actually practice. Ijeoma might have been excited about what she learned in the feedback meeting, but her first time to try it would be in front of kids. In essence, we'd be asking her to experiment with getting better without having tried it out first! By having Ijeoma practice, and doing it precisely, Ashley dramatically accelerates Ijeoma's development by greatly increasing the likelihood that she will be successful when she teaches the next period.

Practice Effectively

Ashley makes practice optimally effective in four key ways:

- **Practice the gap.** Ashley creates a direct simulation of what she and Ijeoma have already agreed Ijeoma needs to do to close the gap in her independent practice.

Ijeoma is using the real exemplar she'll use in class to track students' progress toward mastery, and the work samples laid out on desks are her real students' work from a lesson she taught earlier that day.

- **Practice perfect.** A few moments into the practice, Ashley stops Ijeoma to have her preview the symbols she'll be marking on student work when she kicks off the students' independent practice. Pausing Ijeoma at the moment she stumbles gives her the immediate chance to try it again. This way she'll build muscle memory of success, not failure.

- **Add complexity piece by piece.** If you're working with a newer teacher or on a more complex action step, start the practice simply, then add complexity only after the teacher has mastered the basics: "Let's try that again, but this time I will be [student X who is slightly more challenging]."

- **Lock it in and rename the action step.** Ashley wraps up practice by asking Ijeoma, "How did that align with what we saw in our exemplar?" That lets Ijeoma process her growth on a metacognitive level, leaving her with total clarity about what she's doing differently by the end of this practice session.

Follow Up

Ashley concludes the meeting by identifying precisely how she will follow up—in this case, by observing later that day. Here are a number of follow-up actions that you can take in your own meetings:

- **Set dates.** Both teacher and leader write them down.
  - Completed materials: when teacher will complete revised lesson plan and materials. "When I review your plans, I'll look for _____."
  - Leader observation: when you'll observe the teacher. "When would be the best time to observe your implementation of this?" or "I'll come in tomorrow and look for this technique."
- **Plan for real-time feedback.** Agree on a predetermined real-time feedback cue aligned to the action step you will be looking for during the next observation: "When I come in, I will _____." (See "A Word on . . . Real-Time Feedback" for more guidance on the subject.)

A Word on . . . Real-Time Feedback

Too often while we're observing teachers in action, we're hesitant to speak up at all, let alone deliver feedback. We fear that offering guidance while instruction is occurring will be interpreted as a sign of disrespect—as if we don't trust the teacher to get the lesson right without our aid.

But think of all the other professions in which real-time feedback is, if anything, the utmost sign of respect from a leader. When surgeons begin their residencies, they operate alongside more experienced doctors who let them know how they can complete their work most effectively and safely. When soccer players take to the field, their coaches are as close to them as the rules of the game will let them be, calling out the winning move at every instant. In these careers, real-time feedback from a coach says, "Your success is so crucial in every moment that I would never let you fight for it alone." Why wouldn't we take the same attitude with the professionals who educate our children? Why wouldn't we treat the minutes of a lesson as if they were as critical as the minutes that make up each quarter of a soccer match?

With the help of real-time feedback, we can. Delivering high-leverage feedback in the moments we observe creates immediate opportunities for students to learn more than they could have otherwise. When delivered effectively, real-time feedback does what any feedback does: it gives teachers what they need to grow, and by extension, it gives students what they need to learn. It just accelerates that process so that teachers and students both get what they need faster.

Here's how Nikki Bridges leverages real-time feedback while observing first-year teacher Jackson Tobin.

 WATCH Clip 19: Bridges—Real-Time Feedback

Get Better Faster has much more information—including an extensive bank of video clips—on how to conduct real-time feedback effectively. For now, however, here are two key criteria for determining whether an action step is right for real-time feedback:

- **Will the action step keep the lesson on track and improve student learning?** If giving the feedback right away will improve student learning right away, deliver it right away. If it would interrupt the flow of the lesson that is happening right now, table it; it would probably result in student learning lost rather than student learning gained.

- **Can the action step be implemented immediately without practice?** If the teacher would need to practice the action step outside the classroom to be able to implement it properly, work on it with the teacher outside the classroom. If you could show him or her how to do it right away, real-time feedback is the answer.

Here's a breakdown of the best strategies to use to deliver real-time feedback, ranked from least to most invasive.

Strategy	Degree of Invasiveness	When to Use It
Silent signals	Least invasive	When you and the teacher have already set up a silent signal to prompt the teacher to engage the action step
Whisper prompt	Minimally invasive	When you can deliver feedback quickly in a whisper while students are working independently
Model	Moderately invasive	When the teacher needs to see a quick piece of feedback implemented in order to understand how to do it on his own
Extended model	More invasive	When the teacher needs to see a longer section of a lesson led differently in order to understand how to do it on his own

If you've modeled an action step for a teacher during her class, make sure you continue observing when you've turned it back over to her. Then, debrief her progress either immediately or at your next check-in: "How did that feel? What are your takeaways?" Congratulations: once you've completed all these steps, you've sped up the feedback cycle exponentially!

See It, Name It, Do It. You have the tools at your fingertips to lead effective meetings. To make it even easier, we've consolidated all of that information in one place here. On the DVD, you'll find this in a printer-friendly version that will give you a two-sided "one-pager" for easy reference.

Giving Effective Feedback

See It, Name It, Do It

Prepare during observation	**Prepare**

	• Have your tools in hand.
	  ○ Get Better Faster Scope and Sequence, teacher lesson plan, video tool, Observation Tracker
	• Plan your feedback while observing.
	  ○ Fill out the planning template
	  ○ Videotape while you observe: mark the time stamps in your planning template

See It 2–8 min	**See It: Success, Model, and Gap**

	See past success:
	• "We set a goal last week of _____, and I noticed how you [met goal] by [state concrete positive actions teacher took]."
	• "What made that successful? What was the impact of [that positive action]?"
	
	See the model:
	• Narrow the focus: **"Today, I want to dive into [specific element of lesson, action step area]."**
	• Prompt the teacher to name the exemplar.
	  ○ "What are the keys to [action step/technique/content area]? What is the purpose?"
	  ○ "What did you ideally want to see/hear when ___?"
	  ○ "What was your objective/goal for [activity/lesson]? What did the students have to do to meet this goal/objective?"
	  ○ Connect to PD: "Think back to the PD on [date]; what were the keys required for ___?"
	  ○ Read a one-pager or prompting guide: "What are the essential elements of ___?"
	• (If unable to name it) Show a model—choose one.

See It	See It: Success, Model, and Gap
2–8 min	

- o Show video of effective teaching: "What actions did the teacher take to do ___?"
- o Model: "What do you notice about how I ___?" "What is the impact and purpose?"
- o Debrief real-time feedback: "When I gave real-time feedback, what did I say? What did I do? What was the impact of the real-time feedback?"

See the gap:

- "What is the gap [the model/exemplar] and what happened in your class today?"
- "What was the challenge in implementing [technique/content area] effectively during [lesson]?"
- (If unable to name the gap) Present the evidence.
  - o Present time-stamped video from observation: "What are the students doing? What are you doing?" "What is the gap between what we see in this part of the video and the exemplar?"
  - o Present classroom evidence: "Two students in the front row had their heads down during independent practice. How does this affect student learning?" "What is the gap between [the exemplar] and class today?"
  - o Present student work: "What is the gap between the exemplar and [student work] today?"

Name It	Action Step: What and How
2 min	

Name the action step:

- "Based on what we discussed today, what do you think your action step should be?"
- "What are the keys to closing this gap?"

Punch it:

- "So your action step today is ___"; state clearly and concisely.
  - o *What* the teacher will work on (e.g., What to Do directions)

Name It 2 min	Action Step: What and How
	o *How* the teacher will execute (e.g., 1. Stand still, 2. Give a What to Do direction, and 3. Scan for compliance) • Have teacher restate the action step, then write it down.
Do It (Rest of meeting)	**Plan, Practice, and Follow Up**

Plan before practice:

• Prompt teacher to script the changes into upcoming lesson plans.

  o "Where would be a good place to implement this in your upcoming lessons?"

  o "What are all the actions you need to take/want to see in the students?"

• Push to make the plan more precise and more detailed.

  o "What prompts will you use with students that we can practice today?"

  o "Now that you've made your initial plan, what will do you if [state student behavior/response that will be challenging]?"

• If teacher needs extra development, model for the teacher first and debrief.

  o "Watch what I do and say as I model ____." "What do you notice about how I did ____?"

Practice:

• Round 1: "Let's practice" or "Let's take it live."

  o [When applicable] Stand up/move around classroom to simulate the feeling of class.

  o Pause the role play at the point of error to give immediate feedback.

  o Repeat until the practice is successful.

• Round 2: Add complexity (if teacher is mastering it).

  o "Let's try that again, but this time I will be [student X who is slightly more challenging]."

Do It (Rest of meeting)	Plan, Practice, and Follow Up
	• Lock it in and rename the action step.
	o "How did what we practiced meet or enhance the action step we named?"
	o "Where did our practice fall short or meet the exemplar at the start of the meeting?"
	Follow up:
	• Plan for real-time feedback.
	o Agree on a predetermined cue for the next observation: "When I come in, I will observe for___. If I see you struggling I will [give you a cue]."
	• Set dates for all of the following—both teacher and leader write them down.
	o Completed materials: when teacher will complete revised lesson plan and materials
	o Observation: when you'll observe the teacher:
	■ "When would be best time to observe your implementation of this?"
	■ "When I review your plans, I'll look for _____."
	■ Newer teacher: "I'll come in tomorrow and look for this technique."
	o (When valuable) Teacher observes master teacher implementing the same action step: ID when they'll observe in person or via video
	o (When valuable) Self-video: ID when you'll film the teacher to debrief in future meeting

SYSTEMS: MONITOR YOUR FEEDBACK

The power of feedback is clear; the challenge is staying on top of it, especially if you start to implement far more frequent observations! Ashley and leaders like her make it easier to do so with the help of a powerful tool: an observation tracker. An effective observation tracker measures just two essential pieces of information:

• How often you observe each teacher
• The action step for each observation

In their best iteration, they will give you two views: a tracker for each individual teacher and a school-wide tracker that summarizes all teachers in the building.

Here's what an individual teacher tab looks like.

Observation Tracker—Record of Your Coaching

Individual Teacher Tab

Teacher	Current Instructional Goals	Previously Met Goals
Smith	1. What to Do 2. Radar	Strong Voice

Date	Action Step	Summary
9/4	What to Do: give crisp instructions with as few words as possible	**Areas of Strength** • Opening procedures were very strong! The students got to work right away. **Areas for Growth** • You are giving directions when students are moving (the flip of the page for independent work). Make directions sequential and observable: "Turn the page. You will have five minutes to do this work. You may begin."
9/13	What to Do: check for understanding with three students before beginning the activity	
9/21	Teacher Radar: choose 3–4 "hotspots" (places where students often get off task) to scan constantly	**Areas of Strength** • Oral drill was crisp and urgent! Students were eager to participate.

Date	Action Step	Summary
		• Your pace and urgency were palpable—it was great to see you moving toward kids.
		Areas for Growth
		• For each of your directions, you are getting one or two students who are not responsive. Get to 100% by scanning the room and narrating the positive.
9/23	Teacher Radar: circulate the room with purpose	Areas of Strength
		• Most students are following your directions. It was especially impressive to see all of the students so thoroughly engaged in the independent practice!
		Areas for Growth
		• Only about 75% of students are staying on task during class discussion. You are in a position where you can get 100% if you move among the desks and around the perimeter.
9/30	Teacher Radar: circulate with your hotspots in mind	Areas of Strength
		• The transition out of the room was quick and silent.
		Areas for Growth
		• Stand in a place where you can see all of the students, including the ones directly in front of you. You were missing some students—Brian and Ali most

Date	Action Step	Summary
		notably. Take two steps back from the front desks to widen your view.
	Total Observations: 5	**Days Since Last Observation: 7**

The power of the individual tracker is in your ability to see the progression and frequency of action steps given to a teacher as well as how long it is taking the teacher to master those action steps. From this simple tab, you can see the quality of the action steps the leader has delivered and also whether this teacher is on track to being proficient. In this case, these are Phase 1 action steps occurring in the first month of school, which seems developmentally appropriate if this is a newer teacher.

If you are a principal, in addition to each teacher's action steps, you want to be able to see the trends across the school. A school-wide summary sheet of the Observation Tracker gives you that view:

Observation Tracker—Summary Page

All-Teacher Summary Tab

Name	Total Obs (last date observed)	Major PD Goal	Latest Key Action Step
Smith	5 (Sept 30)	1. What to Do 2. Teacher Radar	• Circulate with your hotspots in mind.
Doe	3 (Sept 23)	1. Habits of evidence	• Ask "Why?" and "How do you know?" after students make generalizations.

Name	Total Obs (last date observed)	Major PD Goal	Latest Key Action Step
Raines	3 (Sept 10)	1. Narrate the positive 2. Engage all students	• Narrate the positive after giving a direction. • Add brief (15–30-second) Turn and Talks after each part of your "I Do."
Antanov	4 (Sept 28)	1. Write the exemplar 2. What to Do	• Script exemplar response to the task into the lesson plan. • Deliver crisp 3–5 word directions for classroom routines like passing out papers.
Beck	5 (Sept 30)	1. Model the thinking, not just a procedure 2. Universal prompts	• Narrow the focus to the thinking students are struggling with.
Avg Obs per Teacher	**4.0**		

In one brief glance, the summary portion of the Observation Tracker can give you powerful insights:

- **Patterns across classrooms.** What are the action steps that are occurring most frequently across the school? Are they limited to new teachers? Just the math department? This information can be invaluable for planning a PD session that meets the needs of a group of teachers, or for training your instructional leadership team on a particular action step that is causing difficulties.

- **Patterns across leaders.** Are all of your instructional leaders observing equally? Are all teachers receiving a similar number of observations? Are there leaders whom you need to push to do more observations, or teachers who need more support?

Now imagine using this with your school leadership team. You can observe teachers to see both where they need to grow and whether the feedback they've received matches what you see. You have a tool for strengthening both your teachers' development and that of your leaders.

TURNAROUND—WHAT TO DO FIRST

A legitimate question to ask is, How do you implement a new observation and feedback cycle like this one with teachers who have never experienced anything like this before? Won't they resist such a change? I look no further than Kim Marshall, who was a pioneer for shorter observations as principal of the Mather School, an elementary school in Dorchester, Massachusetts. Many years later, in his book *Rethinking Teacher Supervision and Evaluation*, he related his personal experience of starting to move to briefer observations. Marshall notes:

> At first, teachers had their doubts about the mini-observation idea. I had introduced it at the beginning of the year, but teachers were still uncertain about what to expect. Several were visibly relieved when I gave them positive feedback after their first mini-observation. One primary teacher practically hugged me when I said how impressed I was with her children's Thanksgiving turkey masks. But others were thrown off stride when I came into their rooms, and I had to signal them to continue what they were doing. I hoped that as my visits became more routine, these teachers would relax and be able to ignore my presence. And that's what happened in almost all cases.[7]

Based on his experience and that of other leaders, there are a couple of key ways to ensure your staff is receptive when you launch this model:

- Make it clear that the purpose is coaching and improvement, not evaluation.
- Frame progress positively.

The greatest source of buy-in? The simplest answer is results, results, results. When teachers see their practice gradually improving and that they are getting consistent feedback, they are much more excited and more inspired to push themselves forward. You will build buy-in as you build a culture of practice.

When teachers see that a culture of practice is thriving all across the school—teachers are practicing reteaching in data meetings, role-playing teacher actions in feedback meetings, and doing the same in PD sessions (Chapter 4)—practice becomes the norm and not the exception. Of course, a small handful of teachers may still remain recalcitrant. At this point, however, the challenge shifts from apathy to intentional pushback. We'll address this challenge—and how to create a culture of practice—in Chapter 6 on staff culture.

When launched effectively, the real turnaround will not be in overcoming teacher resistance but in overcoming your own: resistance to setting foot in people's classrooms far more often, getting out of your office, locking in consistent meetings, and asking people to practice. That's the heart of turnaround, and that is something you can control.

Core Idea

The real turnaround challenge will not be teacher resistance, but your own. Lock in your schedule for observation and feedback meetings, and you will make the turnaround a success.

CONCLUSION

The lever of observation and feedback makes a difference at schools like Ashley's precisely because of the way it normalizes practice and growth in schools. It doesn't operate in isolation: its impact makes the super-levers, data and culture, stronger as well. Want to build a school that grows great—and keeps growing greater? Then get in your classrooms as Ashley did, and coach your teachers to greatness. Bridge the gap between the islands of every classroom, and the sky becomes the limit.

Action Steps for Principals

Observation and Feedback

LEVER	KEY ACTIONS IN SEQUENCE
	PLAN
OBSERVATION AND FEEDBACK	1. **Build weekly observation schedule for yourself and other instructional leaders/coaches:** • Establish and maintain own observation schedule and Observation Tracker. • Establish observation schedules and trackers for leadership team to effectively distribute observation of all teachers. • Adjust the schedule as needed to address trends and/or support struggling teachers. 2. **Prepare:** Stick to an exemplar script (See It, Name It, Do It feedback protocol) to ensure that your prompts are clear, economical, and aimed at the highest-leverage action step.
	EXECUTE

	Action Steps
	
	3. **ID highest-leverage school-wide and individual teacher action steps:**
	
	• Use your tools (Get Better Faster Scope and Sequence, student data) to create action steps that are
	
	   o Highest leverage (will student achievement improve tomorrow as a result of this action step?)
	
	   o Measurable and bite-size
	
	Effective Feedback Meetings
	
	4. **See It—see the success:**
	
	• Prepare and deliver precise, authentic praise rooted in previous action step(s).
	
	• Ask teacher to describe the impact: "What has been the impact of this on your classroom?"

LEVER	KEY ACTIONS IN SEQUENCE
	EXECUTE

<table>
<tr><td rowspan="1" style="vertical-align:middle">OBSERVATION AND FEEDBACK</td><td>

5. **See It—show a model and see the gap:**

- Show a model—video, live model, script, lesson plan—that highlights key actions for the teacher.
- Fully unpack to ID the model: start with the end in mind and ask precise questions to identify all key actions (e.g., What is the purpose of . . . ?" "What did she do next?").
- Ask "What is the gap between what you just saw and what you did?"

6. **Do It—perfect the plan before you practice:**

- Give your teacher time to script out her actions before you start the practice and between rounds of practice.
- Revise the script until it is perfect.
- Use an exemplar to perfect the plan.

7. **Do It—practice the gap:**

- Practice at the point of error: anticipate what teachers or students could do/say incorrectly during the practice and plan for those mistakes.
- Practice the gap: set up practice so that the teacher practices the actions that are most critical for the action step.

8. **Do It—practice. Go from simple to more complex:**

- Practice with upcoming lessons/meetings to apply the skill to multiple scenarios.
- Start with simple practice; when teacher masters it, add complexity (student wrong answers or noncompliance).
- Narrow the practice to repeat it more times and get more at-bats.
- Stop the practice, provide real-time feedback, and redo.

9. **Name It—punch it:**

- Punch the action step by naming the "what" and the "how" clearly and concisely.
- Be bite-size, not book-size: limit the action steps to what the teacher can master in a week.
- Have teacher write it down and check for understanding to make sure she has it.

</td></tr>
</table>

LEVER	KEY ACTIONS IN SEQUENCE
	MONITOR AND FOLLOW UP

<table>
<tr><td rowspan="2" style="writing-mode: vertical">OBSERVATION AND FEEDBACK</td><td>

10. Do It—follow up. Articulate clear next steps:

- Set dates: all deliverables have clear timelines and are written into both the leader's and teacher's calendar.
- Establish follow-up and (when applicable) real-time feedback cues to be used during the observation.

11. Provide real-time feedback:

- Choose highest-leverage moments for real-time classroom feedback.
- Use least invasive method for real-time feedback that is appropriate for the teacher.
  - Silent signal
  - Whisper prompt:
    - Name what to do
    - State the rationale
    - State what you'll look for/how you will support
    - (All in 45 seconds max)
  - Verbal prompt/model
  - Extended model

</td></tr>
</table>

Pulling the Lever

Action Planning Worksheet for OBSERVATION AND FEEDBACK

Self-Assessment

- How frequently are your teachers being observed? _____/year or _____/month

- What is the current teacher-to-leader ratio? _____ teachers per full-time instructional leader

- Review the action steps for principals for observation and feedback (previous box). What are the biggest gaps in your implementation that you want to close first?
  (*Note:* the action steps are listed in priority order, so "think waterfall": start at the top and stop at the first major growth area.)

  _____

  _____

  _____

  _____

  _____

  _____

Planning for Action

- What tools from this book will you use to improve observation and feedback at your school? Check all that you will use (you can find all on the DVD):

  ☐ Get Better Faster Scope and Sequence of action steps

  ☐ Get Better Faster Coach's Guide

  ☐ Giving Effective Feedback one-pager

  ☐ Observation Tracker

  ☐ Real-Time Feedback one-pager

  ☐ Videos of observation and feedback meetings

  ☐ PD materials for observation and feedback

- What are your next steps for improving observation and feedback?

Action	Date

Chapter 4

Professional Development

High school English teacher Laura Palumbo is hard at work preparing for her students to be able to unpack the deeper meaning of a classic: Shakespeare's Sonnet 65.

> Since brass, nor stone, nor earth, nor boundless sea,
> But sad mortality o'er-sways their power,
> How with this rage shall beauty hold a plea,
> Whose action is no stronger than a flower?
> O, how shall summer's honey breath hold out
> Against the wreckful siege of battering days,
> When rocks impregnable are not so stout,
> Nor gates of steel so strong, but Time decays?
> O fearful meditation! Where, alack,
> Shall Time's best jewel from Time's chest lie hid?
> Or what strong hand can hold his swift foot back?

Or who his spoil of beauty can forbid?
O, none, unless this miracle have might,
That in black ink my love may still shine bright.

In the middle of the in-depth discussion, she notes, "Now Kate brought up the concept of beauty. Which of these images that Sarah spoke about most clearly connects to beauty?" The discussion quickly zooms in on the importance of the flower and continues to analyze the meaning.

What's remarkable about this conversation is that Laura isn't actually addressing her students—she's speaking to three fellow teachers. They're attending a professional development (PD) session on close reading, led by Uncommon Schools assistant superintendent Kelly Dowling. The conference room is alive with the sound of dozens of teachers like Laura practicing the techniques they're working to perfect under Kelly's guidance, while their colleagues role-play as their students to make the practice as authentic as possible.

A few minutes in, Kelly brings the room back together. "Now's our chance to give feedback," she says. "What would be the top piece of feedback you would give your teacher to improve his or her close reading instruction?"

After participants spend a minute reflecting, the room grows active again as they exchange high-leverage feedback. Kelly gives them three minutes to debrief before raising her hand to get everyone's attention. "Great," she says. "Partner B, it's your turn."

Practice begins again. By the end of this session, every participant will have had the opportunity to practice these steps to making his or her close reading more effective.

 WATCH Clip 20: Dowling—Do It (Practice)—Leading PD

Take a moment to remember the best PD you've ever attended. Maybe it was a session with a guided reading specialist that finally made sense of all the disparate advice you'd heard previously about teaching your students to read. Maybe it was a diversity workshop that helped you respond to something that had always troubled you in your school community. It may even have been a session on leadership—something you were grateful you got to experience in your career as a school leader, because it made the immense task of leading a school more manageable for you.

Whatever it was, chances are that the reason this PD still sticks in your mind is that it made a difference to who you became as a person, teacher, or leader. The PD that matters is the PD that marks us and changes us.

What if you could lead PD that made that same difference to everyone in a workshop—not just the hungry learners, but the entire staff? Think back again to that session that made such a difference to you, and imagine the impact it would have had if all the participants in that session had gone on to make the same improvements to their practice that you did. If every PD gave every participant the right tools to become better at his or her work, the results would be transformative.

The question is: How can we craft PD that results in that kind of change? We can't do it by relying only on our most avid learners. We have to reach everyone—every time.

Leaders like Kelly say the answer is clear-cut: set up participants to experience success. That's what we saw in the portion of her PD that's captured at the beginning of this chapter. Kelly spent as little time as possible talking to her teachers, and as much as possible letting them practice their new skills in the company of adept peers. "Most PD doesn't make a difference in the classroom," says Kelly, "because you talk about things but you don't tackle the hardest part—doing it! You leave it for the teachers to figure out when they go back to their classroom. But when I give them the opportunity to practice with me right then, we see more results right away."

Her proof is in her results. Kelly's students do more than outperform their neighbors in the economically disadvantaged communities in Newark and Camden, New Jersey, where she manages schools. They also score higher on year-end state exams than their peers across the state (see Figure 4.1).

PD alone will not achieve these results. Nearly every school in the world has some sort of PD at some point, and that does not guarantee improvement. This is why I say that PD is the weakest of all the levers: it only works when in concert with the others. Such was the case with Kelly, who had the other leadership levers in place to make PD stick. Yet PD can play a powerful role in a school. Kelly's experience speaks to a recurring theme that we've already seen play out in every lever we've discussed thus far: the magic of great leadership is tied to what people practice. What teachers can do at the end of the PD determines the quality of the PD. Successful PD isn't about our intent: it's about the quality of what we practice.

Core Idea

Your PD is only as powerful as what you practice.

Figure 4.1 New Jersey PARRC Results: Camden Prep, Percentage at or Above Proficiency in Third-Grade Math

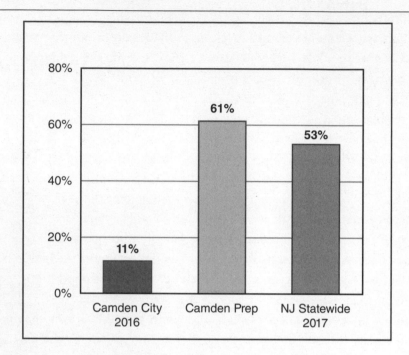

How, then, can you make a practice session with a room full of teachers powerful enough to stick? With the familiar structure of See It, Name It, Do It.

Think about the snapshot of Kelly's PD that opened this chapter: we witnessed the Do It portion of her PD: the driving force of the entire workshop. By giving a large group of people the opportunity to practice a high-leverage action step, you multiply the power of the one-on-one practice that occurs during feedback meetings by the number of participants in the workshop.

This chapter will show you how to put together a workshop that is designed to facilitate practice—and covers material worth practicing. We'll start at the beginning: determining what you'll have participants practice in your PD.

WHAT TO TEACH: FOLLOW THE DATA

Every leader in this book has used PD to support his or her implementation of a key lever. Let's look at two of these leaders—Antonio Burt and Laura Garza—and note how they determine where to focus. As you read the scenarios from each of their leadership team meetings, what do you notice they share in common?

Behind the Scenes: From Paper to Practice

Scene 1

Antonio hunkers down with his colleagues at their weekly leadership team meeting. "Let's look at our observation tracker from this week. Review all the action steps that we gave each of our teachers. What patterns do we see?" His assistant principal and coach lean over, scanning the feedback they've given to their staff.

"We seem to have a group of new teachers who are struggling to identify when the first students go off task. By the time they realize it, they've lost half the class," the coach comments.

"I agree," concurs Antonio. "It sounds like we're talking about radar—scanning the room. Let's plan on making the PD this Friday address that topic. What are the key actions they need to be able to do what we're not seeing in the classroom?"

Scene 2

The members of Laura's leadership team pull out their notes from last week's grade-level team meetings. "OK. Each of you participated in the weekly data meeting of the grade-level teams. What were the most important standards you focused on?" All of Laura's principals recount their meetings, mentioning standards such as base-ten understanding in first grade and fractions of a whole in third.

"OK," comments Laura. "Based on those data meetings, where are the gaps for our teachers—do they need to know the content better, or is the key a part of their instruction?"

Her assistant principal talks about the breakdown that occurs when students get a wrong answer in class. "Rather than letting the students grapple with the error and unpack their thinking, our teachers are consistently stepping in and just telling them the answer."

"I'm seeing the same thing," says another leader. "We should plan our upcoming PD around using universal prompts." Heads nod as they take out their laptops to begin planning.

Stop and Jot

What do Antonio's and Laura's meetings have in common?

_____

_____

_____

_____

_____

_____

_____

_____

Antonio and Laura have never met each other, but they've both landed on the same key principle: PD matters when it responds to a need. You cannot determine that by reading a textbook: you do that by monitoring your school.

The entire purpose of your PD is to close a gap that's impacting learning. Sounds simple, but too often we forget amid the noise of everything we could be doing during PD and prepackaged sessions that are proposed by others.[1]

Core Idea

Effective PD responds to real needs at a real school: yours.
To run PD that makes a difference, give your team opportunities
to practice their gaps.

Like many busy school leaders, Adriana Gonzalez (whom you'll get to know better in Chapter 6 on staff culture) has looked into outsourcing PD to presenters from beyond her campus. Ultimately, however, she's committed to keeping PD "in-house" as much as possible. Why? Because in order to drive a school's growth, PD must meet teachers' needs _precisely_ where they are. Having a company come in and provide a workshop for you may seem like a time-saver, but in the long run, the only way to make time invested in PD time well spent is to figure out what your teachers need. "We make sure our PD is tied to our initiatives as a school for the year," Adriana says. If the PD doesn't reflect where her teachers are on their way to meeting those initiatives, it's not a good use of their time.

Findings from the Field

"What Does It Look Like Inside the Classrooms?"

"Our results took off when we identified the essential components of any successful daily lesson, and built PD around those. We'd train teachers in each of these and then observe them in action. As a leadership team, we'd then look at our observations and ask, 'What does it look like inside the classrooms? What's missing?' That's how we knew what we needed to run PD on next."

—Antonio Burt, assistant superintendent, Memphis, Tennessee

Follow the Data . . .

The first step to identifying a worthwhile PD objective is to determine the highest-leverage actions teachers are struggling to implement. Data from your school is the only way to accomplish this. Here are the three sources of information that leaders like Kelly use in order to craft the PD her teachers need.

Assessment Data and Student Work

Assessments are the first place to look for school-wide areas for curricular or instructional improvement. By analyzing interim assessment data or even daily Exit Tickets, leaders like Kelly are always on the lookout for larger patterns that cut across classes and grade levels. Here is an example of a summary analysis of student work.

ELA Interim Assessment (IA) 7-1—Network Analysis

Most Significant Trend of Errors in Seventh Grade

What?	Why?
Domain and Standard	Which incorrect answer did students choose? Why did students not master this question type?
Choosing the Best Evidence Central Idea II	Across the IA, students struggled to identify evidence to support their views, both in their writing and on the multiple-choice section of the test. Although they

(Determine a theme or central idea of a text and analyze its development over the course of the text; provide an objective summary of the text.)	can sometimes choose just OK evidence, they frequently did not choose the best evidence or picked incorrect evidence altogether. Some examples: • **Question 7—Central Idea II (Part B: 17%)—** Fewer than half of the students who got question 6 correct were able to find the correct evidence to support the answer (53% correct on Q6 dropped to 17% correct on Q7). • **Question 19—Central Idea II (Part B: 20%)—** Again, fewer than half of the students who got question 18 correct were able to find the correct evidence to support the answer (47% correct on Q18 dropped to 20% correct on Q19). • **Writing** ○ **Essay—Evidence (52%):** The nature of this prompt made it difficult for students to choose evidence that was completely without merit, but evidence chosen was often not the strongest possible to support the prompt—or was not analyzed in a way that justified its inclusion. Although it was less pronounced than at this time last year, students were still struggling with chunking a quote of appropriate length.

From this analysis, Kelly has a clear focus for PD for her reading teachers: main idea.

Observation of Teachers and Plans

As noted in Chapters 2 and 3, when you observe effectively, you can review the lesson plan and see the quality of execution at the same time. In doing so, you can more easily determine where the breakdowns are occurring. The observation tracker allows you to see that data as patterns across the whole school. A quick review of the summary page enables a leader to find common or persistent actions where PD could make an impact.

Observation Tracker—Summary Page

All-Teacher Summary Tab

Name	Total Obs (last date observed)	Major PD Goal	Latest Key Action Step
Smith	7 (Oct 26)	1. Engage all students 2. What to Do 3. Strong voice	• Make sure to call on all students. • Give three clear options for polling (thumbs up, down, and side). • Square up and stand still.
Doe	5 (Oct 12)	1. Habits of evidence 2. Economy of language	• Ask "Why?" and "How do you know?" after students make generalizations.
Raines	5 (Oct 13)	1. Narrate the positive 2. Strong voice 3. Engage all students	• Narrate participation. • Add brief (15–30-second) Turn and Talks. • Square up and stand still.
Antanov	4 (Oct 24)	1. Write the exemplar 2. Whole-class reset 3. Strong voice	• Script desired answers into learning plans. • Retrain classroom procedure for passing out papers. Normalize 10 seconds for passing in papers. • Square up and stand still.
Beck	5 (Oct 24)	1. Model the thinking, not just a procedure 2. Universal prompts	• Narrow the focus to the thinking students are struggling with.
Avg Obs per Teacher	5.2		

Walkthroughs for Culture or Rigor

Finally, as you will see in the upcoming chapters on student culture (Chapter 5) and managing school leadership teams (Chapter 7), leaders can use school rubrics to quantify a subjective area such as student culture or rigor—and then to focus on particular aspects of the area that they'd like to improve. Here's one example of a completed rubric after a culture walkthrough. The columns that are shaded represent the score the leader gave the school on the walkthrough:

Culture Walkthrough Data

Scores on Student Culture Rubric

Classroom Systems	Advanced	Proficient	Working Toward	Needs Improvement
Transition Between Activities	• Efficient, time-saving (30 sec) routine. • Teacher initiated using economy of language. (Teacher says "transition" and students move.) • Immediately after the transition, students begin task. • Students know how to adjust the physical	• Efficient, time-saving (up to 1 min) routine. • Teacher facilitated. • After the transition, students are waiting for directions. • Students know how to adjust the physical setting. (MS/HS teacher facilitated.) • Evidence of a routine.	• Inefficient, more than 1 minute. • Off-task talking, too noisy. • Teacher has to repeat directions. • After the transition, students are off task. • Physical setting is not adjusted. • Not a clearly established routine; teacher has to redo the transition.	• Inefficient, more than 1 minute. • Off-task talking, too noisy. • Teacher has to repeat directions. • After the transition, students are off task. • Physical setting is not adjusted. • Not a clearly established routine;

Classroom Systems	Advanced	Proficient	Working Toward	Needs Improvement
	setting (MS/HS teacher initiated). • Evidence of a routine.			teacher has to redo the transition.
Student Joy and Engagement	• Students seem to be joyful and excited to be in school. • 90–100% of students are engaged in classroom activities.	• Most students seem to be joyful and excited to be in school. • 80–90% of students are engaged in classroom activities.	• Although many students seem joyful, there are notable instances of student arguments and/or lack of joy. • 70–80% of students are engaged in classroom activities.	• Students generally seem disinterested in school. • Less than 70% of students are engaged in classroom activities.
Exit	• Class ends on time with sufficient time to line up students. • Teacher uses a consistent system to have students line up that is organized,	• Class ends on time. • Teacher uses a consistent system to have students line up that is organized, quick, and efficient. • Teacher leads students to	• Class ends in a rushed or hurried way or goes over time. • Teacher lines up students in a disorganized way, or does not check to see that all students	• Class ends late or in a rushed or hurried way. • No evidence of a systematic dismissal process is evident. • Teacher does not lead students to

Classroom Systems	Advanced	Proficient	Working Toward	Needs Improvement
	quick, and efficient. • Teacher leads students to the next class.	the next class.	are ready to be lined up. • Teacher does not lead students all the way to the next class.	the next class. • Students are loud and disorganized during the transition.

With these resources in hand, you have the right information to determine what content will make for the highest-leverage PD objective for your staff. Now the question becomes: How much can you accomplish in one PD session?

. . . Then Narrow Your Focus

The natural tendency when designing PD is to try to do too much, which leads to only one outcome: you end up talking too much. Teresa Khirallah, program officer for the Teaching Trust, whom you'll spend more time with in Chapter 6, learned that lesson the hard way. "In the beginning of being a principal, I would talk most of the time and end up with only twelve minutes at the end for practice," Teresa recalls. "That meant when my teachers left the room, I still didn't really know if they could do the skill or not."

So what are some helpful tips to narrow the focus of your PD to what matters most? Start with the opening question of this chapter: What do you want them to practice?

Core Idea

The best way to narrow the focus of your PD is to ask a simple question:
What do you want them to practice?

In the end, what they practice is what they learn. We already learned the key criteria for effective practice in Chapter 3 on observation and feedback: make sure the practice is highest leverage, measurable, and bite-size.

Note: making your PD bite-size depends on the time you have for PD—an hour, a half day, a full day, or even multiple days. What you can accomplish can grow with the amount of time you have.

Now that you know these criteria, give them a try! What follows are three case studies of how to translate the data you collected to a concrete PD objective.

Case Studies

Crafting High-Leverage Actions to Practice During PD

Grab a pen and try these out. We give you the trend that the principal collected from his or her school: your job is to narrow the focus of the PD to what the teachers should practice. After this exercise, we give you some possible answers to check against your own.

1: Teacher PD—Habits of Discussion

Observation trends: Teachers are struggling to lead productive class discussions. Typically, when a teacher opens the floor for class discussion, many students are eager to speak, but they generally just share their point and make no reference to anyone else's argument. When the teacher asks students whether they agree or disagree with one of their peers, the students will start their next sentence with the phrase "I agree with . . . ," but then they will actually say something that is completely different and disconnected from what their peer said.

Weak objective (90 min session):

- Get students to utilize the habits of discussion.

Still too weak:

- Get students to agree and disagree.

Your turn—write the PD objective:
What do you want teachers to practice to improve the habits of discussion in class? Make it high leverage, measurable, and bite-size:

_____
_____
_____
_____

2: Teacher PD—Reteaching Math

Assessment analysis: IA results reveal that fifth-grade math students are struggling to comprehend patterns in the number of zeroes in the products of powers of ten—only 20 percent answered correctly on the last Exit Ticket. They aren't consistently able to write numbers in expanded form, and tend to explain patterns in terms of adding or subtracting zeroes, rather than in terms of place value.

Weak objective (90 min session):

- Reteach place value to lead to a greater conceptual understanding.

Still too weak:

- Model for students how to find the value of each place in larger numbers.

Your turn—write the PD objective:
What do you want teachers to practice to improve their students' achievement with place value? Make it high leverage, measurable, and bite-size:

_____
_____
_____
_____

3: Instructional Leader PD—Weekly Data Meetings

Observation of weekly data meetings: Your instructional leaders are struggling to lead weekly data meetings that drive actual improvements to student learning. As you observe their meetings, you see that the teachers are gung-ho about planning elaborate, detailed reteaching plans, but they often are addressing a superficial part of the student error rather than the root cause that is hindering their achievement.

As a result, students are not doing better on the subsequent reassessments. You want to design a PD session to make your instructional leaders stronger at leading weekly data meetings.

Weak objective (90 min session):

- Lead effective weekly data meetings that follow the See It, Name It, Do It structure.

Still too weak:

- Lead effectively the See It section of weekly data meetings.

Your turn—write the PD objective:

What do you want teachers to practice to improve their students' achievement with place value? Make it high leverage, measurable, and bite-size:

_____

_____

_____

_____

_____

Now that you've taken the time to think of practice-worthy objectives, compare your answers to those we've shown here. Note: there could be more than one possible right answer; it depends on what your teachers or instructional leaders need the most! Spar with these examples to see where your own objectives can be stronger when you plan your own PD.

Spar

Answers for Each Case Study

Case Study 1 (Habits of Discussion)

Strong, practice-worthy objectives:

- Model the proper use of agree/disagree prompts during class discussion.
- Identify when students are not using the prompts correctly.
- Name the inappropriate use of the prompts and ask students to correct their response.

How the objectives meet the criteria:

- **Highest leverage.** They focus on the root problem, which is not the use of the discussion prompts but the *correct* use of them.

- **Measurable.** They are simple to practice and to measure when you observe.
- **Bite-size.** The three objectives are granular enough to be feasible in a single PD session of 60–90 minutes.

Case Study 2 (Reteaching Math)

Strong, practice-worthy objectives:

- Model the thinking, not just the procedure:
  - Narrow the focus to the thinking students are struggling with.
  - Model replicable thinking steps that students can follow.
  - Model how to activate one's own content knowledge and skills that have been learned in previous lessons.
  - Vary the think-aloud in tone and cadence from the normal "teacher" voice to highlight the thinking skills.

How the objectives meet the criteria:

- **Highest leverage.** The key gap here for the teachers is how to model the skill effectively, so improving the quality of the think-aloud will directly impact learning.
- **Measurable.** You can see if the teacher does each of these if you observe the reteach.
- **Bite-size.** The objectives are granular enough to be feasible in a PD session of 60–90 minutes.

Case Study 3 (Weekly Data Meetings)

Strong, practice-worthy objectives:

- Chart the See It:
  - Start with the standard(s): fully unpack the standard to identify what students must know and be able to do to show mastery.
  - Unpack the exemplar: unpack the teacher/student exemplars to add to your chart of what students must know and be able to do to show mastery.
- Name It:
  - Use your chart: identify the parts of the unpacked standard/exemplar that are the root cause of the student error.

How the objectives meet the criteria:

- **Highest leverage.** Unpacking the standard and exemplar is what gives teachers the tools to determine the root-cause error of the students: you need to know your destination before you can figure out where you are!
- **Measurable.** You can observe the charts of a weekly data meeting to see if teachers are unpacking the standard and exemplar effectively.
- **Bite-size.** Instructional leaders could work on these objectives in a single PD session.

Once you know what you're going to practice, you're ready to design your workshop!

HOW TO TEACH: LIVE THE LEARNING

Kelly wasn't born a natural workshop deliverer: she built her skill little by little, workshop by workshop, until she became the nearly flawless presenter she is today. The key to her transformation was her meticulous preparation—and using the See It, Name It, Do It framework. Let's see how.

See It

Leading PD can be incredibly complex, especially when focusing on teaching content. The solution to this complexity is the same as in feedback and data meetings: let participants see it. Take a look at how Kelly does this at the start of her workshop on how to monitor student's comprehension when they are reading independently.

 WATCH Clip 21: Dowling—See It and Name It—Leading PD

Stop and Jot

What does Kelly do to launch her PD? Jot down what you noticed.

_____

_____

_____

_____

_____

_____

_____

Watching how Kelly's teachers respond to the model makes it clear why this strategy works: seeing is believing. Kelly's teachers see an example of a teacher's annotated handout used to prepare to monitor student work, and now they know exactly what it looks like. Just as was the case in feedback meetings, seeing the exemplar sets teachers up to be able to put it into action.

> ### Core Idea
>
> What's good for feedback is good for PD: if you want teachers to get it, get them to see it.

Of all the actions Kelly took, these contributed most to making the See It effective:

- **Choose the best model.** In this case, what teachers most needed to see first was how to prepare to observe students' reading; thus the teacher's plans were the best model. Later, they will need to see the teaching itself, and video clips of exemplary teaching are one of the most powerful ways for teachers to see the model. If you don't have one from your school, you can use one from another campus. There also are many effective teaching clips that you can find in the books *Teach Like a Champion, Get Better Faster,* and *Great Habits, Great Readers.* If exemplary video of an action is not available, an equally strong option is to model it yourself or ask one of your teachers to do so. You can immediately earn your staff's respect when you are willing to model what you'd like them to do: you show that you are "walking the talk."

- **Keep it short.** Kelly knows that a long See It won't hold participants' attention—and will take valuable time away from practicing. Accordingly, she keeps it short: no longer than five minutes.

- **Target the focus.** The goal of the See It is to codify what makes the exemplar great, not to get caught up in its flaws. That's why Kelly kicks off the activity with a targeted question *before* watching the model: "How does Allison prepare for her close reading lessons, and what is the purpose of her prework?" Those questions focus participants' attention on what the master teacher in the exemplar is doing right, not what she is doing wrong. Kelly also keeps these questions visible (on a PowerPoint screen or handout) while the exemplar is being observed. This keeps your participants' thoughts on what you want them to notice—and it will ensure that they remember the questions even as they devote their full attention to the exemplar.

Name It

Once teachers have had time to review the model, Kelly leads them into a discussion as to why each part of the exemplar is important. Once they've mentioned the key concepts, Kelly stamps their understanding—Name It—by showing a Core Idea slide and summarizing the key components that the group mentioned.

Those few minutes are highly valuable. By sharing a key idea with them, Kelly gives the participants a common language with which to remember what they've just discovered. She also makes it memorable and pauses long enough to let it sink in. Put words to what you see, and you see it more clearly.

Core Idea

If you name what you see, you see it more clearly.

Here, again, you'll see a connection to observation and feedback: the steps that made Kelly's Name It effective are similar to those that make a feedback meeting powerful:

- **Prompt the group to focus on the key actions.** Kelly asks a series of prompts that point her teachers to the key takeaways from the See It without giving those ideas away. She starts with a Turn and Talk to allow every person in the room to share and crystallize his or her thoughts. When they then share out in a large group, she uses especially effective universal prompts like "What is the purpose?" or "Why is that important?" By using prompts that didn't reveal the answer she was looking for, Kelly quickly gets PD participants to do the thinking so that they learn on their own.

- **Punch it.** Once the participants have generated all of the most essential cognitive work, Kelly punches the core idea with formal language: "The quality of your prework dictates the quality of your class work." Even at this point, she keeps her language succinct and precise—a one-sentence summary, not a lengthy explanation. By following these steps, Kelly puts the famous advice of Bill Graham into action: she makes the complicated simple, and the simple powerful.

Core Idea

"Make the complicated simple, and the simple powerful."

—Bill Graham

Do It

All that See It and Name It are intended to do is set you up for teachers to have effective practice. Let's see how that looks, this time in a PD at the high school level. In the two clips that follow, Kelly's colleagues Jesse Corburn and Denarius Frazier are preparing their teachers for practice. Jesse is guiding his teachers in the design of effective lesson plans, and Denarius is working with his teachers to develop stronger reteaching think-alouds. Watch what each of these leaders does first.

 WATCH Clip 22: Corburn—Do It (Plan)—Leading PD
WATCH Clip 23: Frazier—Do It (Plan)—Leading PD

Stop and Jot

What actions do Jesse and Denarius take to make their teachers better?.

_____

_____

_____

_____

_____

_____

_____

Anyone who's ever stood up to rehearse a set of actions can testify that if you don't think ahead, you freeze up on the spot. Jesse anticipates this challenge by giving his participants the opportunity to plan before they practice. That sets everyone up to practice perfectly.

Core Idea

The precision of your plan determines the quality of your practice.
Perfect the plan before you practice.

Jesse took three steps to lock in the success of this planning time:

- **Script it.** Have participants script what they will do and say before the actual practice. That way, Jesse knows that when teachers stand up to practice, they'll already have their first moves down.

- **Use your tools.** Utilize resources to make the plan as specific as possible. Jesse prompts teachers to use the resources they already have—guides on lesson planning, exemplar lesson plans, and so on—to optimize their plan's precision and effectiveness on the first go.

- **Tighten it.** Have participants give feedback on each other's plans before they transition to practice. Getting this feedback from their peers gives participants' practice an additional layer of relevance and precision before they dive into practice.

When the plan is in place, it's time for participants to take that plan live. Let's return to Denarius's PD on think-alouds as well as Kelly's PD on monitoring student work in reading class. How do both of these leaders facilitate the practice itself?

REWATCH Clip 20: Dowling—Do It (Practice)—Leading PD
WATCH Clip 24: Frazier—Do It (Practice)—Leading PD

Stop and Jot

What does Kelly do before and during the practice to maximize its effectiveness? Jot down what you noticed.

_____

_____

_____

_____

_____

_____

_____

Kelly and her participants have arrived at the heart of the PD. Let's unpack what they did to make their practice—and their entire PD—powerful.

> ## Core Idea
> Your PD is only as powerful as what you practice.

- **Deliver clear instructions.** When the time comes to begin practicing, Kelly makes sure to deliver clear directions for the practice and post this protocol for the duration of the Do It. PD practice directions should include, at a minimum, the following information: what the main participant who is practicing will be doing, and what the other participants in the group will be doing during that time.

- **Practice the gap.** Kelly makes sure that the practice focuses on the part of the skill participants are learning that will be most difficult for them to master. When you lead this part of a PD session, initially keep the practice simple and straightforward, adding layers of complexity (such as role playing student confusion) in subsequent rounds of practice.

- **Target the feedback.** Kelly prepared a "feedback cheat sheet" to point participants to the highest-leverage areas on which she anticipated they'd need to receive feedback. Other ways to optimize feedback include monitoring practice and responding to what you hear participants struggling with.

- **Do it again.** The goal of the PD is not simply to experience practice: it is to practice perfectly! Kelly therefore makes sure each participant has a chance to do it again to incorporate the feedback and get even better.

Reflect

When we are learning something new, one factor is often overlooked: time. Learning a new skill is just like weightlifting. The real magic of long-term gains is not just in the practice but in the quiet that ensues after. Weightlifters need sleep—physical rest—for the body to actually build stronger muscles. If weightlifters don't get enough sleep, it doesn't matter how much they train—they will not make progress. For learners, that translates to time to think.

For years, PD deliverers have focused on squeezing as much content into one session as possible, thinking that the participants need more knowledge or skill to be effective. This was to the detriment of time to practice or even simply reflect. Yet new research highlights the need for targeted time for reflection. Giada Di Stefano, Francesca Gino, Gary P. Pisano, and Bradley Staats from HEC Paris and the Harvard Business School have looked at models for organizational learning in their recent working paper "Making Experience Count: The Role of Reflection in Individual Learning."[2] One of their core findings is that once an individual has practiced or built experience in doing something, reflecting on his or her experience adds far more value than additional practice without reflection. This helps not only in the cognitive mastery of a skill but also in increasing the participant's belief in his or her ability to master the skill.[3] And adding reflection to our PD takes remarkably little time!

To see how reflection plays out in PD, watch what happens in the final ten seconds of this video of participants completing the Do It portion of a PD led by *Great Habits, Great Readers* author Juliana Worrell.

 WATCH Clip 25: Worrell—Reflect—Leading PD

To lock in learning, Juliana has participants reflect on what they'd learned about the skill they were working on, before diving into practice. Here's how she makes that reflection valuable.

- **Keep reflections brief.** Most individuals only require one to three minutes to reflect on a given topic. Juliana allots one minute for individual reflection, and then a final two minutes for a large-group share.

- **Provide a single place for reflections to be written down.** Juliana provides her participants with a colorful sheet of paper where they can record all reflections. They'll walk away after the workshop with a single, easy-to-find sheet of key takeaways.

- **Share out at key moments.** Juliana has participants share their reflections aloud so the whole group can hear key takeaways.

Reflection takes only a few moments, but it dramatically improves the internalization of the PD. It gives participants time to cement the learning and clears space in the brain for them to learn what's next.

> ## Core Idea
>
> Lock in learning by writing down your reflections.

See It. Name It. Do It. Reflect. When you have these steps in place, PD can produce powerful outcomes. Here's a simple guide for leading PD. (It is also included on the DVD.)

A Word on . . . Preparing Presentations

In keeping with the theme of this book, great PD is about making every minute count. The following are some tips for getting the most out of each session you lead:

Rehearse, rehearse, rehearse. Scripting and practicing the entire presentation will make it far more polished and effective. Even if it feels awkward presenting in front of a mirror or to a colleague, rehearsing will make the final performance much better.

Anticipate tough responses. Because the See It, Name It, Do It model is driven by audience participation, presenters need to be ready to deal with challenging audience responses, such as wrong answers during framing or confrontational reactions. Preparing scaffolded questions to guide your audience back can be invaluable in dealing with these situations. Although these will vary depending on the situation, remember that scripting in advance will help you keep your cool and remain confident even if the questions or responses are challenging.

Build in time for movement. Building in more kinetic activities is a great way to keep engagement high. Movement can be built into presentations by having participants "share out" on bulletin boards, switching groups in the middle of the presentation, or scheduling frequent breaks.

Plan transitions. Taking the time to script and plan for transitions between activities can make a big difference. For example, prepositioning binder supplies rather than handing them out can save several minutes and will make the presentation feel much more dynamic.

Professional Development

An Effective Approach to Leading PD

Objective = Do It	Determining your real objective by what they will practice
	Highest leverage. *Practice the gap*: do the most important skills to increase proficiency. **Clear and measurable.** You can easily evaluate whether they have accomplished the objective. **Bite-size.** You can accomplish the objective in the time you have allotted.
See It	**See It: a model of what the Do It will look like**
	See the model. Let them see the Do It in action (keep it short! < 5 min): • Video clip of teaching/leading • Written exemplar or case study • Live model **Target their focus.** Ask questions *before* the activity to target what they should see: • Focus on the positive. Focus the question on observing the exemplary actions: o What does [teacher/leader] do and say during _____? • Always visible. Keep questions visible during the See It activity.

Name It	Name It: formal language to describe the Do It
	Think-Pair-Share: • Give time to reflect (individual), share with partner (Turn and Talk), and share with the large group. **Prompt.** Focus on the key elements of the model: • "What happened in [certain part of the teaching video]?" • "Why is that important?" "What's the purpose of that action?" "What's the value?" • "What would happen if we didn't do that?" **Punch it:** • Wait until the end. Let participants do the cognitive work first; then name it with formal language: "So we've come to a core idea . . ." • Say the key line, pause, then say, "Think about the significance of this." Then restate. • Limit the words: keep framework succinct and precise (3–5 bullets; one-pager).
Do It	**Do It: putting it into practice**
	Plan before practice: • Give participants time to script prompts/actions/activities before diving into practice. • Leverage the Name It: encourage them to use their tools provided during the workshop.

Do It (con't.)	Do It: putting it into practice
	Provide a clear What to Do: • Name what main participant will do: review protocol timing, where she will practice, and what tools she will use. • Name what the audience will do: cue cards, preprepared student work samples. • (If group is large) Name what small-group facilitators will do: feedback tips, what to look for. **Practice:** • Practice the gap: practice what participants will struggle to master on their own. • Monitor the room with exemplar in hand: ID common errors in implementation. **Give feedback and do it again:** • Give large-group feedback on common errors; model again if necessary. • Peer-to-peer: use feedback cheat sheet to target feedback. • Do it again: each person implements his feedback before moving on. • Add complexity (e.g., student noncompliance) in subsequent practice rounds.
Reflect	**Reflect: lock in the learning by writing it down**
	Brief and written in one place: 1–2 minutes at a time, embedded throughout the PD
Repeat the cycle as needed	

HOW TO MAKE IT STICK: FOLLOW UP

The Impact of Your Levers

How the Instructional Levers Hold Teachers Accountable

A week after her PD session, Kelly conducts her weekly observation of Jacqueline, a sixth-grade teacher on staff. As she does, she is watching to see how the PD is being implemented. Jacqueline does not disappoint; as her students transition from group discussion to independent practice, Jacqueline uses the techniques she just learned in the PD. Kelly nods and writes down confirmation of implementation in her observation tracker. Jacqueline is still struggling with one element of the technique—nonverbal signals—and Kelly writes that down as her key action step for their next check-in.

Kelly knows that however excellent her PD, it may not be remembered. How many times have you learned something only to forget it a few days later? What keeps that from happening is follow-up: someone helps us make those actions a habit.

For school leaders like Kelly, that means seeing the actions in the classroom. A PD without practice won't lead to learning, and practice without follow-up won't make it stick.

Core Idea

A PD without practice won't lead to learning, and practice without follow-up won't make it stick.

The good news is that the other levers in *Leverage Leadership 2.0* give you everything you need to make PD last. Let's take a look at how Kelly does it.

Monitor Implementation . . .

Kelly maximizes the power of PD by utilizing her other leadership levers. Simply observing teachers, leading data meetings, or leading walkthroughs can enable you to collect the data on whether the PD is being implemented:

- **Look at student work.** Because Kelly's top goal when she delivers PD is to give teachers what they need to drive student learning, the first place she looks to see whether the PD is succeeding is at instructional data. Student learning is the clearest indicator of whether a PD session worked: if you deliver PD on guided reading techniques and reading results don't change, the PD isn't being implemented effectively—or you focused on the wrong objective.

- **Observe and/or do walkthroughs.** Whereas some aspects of PD implementation can be observed via a data spreadsheet, others have to be seen firsthand. You can drive PD implementation either by checking for implementation during your regularly scheduled observations or by developing a walkthrough just to check up on one specific set of teacher actions you want to be seeing throughout your school. Chapter 7 on managing school leadership teams will cover the design of a walkthrough that targets a specific area.

. . . and Coach for Results

Once Kelly has collected data regarding PD implementation, she can coach her staff to improve. There are two key opportunities to do this: during a feedback or data meeting, or in real time in the classroom.

- **Upcoming feedback meetings and/or data analysis meetings.** After Kelly gathers data on the quality of implementation, she can make this a focus of upcoming feedback meetings and/or data analysis meetings. That enables a teacher to have a more personalized one-on-one avenue for additional practice on areas of struggle, but it also communicates to the teacher that Kelly cares about him implementing the PD skills and succeeding! That has a ripple effect on his approach to all subsequent PD.

- **Real-time feedback.** Chapter 3 on observation and feedback gave a brief overview of the power of real-time feedback. Real-time feedback is especially valuable after you have led a PD. You can easily establish nonverbal signals to use to communicate with the teacher. For example, if you are working on the habits of discussion, you can simply post universal prompts on a poster in the back of the room and then point to them while observing to encourage the teacher to use them. Given that all teachers just took the PD, they will be attuned to you observing for those skills, which makes the feedback in the moment even more powerful.

- **Practice clinics.** If there is a pattern of teachers struggling to implement a skill, you may choose to deliver another PD session—or you could just target teachers who need additional focused practice. Tildi Sharp, principal of North Star Academy Lincoln Park High School of Newark, New Jersey, has incorporated weekly practice clinics into her school's schedule, and it has sped up improvement across the staff by leaps and bounds. "It's just half an hour with a small group of the teachers with me modeling for five minutes and everyone practicing the rest of the time," says Tildi. "But it makes all the difference." Tildi circulates while teachers are practicing to give immediate, high-leverage feedback to help them get better right away. To see what practice clinics look like in action, see Clip 26, which shows Syrena Burnam leading a practice clinic at Washington Park High School in Newark.

 WATCH Clip 26: Burnam—See It—Practice Clinic

TURNAROUND—WHAT TO DO FIRST

The biggest obstacle to delivering high-quality PD in most school settings is the lack of time to do so. Many schools have only forty minutes with their faculty on a weekly or biweekly basis. What do you do when you have such limited time?

The first thing, quite objectively and pragmatically, is to get data-driven instruction, observation and feedback, and planning up and running before you worry about PD. PD only becomes effective when those levers are working well. Many a leader has devoted countless hours to PD, but without the other systems in place, they did not see in increase in student learning. You can make dramatic improvements without many PD sessions.

Once you are ready to focus on PD, the most obvious strategy is to creatively build in more PD time:

- Acquire a grant to offer PD stipends to be able to have teachers attend more PD sessions.

- Offer voluntary PD sessions that are so impactful that many want to attend.

- Rebuild common planning blocks to include PD workshops.

The second strategy is to leverage your limited time as effectively as possible:

- Remove announcements from faculty meetings and put them in a weekly memo. Make the forty minutes of the meeting purely PD.

- Pick the very highest leverage areas. (See the earlier section, What to Teach; you can also use the Get Better Faster Scope and Sequence in Chapter 3 as a resource.)

- If you need to cut down, go through only one See It, Name It, Do It cycle—rather than showing three video clips on checking for understanding, just show one, frame it, and have teachers spend fifteen minutes practicing.

- Never sacrifice practice, no matter how little time you have.

This list of strategies is only a starting point. The key trait of the leader in a turnaround setting is creativity: always being willing to find creative ways around seemingly insurmountable obstacles.

CONCLUSION

Follow the steps to running PD that are outlined in this chapter, and just like Kelly, you'll shape who your teachers—and their students—become. By creating PD that is relevant to school needs and grounded in practice, you can train as many as hundreds of educators at a time in the skills that take instruction to the next level. In fact, of all the levers in this book, it's probably leading PD that—when rolled out right—empowers school leaders to replicate incredible teaching at the greatest scale. Master the other instructional levers in this book, and you can get any individual teacher to succeed. Master this final one, and you can bring whole schools—even whole districts—to the same level of excellence.

Action Steps for Principals

Professional Development

LEVER	KEY ACTIONS IN SEQUENCE
	PLAN
PROFESSIONAL DEVELOPMENT	1. **Use goals and gaps to plan August PD, yearlong PD calendar, and weekly sessions:** • ID highest-leverage topics for PD based on assessment, culture, or observation data and narrow focus to what matters most. • Develop yearlong PD calendar that identifies the highest-leverage topics that teachers will need. **Plan High-Leverage Individual PD Sessions** 2. **Create the Do It:** • Start from the end: What do participants have to be able to *do* by the end of the session—break it down into the precise steps that they practice (this is your objective!). • Script out precise instructions and scenarios to make practice as authentic and effective as possible. • Build in sufficient time to "practice perfect": plan, practice, and redo each action that the participant needs to master. • Write exemplar script for practice to ID exactly what you are looking for when monitoring. • Develop/adapt monitoring tool to track proficiency during practice. 3. **Create the See It:** • Design effective activities that allow teachers to "see" an effective model (video, written exemplars, models, etc.). • Observe high outliers to ID the strategies and practices that will close the gap. • Align each See It activity to the Do It components: they should reveal what teachers have to do.

LEVER	KEY ACTIONS IN SEQUENCE

PLAN

PROFESSIONAL DEVELOPMENT

4. **Create the Name It:**
   - Ask targeted questions before and after the activity that enable teachers to unpack and discover the best practices.
   - Give clear, concise language that describes the core actions teachers need to take.
   - Develop Core Idea and Name It slides.
   - Design one-pagers of guidance for teachers to help them implement the PD.

5. **Design the follow-up:**
   - Develop clear plans to ensure 90+% implementation of the PD.

Prepare to Deliver—Internalize the Session Plan

6. **Name your exemplar:**
   - ID what you want participants to say in each section of the agenda: ID when you are looking for the right answer (e.g., leading to a core idea) or the right thinking (e.g., thinking of the right action step for a feedback meeting).

7. **Anticipate the gaps:**
   - ID where participants might struggle, and plan your prompts/facilitation techniques to manage.

EXECUTE

8. **Tell a story:**
   - Weave the story between the slides and activities: plan for entry and exit.
   - Say, "We're going to take a journey . . ." or "You hit on many of the key points."
   - Connect each part of the content: "We just looked at _____. The question is how do we do _____? Let's take a look at someone who is doing just that . . ."

LEVER	KEY ACTIONS IN SEQUENCE
	EXECUTE

9. **Make it clear and concise:**
- Reduce your words and cut all extra "throwaway" language.
- Give clear, concise directions, breaking them down to bite-size steps and delivering one at a time. ("Open to page 6 in your handout [wait]. You have 5 minutes to script. Go.")

10. **Punch the core ideas:**
- Create Core Idea slides to drive home your most important points.
- Plan your transition into the core idea—"So we've come to a core idea . . ." Say the key line, pause, then say, "Think about the significance of this." Then restate it.
- Narrate why this core idea is important.

11. **Connect—engage the participants:**
- Use participant names; use the collective "we."
- Break the plane: circulate around the room.
- Honor their expertise (even when it's not apparent): "Just as Keith said . . ."
- Utilize frequent Turn and Talks to get them to participate in the thinking.
- Ask the "why" during large-group sharing: "Why is this important?" "What is the purpose?"

12. **Bring it:**
- Keep an open face.
  - Watch your eyes: look at the audience.
  - Keep your eyebrows up: don't let them furrow!
- Modulate the inflection in your voice to convey excitement.
- Be all in: believe that this is the greatest thing to practice and get right. Don't let your energy drop even if participants aren't excited.
- Use calm, slow hand movements.

Lever	Key Actions in Sequence

	EXECUTE

13. **Create the illusion of speed with appropriate pacing/time management:**

- Before session, determine which activities can be shortened/skipped to account for pacing issues.

- Tightly manage transitions, sharing clear instructions for each activity.

- Make strategic on-the-fly adjustments to the agenda based on the pulse or needs of the group.

- Intentionally design reflection time to capture takeaways and help participants write their action steps.

14. **Facilitate discourse when the comments go off track:**

- Roll back: repeat the participant's answer so that she can self-correct.

- Say, "Reactions? What do you think?" Then call on someone who will give a strong answer in response to the off-track answer. Ask that person, "Why is that important?"

- Redirect them back to the core question.

   o "The key question is how are we increasing student achievement with ___? We have to justify our answer with that in mind."

   o (If the question/comment is about an unrelated subject): "Hold that question. You and I can talk about that at the break. But first I want to answer the question on the PowerPoint slide."

- Wait until the right moment (if the question/comment will be addressed later in the PD): "Great question: we will address that directly in the next part of the PD."

MONITOR AND FOLLOW UP

15. **Actively monitor and follow up to achieve 90+% implementation:**

- Conduct school walkthroughs post-PD and provide real-time feedback on PD objective.

LEVER	KEY ACTIONS IN SEQUENCE
	MONITOR AND FOLLOW UP
PROFESSIONAL DEVELOPMENT	• ID individual teachers who have not mastered/are not implementing the PD objective. • Plan additional follow-up (modeling, focused observation and feedback, practice, recurring small-group PD).

Pulling the Lever

Action Planning Worksheet for PROFESSIONAL DEVELOPMENT

Self-Assessment

• Review the principal action steps in the previous box. What are the biggest gaps in your implementation that you want to close first?

   (*Note:* the action steps are listed in priority order, so "think waterfall": start at the top and stop at the first major growth area)

_____

_____

_____

_____

_____

_____

Planning for Action

• What tools from this book will you use to improve PD at your school? Check all that you will use (you can find all on the DVD):

   ☐ Professional Development one-pager

   ☐ Professional Development Rubric

   ☐ Videos of effective PD

   ☐ PD materials for training leaders to lead PD effectively

- For what key topics do you want to use the See It, Name It, Do It framework to deliver upcoming PD?

_____

_____

_____

_____

_____

- What are your next steps for leading PD effectively?

Action	Date

Part 2

Culture

Chapter 5

Student Culture

Student Culture: An Environment Where Learning Grows

On a crisp December morning in Dallas, Texas, hundreds of students make their way through the front doors of Annie Webb Blanton Elementary School. Any child who looks less than enthusiastic about starting the school day quickly perks up when Edgar Jamarillo, one of Blanton's assistant principals, offers them a quick handshake. "Good morning, good morning, good morning! Happy Thursday!" he greets one group of children. "Good morning, Emelio!" he tells another student as Emelio grins back at him. Then he pauses while shaking hands with a student named Elena. "I'm going to stop you," Edgar says, and Elena looks up to engage fully with him as they greet each other. "Thank you so much for the eye contact," he affirms. "I appreciate you."

Emelio and his peers walk down the hallway with renewed confidence as soft music emanates from each of the classrooms. In Mrs. Belchi's fourth-grade classroom, a morning meal is waiting for each student as well as a "brain breakfast"—an engaging quiet activity for everyone to complete. The learning has begun even before the morning bell has rung.

A few minutes later, morning announcements begin over the loudspeaker. "Good morning, Blanton Bruins!" the warm voice of Blanton's other assistant principal, Derek Thomas, echoes across the campus. Derek shares, "Our Character Counts word of the week is 'equality.' Equality is when all people have the same rights and privileges. Equality is another word for fairness:

whether you are a boy or a girl, African American, Anglo, Hispanic, Asian, or Indian, rich or poor, you should always have equal rights."

As the announcements draw to a close, teachers throughout the building launch the first lesson of the day. Every child has been welcomed and nourished, and they are ready to learn.

 WATCH Clip 27: Garza—See It (Model)—Morning Routines

The first time Laura Garza visited Annie Webb Blanton Elementary School, she saw children who looked deeply discouraged. "Students were putting their heads down in the middle of class, or dragging their feet during transitions," she remembers. "I wondered, 'Why do they think it's OK not to be learning?'" Laura realized that students were checking out because they were in an environment defined by low expectations. At a school where more than 80 percent of the students qualified for a free or reduced lunch, 80 percent were Latino, and 58 percent were English language learners, many adults felt that the challenges were too steep to overcome. No one was showing what was possible, and, in turn, the students didn't expect to learn.

When Laura became principal of Blanton, she knew her starting point had to be changing the culture. The key for her was not long talks about having high expectations; those rarely work. Instead, she got the staff practicing—taking the actions that can change a school's culture. Every moment our students and adults practice the right things is a moment that builds habits of excellence. By contrast, every moment in which we as adults allow our students to do less than their best is when we unintentionally are the authors of their bad habits.

Core Idea

Culture is not formed by motivational speeches or statements of values.
It is formed by repeated practice—
using every minute of every day to build good habits.

At first, many teachers were reluctant to embrace this idea of practicing. "Why do we need to practice breakfast? That doesn't have anything to do with the instruction." But Laura smiled and persisted. Together, they practiced not only morning routines but also hallway transitions that took five minutes instead of fifteen, and welcoming students into class in a way that would engage them. "Not everyone was sure we could fix our culture quickly," Laura says. "But I kept reminding them: This is why we're here. We're passionate about teaching and we want to make a difference. We're going to show children they can learn."

You could see the difference from Day 1. Teachers were acting completely different, and rather quickly students followed suit. Laura recalls watching her teachers greeting children at their classroom doors and sharing in their joy. "By a month in, our students really got it," she says, "that we weren't going away, and we expected them to learn."

The evidence of the importance of student culture can be seen in Laura's results. "Culture and data-driven instruction—that's what it took," she recalls. In just a few years, she set the highest bar for what is possible—not only in Dallas but for all of us (see Figure 5.1).

Laura transformed Blanton by recognizing something incredibly important: you can't blame your students for your school's culture—they simply follow the adults.

Figure 5.1 Texas State Assessment (STAAR): Blanton Elementary School, Percentage at or Above Proficiency

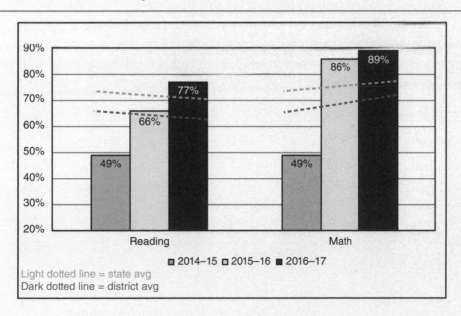

Light dotted line = state avg
Dark dotted line = district avg

2014–15   2015–16   2016–17

Laura had been told—as many of us have—that her students had "behavioral problems," that their second-language gaps were too large, and that they were not really teachable. But the more important problem at Blanton was that adults weren't giving students consistent messages about what to do or how to do it. Children will rise to the level of our expectations; it's our job to set those expectations—and teach them.

Core Idea

Children will rise to the level of our expectations. It's our job to set those expectations—and teach them.

Laura's success is not an isolated case. Rebecca Utton experienced the same thing in turning around her school in Denver. She replicated what every other leader highlighted in this book will affirm: student culture is a super-lever. But the truly good news we take from the work of these leaders is that as adults, we can fix student culture. You don't have to look as far away as Dallas or Denver to see the proof: you can see it in the automatic ways children adjust their behavior when they enter your local library or place of worship. They know they are expected to speak in a respectful tone of voice, to walk rather than to run, and to treat property gently in these spaces. So they do so—and whole worlds of opportunity to learn, discover, and grow open up. As adults, we can build those opportunities in our schools, too. The question is, How?

The answer lies in a single powerful idea: if you want a culture of excellence, you build it through repeated practice—performed by both children and adults. What follows in this chapter are the steps Laura took to build that culture:

- Set your vision.
- Roll it out to your staff.
- Roll it out to your students.
- Monitor and maintain.

Let's dive in.

SET THE VISION

You can tell a lot about student culture just by how a school feels. Imagine that you want to walk into a high school classroom and see students passionately engaged in a rigorous college-level seminar. Without a doubt, this ideal is worth working toward. But consider everything that needs to be in place in order for that seminar to take place. You could get to something that resembles what you imagined by handpicking top students from your debate team who already thrive in these conditions. Yet that would only give those particular students the exciting intellectual experience; it wouldn't provide such a culture for *all* students. What needs to occur for that to change?

First of all, you need the seminar to be happening: a solid lesson plan that sets up a productive seminar, and a unit that has provided the background material students need to participate in it. All students need to have completed any necessary prework, to be seated, and to listen respectfully to whoever is speaking.

Even with this groundwork for an academic seminar in place, you also need to have established rules for everyone in the room to follow during the seminar. The teacher needs to prompt when necessary without doing the work for the students; and the students need to ask good questions, express disagreement—and agreement!—constructively, and hear each other out without interrupting. Finally, the teacher needs to be ready to jump in when students go off track, using intervention strategies designed to halt whatever's derailing the conversation and pull it back on course.

What do all these factors have in common? *Visibility.* The seminar provides some of the greatest things we hope our students will have—intellectual rigor, a safe environment where they can learn—but those hopes alone don't make a culture. What makes a student culture is what we can see—as evidenced by this video of Emelia Pelliccio's AP Physics class, in which she has successfully set the stage for rigorous discourse supported by strong student culture.

 WATCH Clip 28: Pelliccio—See It (Model)—Academic Discourse (Teaching Clip)

Student culture is what you see, not what you hope for.

Core Idea
Student culture is what you see, not what you hope for.

In order to build a strong student culture that you can see every day, you first need to articulate in crystal-clear terms what you want it to look like. The best way to set that vision for a great student culture is to answer a few simple questions. At every moment in your school day (be it breakfast, classroom discussion, dismissal), what ideally would be happening?

- What are students doing?
- What are teachers and leaders doing?
- What are teachers and leaders doing when students aren't doing what you want?

These are the questions leaders like Laura ask themselves when they set out to lead student culture—not just for the first hour or the first day of school, but for every minute of every school day. Think back to the scene from Laura's school that opened this chapter. How does what you see in that video tell you about Blanton's culture?

 REWATCH Clip 27: Garza—See It (Model)—Morning Routines

Stop and Jot

Based on this video of morning procedures, what are Blanton's values? How can you tell?

_____

_____

_____

_____

_____

_____

_____

Laura wants to lead a school where students are joyful, respectful, and dedicated to learning. She doesn't just dream about it; she makes it happen by beginning their day with a warm welcome that sets them up to receive great instruction. In this context, Blanton is also able to build a strong moral foundation in the application of a set of core values. The culture doesn't just use these as platitudes; they are living parts of the school's cultural systems. When students don't do what they are supposed to do, school leaders talk about not living up to the school's core value of responsibility. However, when a student helps a peer up the stairs, that action is praised as an example of responsibility. Morning announcements and assemblies are geared toward teaching and presenting these values as essential. Time and time again, this commitment to moral values in student culture reasserts itself.

In building from these core values, top leaders reveal something important: ultimately, a culture of making every minute count and of constantly improving practice is not an end in itself. It matters insofar as it prepares students to be fully formed individuals. Without a school that builds culture meticulously and relentlessly, students will not have what they need to fulfill this vision. Values without cultural systems can never be put into practice. Cultural systems without values are truly meaningless. Only together can they build the schools our kids deserve: a foundation on which students develop virtuous action.

Core Idea

Cultural systems are the foundation on which students develop virtuous action.

How can you accomplish what Laura did at your own school? The keys are to see and name what you're striving for: seek out and define exemplary routines, identify the gap that separates those routines from the way your school looks now, and craft minute-by-minute action plans that will make your vision a reality throughout the school day. Let's address these keys step-by-step.

Find Your Model

When Laura set out to reshape school culture at Blanton, her first step was to identify model school routines to replicate school-wide. "Before school started, I met with my leadership team almost every day so we could decide exactly what we were going to strive for," says Laura. Without selecting a model to follow, Laura and her team wouldn't have known how to pass on their vision for Blanton's culture to their teachers—a sure way to prevent it from ever becoming a reality.

Here are the steps Laura and her team followed to identify exemplar routines for every part of the school day.

- **Find bright spots in-house.** Your most successful teachers may well have already created routines that are driving their results effectively. By observing them and noting what they say and do, you can discover actions that can be replicated throughout your school, rather than having to teach everyone in your school a new routine from scratch.

- **Find bright spots beyond your school.** Any time your school doesn't already have an exemplary routine you can build into the whole campus's culture, you can look elsewhere to find one. Laura found two key strategies especially constructive: visiting high-performing schools to record what teachers, leaders, and students say and do; and seeking out videos of school culture run well, such as those included in *Teach Like a Champion* or *Get Better Faster*.

- **Define teacher, leader, and student actions for whole-school and in-class procedures.** Naming the concrete actions that will make each routine successful is how Laura and her team translate their hopes for their school not only into something they can see but also into something they communicate. "A Sample Vision" is an example of what this might look like for the system that sets the tone for the remainder of the school day: the students' arrival on campus.

A Sample Vision

Blanton School Morning Arrival

- What is the *leader* doing?

   Before doors open, the school leader (SL) is doing a quick school walkthrough to ensure that all teachers are transitioning to their morning stations and to check whether there are any items for follow-up. The custodian is putting out the breakfast crates in the commons room and setting up the breakfast scanning stations.

   The SL opens the door at student arrival time and stands outside the front door. The SL squares up (stands up tall) and scans for uniform compliance. The SL has a bright smile to greet students and shake their hands. If a student doesn't shake her hand or greet her in return, the SL has students "do it again."

   Once breakfast finishes, the custodian posts the late sign, and the SL enters the building and does the all-school clap for students' attention. The SL greets the students and promptly begins morning meeting. The SL quickly transitions students to classrooms or morning circle.

- What are the *teachers* doing?

    Lead teachers transition to the cafeteria tables before doors open and set out "bright work" (engaging mental math activities and challenges) and pencils. Assistant teachers transition to the homework check-in station and set out homework bins and the check-in binder.

    Once students arrive, the lead teacher greets each student with a bright face and circulates to ensure that they are either eating their breakfast or working on bright work. The lead teacher ensures that all breakfast is thrown out when students finish. The assistant teacher ensures that all students place their belongings in their cubby, deposit any snacks or lunch, and hand in their homework. The assistant teacher checks student homework. Performing arts teacher plays CD of soft background music.

- What are the *students* doing?

    Students greet the SL upon arrival at the door. Students shake hands with a smile and wear a compliant uniform. Students then walk to the cafeteria if they are eating school breakfast. Then they walk straight to their cubby to greet the assistant teacher and deposit their book bag and any snack and lunch from home. Students hand their homework to the assistant teacher and then walk to their cafeteria table and greet the teacher. Students eat breakfast or begin working on their bright work. Students signal hand on head when finished eating.

    If a student is late, he or she goes to the main office with parent to sign in, then reports to the cafeteria or classroom depending on time.

- **Define actions to take when a student doesn't follow directions.** Even the schools that have established the most excellent student cultures have students who don't follow directions. What sustains the school leaders' success is that they've planned responses that are effective—and immediate. Laura plans those responses from the beginning, knowing they're an integral component of a school culture that runs smoothly. Again, see how this looks for morning arrival.

Plan Your Vision: Morning Arrival

- What will happen immediately when a *student doesn't follow instructions*?

    The teacher will first try the least invasive redirect (proximity, nonverbal, modeling what to do). If the student is still nonresponsive, the teacher repeats direction and has the student do it again, and provides a countdown. If the student is still nonresponsive, the teacher pulls the student aside to redirect or sends the student to another teacher. If the student still refuses to follow instructions, the teacher refers the student to the assistant principal, and the assistant principal will follow up.

- **Create a tool to evaluate success.** Finally, Laura defines what each routine in her school will look like when it's implemented at an advanced level, a proficient level, a working-toward level, or a needs-improvement level. She compiles those parameters for success in a single school culture rubric that will make it significantly easier for her to evaluate Blanton's culture as a whole once the year is under way. The next "Plan Your Vision" box shows how the Morning Circle section of the rubric looks.

Plan Your Vision: Morning Circle

School-Wide Systems	Advanced	Proficient	Working Toward	Needs Improvement
Morning Circle	• Circle is organized such that all students can see and actively participate in circle activities. • All circle topics address core values, college, or community needs. • All students are silent and tracking the speaker. • Students are engaged and participate enthusiastically. • Leader encourages student participation through relevant questions and/or student presentation. • Leader provides opportunity for teachers to present or give input. • All transitions within circle are	• Circle is organized such that almost all students can see and actively participate in circle activities. • Almost all circle topics address core values, college, or community needs. • 95% of students are silent and tracking the speaker. • Students are engaged and participate. • Leader encourages student participation through relevant questions and/or student presentation. • Leader provides opportunity for teachers to present or give input.	• Circle is somewhat disorganized, such that some students are unable to see and participate in circle activities. • Circle topics may not be connected to core values, college, or community needs. • There are some side conversations, and not all students are tracking the speaker. • Students participate begrudgingly. • Leader does not encourage student participation with questions or student presentation. • Leader infrequently opens	• Circle is poorly organized, limiting students' ability to see and participate in circle activities. • Circle topics are not connected to core values, college, or community needs. • Side conversations disrupt the flow of circle. • Students do not participate. • Other adults do not participate. • Transitions within circle are almost always noisy and take too long. • Leader does not model taxonomy techniques (cold call, CFU, positive framing).

School-Wide Systems	Advanced	Proficient	Working Toward	Needs Improvement
	silent, smooth, and efficient. • Leader always models taxonomy techniques (cold call, CFU, positive framing).	• Transitions within circle are mostly silent, smooth, and efficient. • Leader consistently models taxonomy techniques (cold call, CFU, positive framing).	the floor for other adult voices. • Transitions within circle can be noisy or take too long. • Leader occasionally models taxonomy techniques (cold call, CFU, positive framing).	

A complete sample student culture rubric is available on the DVD that accompanies this book, as are templates you can use to complete each of the steps we've described in this section.

Find the Gap

Once Laura has set the bar for culture at Blanton, her next step is to see the gap between the vision she's defined and the way each routine looks currently. Evaluating the gap looks slightly different depending on whether Laura is introducing a new system or relaunching an existing one. If the routine has never been implemented at Blanton before, Laura has to anticipate what the gap might hypothetically look like when she rolls it out, asking herself these questions:

• **What would the students be doing that would indicate the system was being implemented poorly?**

• **What would ineffective leaders and/or teachers be doing?**

If Laura is revising or relaunching an existing system, her goal is to pin down the actions that are currently causing the system to break down:

• **What student actions or inactions are indicators of the problem?**

• **What teacher actions or inactions are causing the problem?**

• **What leader actions or inactions are causing the problem?**

Identifying the actions that would define ineffective implementation of school routines, as well as those that would show it had been implemented successfully, prepares Laura for the final phase of setting her vision for culture at Blanton: crafting a minute-by-minute system for each of these routines.

Move Beyond Superman—Craft Minute-by-Minute Systems

Too often when we think of transforming student culture, we envision Superman or Superwoman: a charismatic, show-stopping leader who gets all students to be invested. Yet everywhere I travel, the school leaders who drive strong culture are not superheroes in the stereotypical way (although they certainly should be admired!). Rather than lead culture by the sheer force of their personality, they build systems that make culture a habit. Your vision won't become a reality until you have a system to lock it in.

Core Idea

You don't make your vision a reality by the sheer force of your personality; you build systems to lock it in.

Findings from the Field

Lock in Culture with Systems, not Superheroes

"We used to manage student culture by trying to be magical, but there aren't that many magicians. We used to tell the Superman story, but how many superheroes are there? Having minute-by-minute systems has given us the ability to systemize culture. This way, I don't need to be standing right there every moment to make sure it gets done."

—Mary Ann Stinson, principal, Truesdell Education Campus, Washington, DC
(See Mary Ann's more complete story in Chapter 1.)

Laura epitomizes this mantra. Quiet and unassuming, Laura leads by example and by building systems that allow everyone to do the same. Her work in setting Blanton's culture isn't complete until she's named what leaders, students, and teachers will do during each school routine, laid out in a comprehensive, sequential, minute-by-minute plan, including materials she'll need and actions that will be taken when students do not follow directions. If she's revising or relaunching a procedure, she makes sure to account for the breakdowns identified. To give you a sense of how detailed this plan needs to be, here is a sample. A template is available on the DVD.

Sample Minute-by-Minute Student Culture Plan

Elementary School Morning Arrival

Prior to doors opening:

7:15 a.m.

- Custodian puts out breakfast crates and computers for breakfast sign-in
- School leader (SL) does a walkthrough of the building, making sure to stop by the teacher work room, copy room, and commons room (with notebook in hand to record anything that requires follow-up)

> **Materials:** crates with breakfast already in them (pick up from walk-in refrigerator), notebook, and the breakfast computer stations

7:25 a.m.

- SL goes to front door for morning arrival
- All lead teachers report to their breakfast tables and set out bright work on stools, and pencils on table tops
- SL greets students as they arrive; all teachers make sure students pick up their breakfast
- All assistant teachers report to their morning homework check-in station
  - Prepare to greet students as they arrive
  - Prepare to collect homework

> **Materials:** bright work bins with bright work folders and pencils, empty homework bins for collection of homework, check-in binder, and notebook (each teacher)

Doors open and students enter:

7:30 a.m.

- SL opens the door, begins to greet students and parents
- Performing Arts teacher puts on music (calming) and gets out materials for circle

Materials: CD with calming music

- Students square up/stand still and greet SL by shaking her hand with a bright face and saying good morning
- SL does a quick scan of each student's uniform to ensure compliance and has any noncompliant students "do it again." SL gives 5-second pep talk for certain students to set them up for success.
- Students enter the building and walk quietly down the steps (holding on to the railing)
- When students reach the bottom landing, they are greeted by a teacher
- Students stop by the computer station to scan their hand for breakfast or keep going if they are not eating breakfast
- Students enter the commons room and go to their cubby
- Students greet assistant teacher
- Students put their belongings in their cubby, submit homework binder, and put snack in yellow bin and lunch in red bin (if they brought their snack or lunch)
- Students then walk to their table with hands by their sides and greet the lead teacher
- Students sit down and begin to eat their breakfast (if they already ate, they begin their morning bright work)
- Lead teachers are circulating, monitoring, and interacting with students (low tone of voice)
- After eating breakfast, the student gives the nonverbal signal (hand on top of head) to signal he/she is finished eating and ready for cleanup
- Teacher will respond to the student by doing one of the following:
  - Go to the student and pick up the finished breakfast and throw it in the trash
  - Give the student a nonverbal signal (head nod) to throw the breakfast away
  - Assign student helpers (2) who circulate during breakfast and respond when they see the nonverbal cue signaling a student has finished his/her breakfast

Materials: yellow snack bins, red lunch bins, morning bright work, and pencils

7:55 a.m. SL enters the building

- SL goes to the commons room in preparation for morning meeting
- Custodian puts out the late sign, closes the door, and reports to the commons room for morning meeting

> **Materials**: late sign stand

8:00 a.m. Performing Arts teacher gives the signal (cleanup song) for teachers and students to begin final cleanup and prepare for morning meeting or dismissal
8:05 a.m. SL greets student body

- SL does the all-school clap, and students respond (if SL does not get 100%, they "do it again")
- SL verbally greets the student body and circulates
- SL gives signal for students and teachers to begin transition for morning circle

Late arrivals:

- Any student who arrives after 7:55 must report to the main office with an adult to be signed in
- Office manager gives the student a pass, and the student reports to the commons room (if it is prior to 8:20 a.m.) or to the classroom (if it is after 8:20 a.m.)

All adults should use the least invasive form of redirects:

- Nonverbal redirects
- Use of proximity—stand beside or behind the student
- Modeling what to do

Students who do not follow directions during arrival/breakfast:
Step 1

- Teacher goes through the set of nonresponsiveness strategies (e.g., give the direction again using a strong but low voice, provide students with a countdown to do what is asked, give a consequence, pull to the side for a discussion, send to another teacher).

Step 2

- Student is sent to the assistant principal, and that person will do the follow-up.
- If assistant principal is out of the building, the student goes to the instructional leader for that grade level.

Measure It

Only once she's planned the system at this level can Laura define how to measure whether or not she is successful:

- **What is the outcome?** Laura always sets a concrete, measurable goal that she'll use to determine when the system has been successfully implemented—for example, "Hallways transitions will reduce to one minute," or "One hundred percent of students will turn their full attention to whoever is speaking in every classroom."

- **How will we measure it?** There are a number of different tools to measure student culture. Either you can create a student culture rubric (see the DVD that accompanies this book for an example), or you can create a checklist of actions you are looking for when observing. (*Get Better Faster* is a fruitful tool for observing in-class student culture. Make this tool transparent for the leadership team and the staff will make the goal the school is setting for culture clear to all.

It's one thing to set your vision as a leader, and another thing to get everyone else in your school to follow it. Leaders like Laura translate their cultural systems from paper to practice in two steps: they roll the systems out to their staff and then later to their students. Let's first see what a staff-facing rollout looks like.

ROLL IT OUT TO YOUR STAFF

For most marathon runners, preparing for a race follows a fairly simple course: doing practice runs of a certain prescribed length each week, getting enough sleep, and eating right. Through these efforts, the runners will get in shape, improve their form, and earn good times. For the elite marathoners, however, training looks very different. In the months before race day, elite marathoners plan *obsessively,* creating strategies for each hill, each turn, and each drink station. In the hours before the race, they don plastic bags to reflect sunlight, working to save every single calorie for competition. These runners aren't training to participate; they're preparing to win. And when the goal is victory, it's the details that separate contenders from weekend warriors.

Core Idea

It's the details that separate contenders from weekend warriors.

How does this apply to school leadership? Enter Tera Carr. As principal of Hamilton Elementary School in Tulsa, Oklahoma, from 2014 to 2016, Tera led the school to a 16-point gain in math and an 11-point gain in reading on the Oklahoma Core Curriculum Tests (OCCT). A lot of that had to do with resetting the student culture. Let's consider how Tera Carr's rollout of student culture differs from that of a traditional school leader, whom we will call Ms. Smith. Both Tera and Ms. Smith want to put strong school culture into place. To prepare, both lead a PD session for their staff. Yet the similarities end there.

Case Study

A Tale of Two Leaders Launching Student Culture

Leader 1: Ms. Smith

Ms. Smith begins her staff PD with a presentation on the general principles of the culture she wants. The slideshow is elaborate, containing instructions on a variety of classroom and school-wide norms. In pairs, Smith has her teachers read a recent article on the "achievement gap" in America before partner groups discuss how this work connects to the school's overall mission. After narrating what each procedure might look like, Smith leaves her teachers to determine how each procedure will be applied to their individual classrooms. During the two weeks that follow, leaders create templates of their student rules and make them available to the school leader for feedback and suggestions.

Stop and Jot

What pitfalls might keep Ms. Smith's culture launch from succeeding?

_____

_____

_____

_____

_____

_____

_____

Leader 2: Tera Carr

Here's what it looks like when Tera Carr rolls out culture with her staff.

 WATCH Clip 29: Carr—Do It—Roll Out to Staff

Stop and Jot

How does Tera's rollout differ from Ms. Smith's? What makes it more effective?

_____

_____

_____

_____

_____

_____

_____

Tera's talk was brief, but the change was real: the staff practiced the vision, and in doing so made it a reality. In the marathon that is building strong student culture, Ms. Smith is a weekend warrior. She has good ideas, works hard, and may make a positive impact. But she will not build an extraordinary school.

Tera, by contrast, is a champion. She has built an exceptional school like Laura Garza's, and this video makes it clear how. Like an elite marathon runner, she trains her staff down to the smallest details. They set a meticulous vision and work relentlessly to achieve it. In short, leaders like Tera and Laura do not leave learning to chance. Let's break down how they do this.

See It and Name It

Take a look at this video of Eric Diamon, the principal of Vailsburg Middle School in Newark, New Jersey (whom you'll see again in Chapter 8), another leader who has built a strong student culture that has led to strong results. He is introducing a new routine to his staff. As you watch, try to note as many as possible of the actions Eric takes to introduce the routine effectively.

 WATCH Clip 30: Diamon—Do It: Roll Out to Staff

Stop and Jot

What did Eric say and do to lead an effective See It when he rolled out his cultural routine to his staff?

_____

_____

_____

_____

_____

_____

_____

The actions of Laura, Tera, and Eric are strikingly similar, and they follow the principle we saw in previous chapters: if you want them to get it, get them to see it. Here's how:

Hook. Eric inspired and empowered his staff to learn this routine by letting them know up front why it mattered and what it looked like. As you can see, there is a place for motivational speeches! He just keeps it short and sweet to allow him to focus most of his time on the model.

Frame. Before transitioning to a live model, Eric took an important step to ensure that his staff was prepared to master the routine: he named what would happen sequentially during the model his teacher was about to perform. He told them what to look for, which allowed them to see it more clearly.

Model. For her part, Eric's teacher Julia didn't model the routine halfway: she dove in completely. She took on the full actions as if students were in front of her, and she exaggerated the actions she wanted to see teachers replicate so that they couldn't possibly be missed.

Debrief. Finally, Eric stamped his staff's understanding of the model by asking them to unpack what they had seen. (Verbal cues leaders can use to complete this step include "What did you notice? What actions did I take, and what did I say?") Just as important, he pushed them to name why those actions had been part of the model. In short, the modeling is the method by which your vision comes alive.

Core Idea

Modeling is the method by which your vision comes alive.

Do It

Just as with leading PD, the value of a student culture rollout comes with the practice. The first step is to let your staff know exactly what actions they'll be practicing. Take a look at this video to see how Tera introduces practice.

 WATCH Clip 31: Carr—Do It—Rehearsal

Stop and Jot

What does Tera say and do to lead an effective practice of the routine?

_____

_____

_____

_____

_____

_____

_____

_____

Plan

To set practice up for success, Tera delivers clear What to Do directions to her staff that let them know the following:

- **What the main participant will do.** Tera makes sure to delineate the tasks of the key person in each group who is taking on the main practice role during the role play. Multiple participants are shown practicing in the video. She also gives her teachers time to plan and script their actions, which will make them far more successful during the practice than if they went off the cuff.

- **What the audience will do.** Tera also sets clear roles in place for the members of her staff who will be playing the role of students while someone else practices the teacher role in the routine. Having prepared student roles for them to emulate makes the practice that much more relevant to what it will be like for teachers to roll out this routine on the ground.

Practice

All of the planning sets the teachers up for effective practice.

- **Round 1: Build muscle memory—start simple.** Tera starts by having participants rehearse the routine at its simplest from start to finish. To ensure that her staff spends this time building the muscle memories of what it feels like to rehearse the routine correctly, Tera delivers feedback in real time when staff make an error, and has them try again, starting at the point where they stumbled. Remember, you need to know how to lift a bar before you add the weight.

Core Idea

Keep the first practice simple to build muscle memory: you need to know how to lift a bar before you add the weight.

- **Round 2: Add complexity.** Once the basics are mastered, Tera could add complications like student misbehavior to the practice. This is the heart of the most effective practice: add the complexity once a participant is ready for it.

  Practice is so simple in its concept; all it requires is a commitment to make it happen with your staff.

A Word on . . . the Day 1 Dress Rehearsal

When you participate in a play, most of your practices leading up to it focus on one scene, one act, or even just an individual song. But as you get closer, it becomes essential to put it all together for a dress rehearsal. As any actor or actress will tell you, it's one thing to know each individual part, and it's another to string them all together in a full performance!

Many of the most successful school leaders imitate this by engaging in a full "dress rehearsal" a few days before school begins. The dress rehearsal is a minute-by-minute walkthrough of the school's entire day, from morning breakfast to detention dismissal. Teachers and leaders walk through what they will be doing in each part of the day, finishing the exercise by rehearsing their systems in pairs, offering critiques and suggestions as they refine their systems. For example, they stand in the hall outside their classrooms "watching" students enter, and they teach students to sharpen pencils and how to put away books.

Don't underestimate the power of a rehearsal. Even if some will protest at the beginning, by the time the real students finally arrive two days later, every teacher knows exactly where he or she is supposed to be and exactly what he or she is supposed to be doing at all times. All the students see is a fully coordinated, united front: the first strong message of what to expect for the rest of the year.

ROLL IT OUT TO YOUR STUDENTS

After the staff is prepared to roll out culture as a team, it's the students' turn to learn the routines. What works for adults works for children as well: hook, frame, model, debrief—and then get them to practice. The two structures for rolling out student culture, then, are nearly identical.

Core Idea

What works for adults works for children: hook, frame, model, debrief, practice.

Here are the key nuances Laura adds to the hook, frame, model, and debrief process when she leads a student-facing rollout.

- **Challenge and affirm.** The magic of Laura's rollout to students is in how she challenges them into doing a task that could otherwise be menial (i.e., raising your hand). She makes it an exciting opportunity for them to show leadership. To do so, she speaks with urgency and importance that makes it hard for the students not to follow suit.

- **Lightning-quick correction.** Laura doesn't wait until multiple students are off task: she corrects the very first instance. For Laura the reason is simple: all the other students redirect themselves when they see a peer redirected. She's sending a message to all about the standard for engagement.

- **Leaders and teachers together.** Laura knows that if she asks the students to do something and the teachers don't make the same request, the culture will not work. Therefore, Laura and her teachers work together to give feedback to students as they learn each part of a routine.

MONITOR AND MAINTAIN

Imagine that you tell a child to brush his teeth every night before bed, and monitor him only the very first evening after you give him these instructions. That first night, the child will go to bed with clean teeth. Tell any parent that the child now automatically brushes his teeth every night, however, and you'll be met with justifiable laughter. The reality is that people of any age need to be monitored and supported in the process of making routines into habits.

By the same token, the rollout of student culture will only be as successful as your maintenance of it. The steps in this section will show you how. They'll prevent you from having merely a "honeymoon period," keeping the celebration of strong culture going all year long.

Lead Publicly

Whenever I visit a school that has a strong student culture, I immediately get the impression that the school leader is everywhere. This is not by accident. School leaders like Laura make sure they're visible at key times and places during the school day—such as lunch, troubled classrooms, or hallways—after her staff- and student-facing rollouts. "When our first day of school went well, I thought, 'OK, let's not jinx this!'" Laura remembers, laughing. "I kept up the success by making sure my leadership team and I were very visible."

How can Laura do that and still stay on top of all of her work? She is relentlessly intentional about how she manages her time. She knows when she'll be walking around, when she'll be observing or leading meetings, and when she'll do other things. And she coordinates with her leadership team to make sure someone is present when she is not. (More about that in Chapter 8, Finding the Time).

A Word on . . . the 30-Day Playbook

Bill Walsh was one of the most successful professional football coaches of all time. One of his many legacies was the way he called plays for his offense.

At the time Walsh was coaching in 1980, every coach made a decision in the moment of which play his offense should run. This would happen roughly sixty-five times a game. Each team had hundreds of plays to choose from, and each coach needed to decide within a few seconds.

At one point, Walsh realized that he wasn't at his best when trying to make decisions this way. So one night he decided to script the first seven plays of the game. No matter what the defense did, he told himself, he would stick with those plays.

His strategy worked. The team looked better, advanced the ball further, and had more success in those first plays than later. Walsh kept expanding the number of scripted plays until he reached twenty-five, or the equivalent of nearly the entire first half. And his teams were wildly successful on offense.[1]

In many ways, leading student culture is like coaching a football team. There are at least sixty moments in a day when a leader has to decide rapidly what he or she is going to do: what to say during breakfast, how to talk to a student who's upset or angry in the hallway, whether to restart a routine or not, and so on.

To help leaders who aren't instinctually good at leading culture, we have experimented with our own version of Walsh's success. Rather than a thirty-play script, we established a thirty-day playbook. Given that the first thirty days are essential to establishing culture, the leaders we worked with made a minute-by-minute script of what they would do throughout those first thirty days to set in place the right habits.

- 7:00: Arrive at school and quickly check emails: Anyone sick? Any emergencies?

- 7:15: Walk around to greet the early-arriving teachers: How are they? Any concerns?

- 7:20: Go to stand outside to greet students and parents. Look for the fifteen students who need extra "love" to start the day strong—make sure to give them a particularly positive message.

And so on.

What was the impact? Hear it from Christine Algozo, principal of Uncommon Preparatory High School, who admitted to having struggled with student culture in the past:

> Sustaining strong student culture has been a key area of my own growth as a principal, and the 30-Day Playbook was a significant game-changer for me. For the first time, I had a game plan for everything I and my leadership team needed to do. It freed my mind from overthinking and allowed me to focus on simply acting: taking the steps that would build the culture, one

action at a time. By the end of thirty days, we had in place the strongest culture we've ever had, despite being larger than ever and with new leadership team members. It built habits that made it easy to sustain what we had worked so hard to establish.

For any principal who is working on changing or improving his or her student culture and building new habits, a playbook frees your mind to look at the big picture while your playbook moves your feet in the right direction. We have a sample segment of a 30-Day Playbook here and a complete version on the DVD. You have to adjust the playbook to how your school runs and to your own vision.

The 30-Day Playbook: High School Version

Between 7:40 a.m. and 7:58 a.m.: Student Breakfast

- **Student Culture Observation—Breakfast**
  - Observe student behavior at breakfast and note gaps in teacher presence or teacher actions
  - If needed, pull aside a student who is not following the norms: model for teachers a quiet correction

  What to Scan for and Fix
  - Staff not present in the lunchroom, not seen looking
  - Students too loud or shouting
  - Students blocking the entrance to the cafeteria or going to different rooms without approval
  - Students standing, wandering
  - Students leaving without permission or pass

- **Real-Time Coaching**
  - Note any teachers not coaching students for 100% behavior. Real-time coach using whisper prompts and/or modeling if necessary
  - Debrief quickly: "What did you notice me do? Why did I do that? What was the impact?"

- **Public Leadership Moment**
  - With 5 minutes remaining in breakfast, model the hand-raise procedure with all students; expect 100% of hands raised and silent within 3 seconds. Use *Do It Again* technique until success is achieved

---

- Give public, precise praise to key students to build positive culture. Clearly state the expectations
- **Cue the Transition**
  - Restate the expectations for hallway transitions and let students know that staff will be watching them to ensure success:
    - Moving with purpose, not lingering in the hallway
    - Talking quietly, no shouting
    - Lining up at classroom doors (grades 9/10) or entering quietly (grades 11/12)

While on the ground, Laura takes the following actions to make the most of her presence:

- **Communicate urgency.** Leaders can communicate so much about what matters to the school just in the way they stand and talk. When Laura is on the scene, she makes sure to stand up straight, walk calmly and with purpose, and smile. She tries to make others feel at ease while also establishing that her school is a cathedral of learning.

- **Provide immediate feedback.** When Laura sees something not working (a student or teacher who is struggling), she doesn't simply observe and wait until later to address it—she jumps in right away. Sometimes, nonverbal cues are all it takes, such as looking at a student who needs redirecting, or gesturing to a teacher to notice the students in the back of the line. Other times, Laura will whisper something to a teacher or student. Or she might communicate verbally by having students do a routine over that they aren't performing correctly, or issuing a challenge like "The fourth graders already learned this. Can you do it too?" All of these actions communicate a singular message: I care about you and your learning, and I'm not going to let you fail.

Manage Individually

No organization runs perfectly, and that is the same for schools. Regardless of how well Laura rehearses, occasionally she needs to have a conversation with an individual teacher or student who is struggling to meet cultural expectations. During these conversations, Laura makes clear not only what concrete actions the individual needs to begin performing but also what the constructive impact is on the community when everyone works to perform these actions consistently. (We dive more deeply into these types of conversations in Chapter 6 on staff culture: accountability conversations.) She closes the loop on implementation by working with the individual to set a prompt timeline for him to begin performing those actions himself.

Evaluate Progress

The power of a school culture rubric (which we showed how to design in the first section of this chapter) is that it makes it a straightforward matter to conduct a student culture–specific walkthrough. Laura and her staff can simply monitor each cultural system in action, give their school a score on the rubric, and make an action plan to close the gaps. We'll cover the process of conducting walkthroughs in greater detail in Chapter 7, Managing School Leadership Teams.

Lead a Whole-School Reset

Occasionally, monitoring student culture leads Laura to discover that a school routine needs to be reset; the habits have slipped, and the routine is no longer functioning effectively. A reset has much in common with a rollout; the small adjustments we describe here will make the steps we covered in the rollout sections of this chapter applicable to a reset.

Clip 32 shows how Nikki Bridges approaches the process of resetting a routine.

WATCH Clip 32: Bridges—See It—Student Culture Reset

Let's break down how Nikki makes her reset effective.

- **Execute a walkthrough to monitor the targeted action steps.** After revisiting the routine, monitor its implementation daily until it has become habit. Look specifically for the actions that you targeted during the reset to ensure they are being performed. As you can see in Nikki's model, she has all the staff participate in evaluating the culture: that is a powerful investment strategy that makes everyone feel like leaders of culture. Don't be afraid to do this; teachers are wonderfully self-reflective and often will be even more critical than leaders themselves!

- **Revisit the model.** If members of the school community are repeatedly not following a system, it's an indication that the community needs to revisit the exemplar that shows what the routine should look like. Start there, either by showing a video of the model or by performing it yourself.

After members of the school community have seen the model and the gap, give them time to practice.

 WATCH Clips 33 and 34: Bridges—Do It (Plan and Practice)—Student Culture Reset

- **Repractice the broken routine.** After just a few minutes, Nikki has the staff spend the rest of their session repracticing the techniques needed to reset the routine. Teachers walk away with not only a sense of the gap but also actions to close it—and they know everyone else will be doing the same thing in their classrooms. That creates collegiality as well as results.

- **Communicate to staff the progress until the goal is met.** As you monitor progress, keep your staff in the loop. Celebrate progress and stamp next steps each day until the routine in your school looks the way it does in the model!

TURNAROUND—FIXING A BROKEN CULTURE

Sometimes culture faces more serious problems. If normal "wear and tear" in culture can reduce performance, sometimes the culture frays so completely that it breaks down. Whether you come into a new situation where the culture is completely broken or it has deteriorated to that point, major repairs are needed just to get the culture up and running. In short, you have to reset the culture.

When I first wrote *Leverage Leadership* in 2012, I thought that the actions taken to fix a broken school culture were notably different from those taken by school leaders who have established incredibly strong culture. As I have had the opportunity to study even more leaders who implemented successful culture turnarounds and to compare them to leaders with steadily solid cultures, I have been struck that the leader actions are nearly identical. Laura had to fix the culture when she first arrived at Blanton Elementary School. Yet she followed the same actions as Eric Diamon, who inherited a solid culture: they both set their vision, rolled it out to staff and students, and then monitored and maintained—all the steps we broke down over the course of this chapter. (That is why the actions of leaders who turned around culture are mixed in throughout the chapter with the same actions taken by leaders with stronger cultures.)

If the actions you need to take to turn around a culture are the same as to set one, what is the difference? The difference lies in your having to get your staff invested in the turnaround—and to manage the initial pushback from those who aren't.

Core Idea

The biggest difference between setting and fixing student culture is getting your staff invested and managing the pushback from those who aren't.

A Parent's Testimonial on Student Culture: "My Third Grader Talks About Going to College"

Tanya Wheelington

What's the school turnaround process like for the families who live it every day? We asked someone who knows firsthand: Tanya, a mother of three students enrolled at Blanton. Here's how she described the transformation she witnessed when Laura began to lead her children's school.

In 2014, I was planning to take my three children out of Blanton. It was a bleak, unwarming place where you couldn't feel at home or comfortable. When I asked my kids what happened at school, there was never anything they wanted to talk about.

But I got a call during the summer from a staff member who said things were going to change. "We're going to challenge students more," they said. That sounded great to me! I said, "Okay, we'll stay."

I'm so glad they called, because I wouldn't trade the Blanton my children attend now for any other school. It just feels more bright, more welcoming. Everyone on the staff acknowledges you and your kids. My son, who's in second grade, has really opened up to his teacher. I understand why he trusts her, because whenever I need to speak to a teacher, a counselor, or even the principal, it's like I'm the only person who exists in that moment. I get their full attention. Meanwhile, my third-grade daughter just went on a field trip to the Southern Methodist University, and now she wants to go there. My third grader talks about going to college!

At Blanton, they know what our kids are capable of, and they tell us how they're doing. They listen to all of us—you can see it in their eyes. We all work together to give our children the education they deserve. That's what I love about this school.

Face the Brutal Facts—of Students and Staff

In *Good to Great,* management guru Jim Collins famously says that we must face the "brutal facts" of our situation before we can improve it. In a broken culture, the most crucial facts to define are twofold: what brokenness looks like for your students, and what it looks like for your staff.

In many schools, the brutal facts of broken student culture look like one of these:

- Mass student apathy
- Students violent or completely off task
- Students not engaged

These are easy to spot: they overwhelm the senses when you walk through the school.

The even more important brutal facts are the adults' actions or inactions that are contributing to this culture. If students rise to the level of expectations placed in front of them, they can sink to meet lower expectations just as easily.

Laura described these actions when she first arrived at Blanton: a passivity from adults which communicated that they did not think there was anything that could be done. Stacey Shells, who leads ReGeneration Schools in Chicago, describes something similar, this time where adults—even the principal—felt it was someone else's responsibility to deal with the culture:

> It was an environment no one would want for their child. In more than half the classrooms, we couldn't find more than one or two students on task. Children were running around, screaming, kicking, hitting, getting up, walking away from adults. No one was paying attention to the teacher. I watched as a six-year-old child blatantly defied a teacher and walked away right in front of the principal. The principal didn't do anything because she considered discipline the job of her assistant principal ("I am the instructional leader, she said. "He manages the discipline.").

Identifying the adults' ineffective actions is the first step toward rebuilding the culture.

Model Constantly—with Constancy

The rollout sections of this chapter highlighted the importance of modeling: showing staff and students exactly what you want them to do. In a broken culture, the modeling doesn't stop during the PD; your staff will be looking to you as a model at all times. Are you consistently following the model you set in the rollout? They are watching you not only to see what to do but also to see if your actions match your words.

In too many schools, teachers have received messages about some initiative that will supposedly improve their school, one that always involves more work. And more often than not, those initiatives don't bring about change, and they are often abandoned before taken to completion. Understandably, then, your staff could be jaded toward a new idea and will be unresponsive to your desire to fix the culture. That reluctance goes deeper.

At our core, we humans are pretty resistant to change. (As I like to quip at workshops, if you don't believe me, just asked your loved ones!) School leaders like Mary Ann Stinson (see more of her in Chapter 1) recognize this, so instead of trying to deny it, they enter their reset with eyes wide open. "I knew that many staff members were not going to be open initially to the change—they needed to see first if it would work," recalls Mary Ann. "So I didn't put much energy into trying to convince all of them. Instead, I focused on remaining constant: unwavering in the setting of a new vision. I didn't expect to be liked; but if I could remain consistent and fair, I hoped at least to earn their respect."

Laura and Mary Ann set their school cultures up to take root over time in the following ways:

- **Set the norm with your leadership team for "all hands on deck."** A root problem in most schools with failed cultures is a lack of support among staff members. To start, all members of the leadership team of the school have to make a commitment to address culture equally. If an assistant principal walks down the hall and ignores the culture issues, she sends a message to the students that school culture is dependent on the individual. The leadership team needs to commit to all taking the same actions if they ever want the teachers to do the same. Note, too, that all hands on deck means that people are paying close attention to culture at critical times of the day and have key look-fors to ground the work in a common set of criteria for success.

- **Start with the staff who are most invested in change.** It is next to impossible to address at once the issues going on in every classroom. Laura sat down with the school leader and went staff member by staff member. They identified those faculty who would be most invested in making a change, and that's where they devoted their energy in the first days. They sat down with those teachers and talked through what routines and procedures they would reset in the classroom.

- **Follow the rollout plan: hook, frame, model, debrief, practice.** Once you've brought on board those whom you can, follow the process for rollout laid out earlier in the chapter.

- **Put aside instruction for one or two days and reset.** Acknowledge that a reset takes time, and give teachers a few days to retrain all of the routines and procedures established in the PD session without having to cover material. Most important, spend all your time in their classrooms, observing and supporting wherever necessary. Note that in some cases this is essential, even though it is not a decision to be taken lightly.

- **Remain emotionally constant.** Turning around a culture is not easy—but it is eminently doable. For your staff and students, you want to be the calm in the eye of the storm. No matter which students still push back at the beginning or no matter which teacher will make a resistant comment, your best action is calm, consistent, repetitive action. Even if you don't always feel it inside, remaining unflappable on the outside sends a message: we can do this—and I will be there with you.

Core Idea

Culture leaders don't succeed because of charisma but because of constancy: always being there, repeatedly, as the calm in the eye of the storm.

A Word on . . . Buy-In to a Culture Change

Building a strong culture is hard work, especially if you are changing a broken one. One of the most challenging issues is dealing with the backlash that can occur with a significant change in school practices. Should you take the change process slowly, one thing at a time? Not so, say leaders who have had consistent success at turnaround.

Jarvis Sanford is the managing director for the Academy of Urban School Leadership (AUSL), one of the most successful organizations in the country at urban school turnaround. Located in Chicago, AUSL has successfully turned around the culture in dozens of public elementary and high schools. What are its lessons learned on this issue?

When a culture is dysfunctional, you need a marked change, not a gradual release. Sanford insists that getting elementary students to line up and enter the school building quietly on Day 1 of school cannot be done halfway. "If you don't start to change habits completely, you won't be successful later on." This is the number one error AUSL staff see in leaders who don't make turnaround stick. "They remain content with the students acting 'better' than before, but because they didn't push for 100 percent compliance, it slowly unraveled later."

There is a consequence to this approach: leaders will get tons of challenging pushback from students, parents, and even some staff members. Weathering this storm, however, is what will make October far more successful.

Brian Sims has seen this play out in multiple countries as the former managing director of AUSL and also the former director of education for Ark, a system of public schools in London. He comments: "Leaders and staff have to prepare themselves for the challenge of the initial shift. If they stay the course, the rest of the year will be significantly better."

CONCLUSION

When Laura took over Blanton Elementary School, she thought that building a new culture would take time. What astonished her was how little time it took for her work on culture to start paying off. "We had an open house before the first day of school," she recalls, "and even then, we had parents telling us that they felt the difference. They immediately felt, 'Wow, this is for our children.'" And what happened when the students arrived? "It just kept getting better," says Laura. The practices she had set in motion during summer PD continued to give students what they needed to learn—on Day 1, on Day 30, and throughout the year.

Student culture matters not only because it gives our students a solid foundation on which to learn but also because it's our opportunity to communicate to our students how much we believe in them, and that we will support them in becoming their best self. Isn't that what we want from all our mentors?

When you stand before your staff and then your students to teach them your cultural routines, remember the "why" behind those actions: we build great school cultures so that our students never forget they are capable of greatness.

Action Steps for Principals
Student Culture

Lever	Key Actions in Sequence
	Plan

Student Culture	**Set the Vision**
	
	1. **Define your vision for student culture:**
	   • See a model.
	     o Review videos of implementation (e.g., from *Get Better Faster, Leverage Leadership, Teach Like a Champion*) and/or visit high-performing schools or classrooms.
	     o Record what teachers, leaders, and students say and do.
	   • Define the model for your own school's routines and procedures.
	     o Write what the leaders, teachers, and students should be doing.
	     o Enumerate what will happen if a student doesn't follow directions.
	     o Create a school-wide culture rubric that defines the following:
	       ■ Common language that teachers and leaders will use
	       ■ Vision for all school-wide and classroom routines and systems
	   • Anticipate the gap.
	     o Determine what it would look like if student culture was executed poorly.
	     o What would ineffective leaders and teachers be doing?
	     o What would the students be doing if it was implemented poorly?
	
	2. **Name It—build a minute-by-minute plan for every routine, procedure, and all-school culture moment:**
	   • Craft minute-by-minute systems for routines and procedures.

LEVER	KEY ACTIONS IN SEQUENCE

STUDENT CULTURE	**PLAN**
	
	    o Name what leaders, students, and teachers will do in a comprehensive, sequential, minute-by-minute plan.
	
	        ■ Describe every part of the day: arrival/breakfast, hallway transitions, in-class routines (including first and last 5 min of class), lunch, dismissal.
	
	        ■ Include what will happen when students do not follow directions.
	
	  • Set goals and deadlines.
	
	    o Set a concrete, measurable goal—e.g., hallway transitions will reduce to 1 min; increase all hands raised to 100%.
	
	    o ID when the system will be *introduced* and when the goal will be *met*.
	
	    o Determine the tool for measurement (e.g., Student Culture Rubric).
	
	3. **Name It—build systems to manage student discipline (asst. principal, dean of students, etc.):**
	
	  • Set up effective systems and routines for the leader who will drive student culture.
	
	  • Set a weekly and daily schedule for that leader.
	
	  • Create a clear protocol for responding to specific student discipline situations.
	
	  • Build a standing agenda for principal–culture leader check-ins that includes:
	
	    o Data review of student discipline issues and most pressing student issues
	
	    o Feedback to the leader and to teachers who need support
	
	    o Review of send-out or suspension data to problem-solve ways to prevent the behavior
	
	ROLL OUT
	
	4. **Plan the rollout/rehearsal:**
	
	  • Plan the rollout.
	
	    o Script a hook:

Lever	Key Actions in Sequence
	Roll Out

- Frontload school values/mission—short and sweet speech that states rationale and purpose.

  o Script the model.

    - Using clear and concise language, tell them the procedure and the sequence of the procedure. Everyone needs to know what it will look like.

    - Script what you will narrate as you model to highlight key takeaways.

  o Plan the staff practice of the routine/procedure.

    - Script what you will say and do and script what teachers will say and do (roles, timing, etc.).

    - Script what real-time feedback you will give during practice, with associated prompts.

5. **Roll out/rehearse:**

  • See It—model the routine/procedure.

    o Hook: deliver a hook (short and sweet) that gives them the "why."

    o Frame: name what you want them to observe: "As you watch the model of [routine/procedure], I want you to be thinking about . . ."

    o Model: exaggerate the model to reinforce every action you want to see.

  • Name It—debrief the model.

    o Ask "What did you notice? Teacher actions? Student actions?"

    o Narrate the why: "Why is that [action] important?"

    o Reflect: "Jot down your key takeaways before we jump into practice."

  • Do It—practice the routine/procedure.

    o Give clear What to Do directions:

      - What the main participant will do (time for her to plan/script her actions)

      - What the audience will do (cue cards, prepared student roles)

Lever	Key Actions in Sequence
	Roll Out
	o Round 1—practice the basic routine and procedure from start to finish.
	o Give feedback at the point of error and have them do it again.
	o Round 2 (after teachers have built muscle memory)—add complexity (e.g., student misbehavior, student learning errors).
	o Lock it in and rename the action plan:
	▪ "How did what we practice meet or enhance the action plan we named?"
	Execute
Student Culture	6. **Lead publicly:**
	• Be present and be seen in key areas (lunch, hallways, struggling classrooms, etc.).
	• Communicate urgency (verbal and nonverbal).
	o Nonverbal: point to students who need redirecting; move students along.
	o Verbal: Do It Again until 100%; challenge ("First period did this. Can you do it, too?").
	• Provide immediate feedback.
	o Model concrete phrases and actions that teachers should use (keep it succinct).
	o Address student noncompliance on the spot; follow up face-to-face with teacher.
	o Use precise praise and celebrate success (individual and team) verbally and via email.
	7. **Manage individually:**
	• Teachers—have "course correction" conversations when they are struggling.
	o ID the challenge.
	o State the impact.
	o Make bite-size action plan with prompt implementation on a set timeline.

LEVER	KEY ACTIONS IN SEQUENCE
	EXECUTE
STUDENT CULTURE	• Leaders—implement check-in with the leader in charge of student discipline issues (AP/dean).
	o Model effective student de-escalation and reflection techniques for the AP/dean and have AP/dean execute.
	o Monitor and give AP/dean real-time feedback to ensure AP/dean meets current action step.
	• Students—lead effective discipline conversations by following the model.
	o Listen: ask them to explain their version of what happened.
	o Name the problem and then the consequence.
	o Share why this is important (back to shared mission and long-term dreams for the child).
	o End with shared commitment to work together.
	• Families—lead effective discipline conversations with families.
	o Name the problem and then the consequence.
	o Listen: acknowledge their feelings and their concerns ("open face," eye contact, emotional constancy).
	o Economy of language: keep language concise and precise, and stick to the script.
	MONITOR AND COURSE-CORRECT
	8. **Measure student culture and ID the gaps:**
	• Via a school walkthrough, ID students and teachers not implementing routines effectively and ID the action steps.
	o With Student Culture Rubric in hand, ID where the breakdown occurs:
	■ What student actions or inactions are indicators of the problem?
	■ What teacher actions or inactions are causing the problem?
	■ What leader actions or inactions are causing the problem?

LEVER	KEY ACTIONS IN SEQUENCE
	MONITOR AND COURSE-CORRECT

STUDENT CULTURE	o Bring people outside your leadership team to observe your school and ID the big rocks to move your school culture forward.
	
	• Targeted improvements: choose one row on the Student Culture Rubric and set a specific goal for a score by a specific date. Develop clear action steps and implement. Rescore that row on a regular basis.
	
	9. **Lead a whole-school reset of a specific, high-leverage routine/procedure:**
	
	  • Revisit the model: what the routine should look like.
	
	  • See the gap: have teachers/leaders ID the gaps.
	
	  • Model the reset (follow the actions in the rollout section).
	
	  • Execute a daily walkthrough to monitor the targeted action steps.
	
	  • Communicate to staff the progress and next steps on a daily basis until the goal is met.

Pulling the Lever

Action Planning Worksheet for STUDENT CULTURE

Self-Assessment

• Look at the Student Culture Rubric (located on the DVD that accompanies this book). Select the sections you think are valuable for evaluating your school. For those that you selected, on what percentage of them is your school proficient? _%

• What items on the Student Culture Rubric are your biggest areas for improvement?

_____

_____

_____

_____

_____

- What actions listed in the box "Action Steps for Principals" for leading school culture would you want to implement right away to address the gaps in your school? Choose your top two or three.

_____

_____

_____

_____

_____

Planning for Action

- What tools from this book will you use to lead student culture at your school? Check all that you will use (you can find all on the DVD):

  ☐ Student Culture Rubric

  ☐ Student culture vision samples

  ☐ Minute-by-minute sample plans—in-class and whole-school routines

  ☐ Rollout exemplar scripts—in-class and whole-school routines

  ☐ 30-Day Playbook—HS Sample

  ☐ Videos of effective PD

  ☐ PD materials for leading student culture

- What are your next steps for improving your student culture?

Action	Date

Chapter 6

Staff Culture

Staff Culture: Building Trust

"Take another minute to wrap up," shares Adriana Gonzalez, principal of Lenore Kirk Hall Elementary School. It's the beginning of Adriana's weekly faculty meeting, and they start as they often do—by celebrating their peers. "They can be great without being long!" she says with a smile. A few laughs emanate from the staff who are finishing their notes.

"OK: give your peer a shout-out!" The noise and energy pick up in the room as teachers turn toward a colleague and read off of the note card what they thank their partner for. Smiles abound as teachers share their quick notes of affirmation.

After a few minutes, Adriana raises her hand, and the faculty turn back toward her. "Before we begin our practice clinic, let's remember our norms for today." The staff turn toward the chart on the wall where the school norms are always visible: Take ownership of results and learning for self and others. Assume the best. Listen well. Be respectful and engaged.

After seeing a model and receiving precise directions, the faculty break up into groups of four and start practicing their guided reading conversations. Adriana floats around the room, affirming teachers and providing feedback on where they could improve. She notices one teacher who is more flustered than normal and another who seems disconnected. Her groups leaders note them as well. As they transition between practice rounds, a group leader leans in to whisper to Adriana, "Something is off with Katie today. I'm going to talk to her so we can figure out what's wrong."

"Excellent," replies Adriana. "I was noticing the same thing. Let's touch base when we debrief at our leadership team meeting."

The year Adriana became principal of Lenore Kirk Hall Elementary School, she encountered some significant challenges. For one, twenty-one of her thirty teachers were new to the school—and fifteen of those new teachers were new to teaching altogether. But just as big of a challenge—if not bigger—was the lack of connection and trust among them. Adriana quickly found that the systems she'd planned to use to drive achievement at Lenore Kirk, such as data-driven instruction and weekly observations, wouldn't work unless all of these staff members trusted each other. "In my second year, we worked really hard to build trust on our team," Adriana says. "My teachers have to trust that I give them feedback to help them improve—not just to tell them what to do."

By the end of Adriana's second year at Lenore Kirk, it was clear she was on to something. Her students saw double-digit gains in math and reading (see Figure 6.1). And her staff? They were thriving. Kirk had double-digit gains in the district climate survey in the categories of "culture of feedback/support" and "positive culture/environment," and staff turnover dropped from 29 percent to 8 percent.[1] Adriana gave teachers opportunities to give her feedback, and her teachers welcomed the feedback of instructional leaders in return. Mutual support has become the norm, Adriana says. "We all work to help each other."

Adriana is one of a growing cohort who have cracked the code on staff culture—and discovered that it makes all the difference in the world. Teresa Khirallah, program officer at the Teaching Trust in Dallas and a former principal, has led teams of school leaders in Dallas to dramatic gains in achievement, including Adriana.

Without question, Teresa will tell you that student culture and data-driven instruction are the key levers that drove results. What staff culture does is make sure that those levers can be implemented to fruition. "Your people have to learn how to do it," comments Teresa, "and they also have to want to." If coaching and leading professional development are about giving your staff the ability to succeed, staff culture is about making sure they want to. Staff culture is to teaching what student culture is to learning: it creates an environment where sustained growth is possible.

Figure 6.1 Texas State Assessment (STAAR): Lenore Kirk Hall Elementary School, Percentage at or Above Proficiency in Math

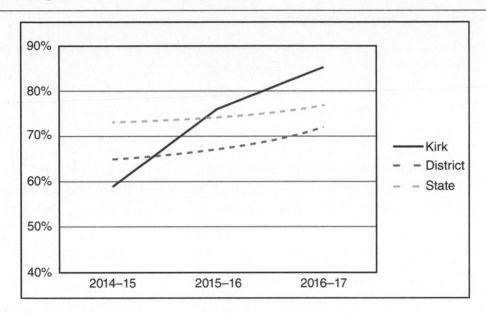

> ## Core Idea
>
> If instructional leadership is about giving your staff the ability to succeed, staff culture is about making sure they want to.

Research confirms this. Authors from Judith Warren Little to Ron Edmonds to Michael Fullan have proven that strong adult culture creates more teacher expertise and higher achievement.[2] Although the research is solid, schools have been slow to implement it. Part of the reason is that even though it is easy to spot a strong culture, it is hard to know how to build one.

When you observe a strong family from afar, you are struck by the unity they display and the closeness of their relationships. You see the joy and the love. What you probably don't see, however, is the hard work that is done on a daily basis to create that unity. The same holds true for schools.

A great team isn't built on superficial happiness but on concrete habits that bond a team. In this sense, leading staff culture is not a soft skill—on the contrary, it's the toughest steel that keeps your school's foundation permanently rooted.

> ### Core Idea
>
> A great staff culture is built on love—but that doesn't make it "soft."
> It's the steel that keeps your community strong.

In this chapter, we'll show how leaders like Adriana take concrete action to build a strong, united team among their staff. The process starts with setting a vision and then rolling it out and maintaining it. Let's read on.

SET THE VISION

If you've ever made Thanksgiving dinner with a large family, you know the challenges that can arise! If some members of the family have now started families of their own, you have to find a way to merge the different visions to make everyone feel a part of it. Then you have the challenge of how to prepare the meal once you agree on it. One person doing all of the cooking can create exhaustion and tension over the course of the holiday, but having several people in the kitchen at once without clearly defined roles will create tension in about an *hour*. The only way to share the work so that the food is excellent and everyone feels loving toward each other is to split up the work explicitly, so that everyone knows what his or her job is.

The same is true of working with people you care about to build a school. You need to know what you want from the adults and to make that clear. Research from the New Teacher Project confirms it. In their national survey of teachers, researchers have discovered three statements that separate high-achieving schools from the rest. "The responses to three questions on our survey had the strongest connection with greater retention of successful teachers and higher student achievement in reading and math."[3] The three statements were

- "My school is committed to improving my instructional practice."

- "Teachers at my school share a common vision of what effective teaching looks like."

- "The expectations for effective teaching are clearly defined at my school."

The first two are pretty clearly addressed by Chapters 1–4; the third merits additional attention.

A clear vision and consistent role clarity are the cornerstones of a team that can build something awe inspiring—and function harmoniously. Put another way, when it comes to staff culture, warmth grows from clearly defined expectations, not the other way around.[4]

Core Idea

Warmth grows from clearly defined expectations, not the other way around.

To hold your staff to these high expectations, you'll have to create an environment where you can set those high standards in the first place. Here's how.

Name the Behaviors You Wish to See

When educators think about their dream school, they often describe what they want to see in the students: investment in their learning, curiosity, and high engagement. It is just as valuable to ask what you want to see in the adults in the building. Although there are many pathways to defining what you want to see, Adriana has two nonnegotiables that she shares in common with other leaders who have the same sort of success as hers.

Belief in Your Mission

Every school leader can establish her own core mission and vision for the school. Yet successful schools have three essential keys embedded within that vision. In their 2006 article "Three Strands Form Strong School Leadership," Jon Saphier, Matt King, and John D'Auria noted those three keys as

- "The belief that all students are capable of working on rigorous material and meeting high standards, even if they currently are behind grade level."[5]
- Academic focus (which you cover by rolling out the other levers of this book!)
- Honest and nondefensive communication (which we'll address later in this chapter)

Laura Garza remembers screening prospective teachers for aligned vision as a key to the success of her first year at Blanton Elementary. "I laid out all my expectations for what I wanted to accomplish that first year," Laura says. "I was looking for reactions, to see if they thought it could be done. Some didn't, so they chose not to join our team—but those who did join us were committed to making these changes."

Hunger to Learn

At Lenore Kirk, feedback is a fact of life—it is at the heart of every lever in this book! For Adriana, the ability to accept such feedback openly—even more, to yearn for the opportunity to grow—is nonnegotiable. Accordingly, Adriana always looks for a chance to see the teacher in action, in a sample lesson, before hiring. As she observes him or her, Adriana focuses less on the skill of the teacher in the classroom at that specific moment—we can always develop that!—and more on his or her enthusiasm to grow. Put another way, Adriana prioritizes a teacher's will over his or her skill. Sample lesson feedback gives her a sense of a teacher's willingness to join her professional learning environment. There is a big difference between asking, "Are you open to getting feedback?" and actually giving someone feedback on a lesson and seeing how he or she reacts. A hungry learner will lean in and start taking notes. By contrast, someone who is not interested might smile and nod his or her head and graciously receive the feedback, but he or she won't show any interest in actually implementing it.

The beauty of these two character traits is that they require only will, not skill. To be certain, hiring people to live by these traits isn't always easy. As former CEO of General Electric Jack Welch and former *Harvard Business Review* editor Suzy Welch write in their book *Winning*, "Hiring good people is hard. Hiring great people is brutally hard. And yet nothing matters more in winning than getting the right people on the field."[6] The upshot, for leaders like Adriana and Laura, is that time invested in carefully naming what they are looking for in staff will pay enormous dividends in building a team that will accomplish great things for their students.

Core Idea

Hire for will more than skill.
If your teachers believe in your mission and are hungry to learn, you can coach the rest.

A Word on . . . Content Knowledge in Hiring for High School

Adriana leads an elementary school, but many of you reading this book work at the high school level. From my experience working with high school leaders across the country, a third key criterion emerges when hiring for high school teachers: content knowledge. To be certain, content knowledge is important at every grade level; I never knew how complex kindergarten was until I looked at the art of teaching reading! At the same time, it is easier to develop an elementary school teacher in that content knowledge after you hire him or her: we show that in *Great Habits, Great Readers*. The same is not true at the high school level. If a teacher doesn't know calculus pretty deeply, he or she cannot teach it effectively.

Because of this, high school leaders also find content expertise an essential element of hiring. What is challenging about this criterion is that finding someone who deeply knows the AP content or HS-level content is a challenge. Particularly in the STEM fields, not enough college graduates are entering the teaching field. Even when you do find a STEM teacher, assessing content expertise is not quite as easy as looking at someone's transcript. If you have a teacher who majored in chemistry, she likely hasn't even looked at the content of AP Chemistry since she was in high school!

These challenges leave us without easy answers. Watching guest lessons and asking teachers questions about their content knowledge can help assess expertise. For those who don't have that knowledge and we need to hire them anyway because of a lack of options, utilize the resources available for them to learn the content as they teach.

Set Clear Roles

When you look at surveys of children of their favorite teachers, and surveys of teachers of the leaders they respect the most, a common pattern emerges: consistency. It matters less the type of personality the teacher or leader has than whether he or she is consistent.[7] Standard routines and clear understanding of what to do bring stability to a teacher's job, and they enable teachers to spend mental energy on their craft and not on negotiating uncertainty. How do leaders do this?

Mike Mann (whom we met in Chapter 2) creates a detailed list of all teacher roles and responsibilities at the start of each year. It includes everything: your teaching load, your coaching load (if you are coaching a peer), your duties, your standing weekly meeting with your instructional leader, and even what prep periods you will be occasionally asked to give up to cover for an absent teacher. Here's an example of what Mike's document looks like.

Setting Clear Roles

Creating Equitable and Transparent Schedules

| Teacher | Teaching Hours | Duties | | | | | Other Responsibilities | | Total Hours |
		Mon	Tues	Wed	Thurs	Fri	Hours	Description	
John	20	0.5	1.5	1.5		0.5	2	Journalism—newspaper	**26.0**
Mary	20	0.5	0.75	1.5		0.75	2	Yearbook	**25.5**
Derek	16	0.5	1.5	0.5	0.5	1.5	5	Curriculum and Assessment Development	**25.5**
Katrina	20	0.5	0.5	0.5		0.5	4	Dept. chair	**26.0**
Tom	26			0.5					**26.5**
Meghan	22	0.5		0.5	0.5	1.5			**25.0**
Amy	19						8	Writing Ctr/ Support teacher	**27.0**
Thomas	17	2	1.5	1.5	0.75	1	2	Curriculum and Assessment Development	**25.75**
Ashley	24		0.5		0.5	0.5			**25.5**
Sam	18						8	Dept. chair	**26.0**
Brittany	26	0.5			0.5				**27.0**
Tiara	26	0.75	0.5						**27.3**
Michael	21	0.5	0.5	0.5	0.5		3	Senior Research Project	**26.0**

This seems simple, but it adds so much value to staff morale. For one, when teachers know all of this in advance, they can schedule their time and plan accordingly. But they also benefit from knowing that everyone in the school is carrying his or her weight: we are in this together.

Set Clear Weekly Schedules

We all know that school life is turns and changes: one week there is a field trip, the next week a fire drill, and so on. After the roles chart, the second key structure that keeps staff duties clear is a simple weekly email to all staff that has all the changes to the standard schedule. Here is Mike's example. He starts with a bit of inspiration and then brings clarity to the upcoming week and month.

Sample Weekly Email

Above and Beyond . . .

All of us who know Jared's story are proud of the young man he has become. Amir, who has known him and taught him since middle school, went out of his way this weekend to help Jared with a college visit: "Jared asked if I could help him with a college visit, because his mother wasn't going to be able to take him. So I volunteered. Today we want to Franklin & Marshall, and Jared was so impressive. His interactions with folks at Admissions were the epitome of professionalism. When he talked with Dr. Penn, professor of neurophysiology, he made our community proud!" Thanks, Amir, for going above and beyond!

On the Calendar This Week . . .

- Monday: Advisory Spirit Competition (attached)
- Wednesday: Advisory video #1 on the International Day of the Girl
- Friday: Whole-faculty PD, 1:30–4:30 p.m.

Of Note . . .

- **Advisory Spirit Competition:** Please see the attached flyer and be prepared to share this with your advisory on Monday. Each advisory is asked to create a video this week showing their spirit. Students will have a chance to work on this on both Monday and Tuesday. Thank you for your help with this!

- **International Day of the Girl:** Last Wednesday, October 11th, was the sixth annual International Day of the Girl, as declared by the United Nations. **All advisories are expected to view the videos linked in the handout and to discuss the questions listed.** Advisories that are still not finished with their spirit video by Tuesday will still have a chance to work on the video next week.

- **Fire drill, October 17th:** We will be having a fire drill on **Tuesday, October 17th.** Please review the Emergency Reference Guide located in the operations manual or on your classroom wall in advance of this drill. If you have any questions, please reach out to Connor before the drill takes place.

Kudos!

- **Boys Soccer:** Good luck in the county tournament Friday!
- **Girls Varsity Volleyball:** It was "pretty in pink" this week as both teams rocked pink socks for breast cancer research. Great cause and well done, girls!!!

Month at a Glance

Week	Monday	Tuesday	Wednesday	Thursday	Friday
Oct 16–20	Advisory: Spirit Competition	Advisory: Connections Fire drill	Advisory: video and discussion	Advisory: video and discussion	Faculty PD: Predicting IA performance
Oct 23–27	School Forum: Fastest Improvement	Advisory: Connections Tag Day	Quarter 1 Exams	Quarter 1 Exams	Quarter 1 Exams Faculty PD: Complete IA grading and begin analysis
Oct 30–Nov 3	School Forum: Personal Improvement Plans 9th-grade hike (group 1)	Advisory: Connections 9th-grade hike (group 1) Instructional Ldr PD: Leading Data Meetings	Advisory: reading and discussion	Advisory: reading and discussion 9th-grade hike (group 2)	Faculty PD: IA data meetings 9th-grade hike (group 2) Quarter 1 grades due
Nov 6–10	School Forum: Latinx Cultural Celebration	Advisory: Connections	Advisory: reading and discussion Quarter 1 Report Card Night	Advisory: reading and discussion Senior Class Tag Day	Half day: No faculty PD

Notice the power of Mike's memo. First, it is pretty short: no one wants to read a long essay! Second, it gives a clear calendar of what is coming up in the week and the month ahead so staff can plan accordingly. Finally, it includes a few accolades from that week.

Everyone gets excited hearing about the athletic teams' success—and it also makes it easier for teachers to feel better about the student who missed their class that Friday traveling to the tournament.

Clear roles and clear schedules mean a clear mind: you drive out the clutter and allow a teacher to focus on teaching. When they can do that, your students will fly.

> ## Core Idea
>
> Clear roles and clear schedules mean a clear mind:
> you drive out the clutter and allow a teacher to focus on teaching.

ROLL IT OUT

Once you've set your vision for staff culture, the next step is to roll it out.

Lead by Example

Whenever Teresa Khirallah sets out to lead a group of educators to excellence, she begins by modeling vulnerability. Sometimes, she talks about her own experience as a principal; other times, she uses a story about how meal planning helped her meet a health goal to illustrate the power of planning. No matter what personal story Teresa chooses to share, though, one thing remains constant: she always shows her staff she's had to work hard, and sometimes struggle, to master something she excels at now.

Why does Teresa do this? Because she wants people to be vulnerable about their own stumbling blocks, too. She needs them to embrace their own points of error so that, through coaching and practice, they can close the gap between challenge and triumph. "In an environment where being vulnerable—that is to say, sharing where your gaps are—is openly encouraged," Teresa affirms, "that's the perfect place to go in with a technical skill set and show someone how to close their gaps." To create that ideal environment, Teresa models embracing the point of error herself, recognizing that those she leads won't do what she says: they'll do what she does.

> ## Core Idea
>
> People will do as you do, not as you say.

This type of leadership by example is necessary to get your staff to replicate any behavior you need them to emulate. If you want your staff to be kind to each other, be kind to them. If you want them to be receptive to feedback, receive feedback constructively. If you want them to act as one school with one mission, model that you are part of that one school and hold yourself to the same high standards. By leading by example, you model the ethos that is the heart of any effective staff culture: "My success is your success." You won't create a common culture if your school operates as every individual for himself or herself; and you won't create an environment where everyone is in it together unless you show you're in it, too.

Core Idea

"My success is your success."
You won't create a common culture unless you show you're in it, too.

Create a Culture of Practice

You will not find a single professional athlete or musician who didn't have a deep commitment to practice. An ethos of practice is also central to successful schools. Judith Warren Little and Jon Saphier—and a host of other authors—have defined this as one of the key characteristics of a high-achieving school.[8] Every previous leadership lever has driven home the importance of practice, yet that culture isn't always apparent in schools. What do you do when your staff doesn't have a culture of practice? You show them.

In our conversations with leaders who have successfully changed the ethos of their school around practice and feedback, they describe three pretty simple steps that make the difference:

- **See It.** Show teachers an example of the power of practice, both in another profession and also in education. Most of the videos highlighted in this book would be good examples!

- **Name It.** Make practice and feedback a norm. Plain and simple.

- **Do It . . . consistently . . . and with emotional constancy.** The first time you ask a teacher to practice who has never practiced before, she might balk or have an attitude. The second time you do it, she'll react a little less. By the time you've done it for the fourth time in a row, she will understand that this is the way you do things, and your culture has been established. You just have to stick with it even if it's awkward at the beginning, and you have to remain emotionally constant. If teachers sense that you are uncomfortable with practice, they will be, too. If this is natural for you, they will embrace it.

Build Relationships

When you devote the amount of time to be an educator that it takes, the school becomes more than just a place of work—it is one of your communities. At the heart of a community are the relationships between people within them. Your relationship with your teachers will always be different because as a principal, you are also the authority. But that doesn't mean you cannot strengthen relationships—and use those as a foundation to lead.

Leading by example is the right way to start, and building a culture of practice will build bonds among the staff. A few more things that help are the little things—namely the small moments of every day when you can connect. In many ways, small talk is big talk.

Core Idea

Small talk is big talk.

Engage in Small Talk

The art of small talk is often underrated. For some, it comes naturally. If that is the case for you, you can skip to the next section! If this is unnatural, there are concrete actions you can take to get better at the art of small talk to make a bigger impact:

- **Deliver a warm greeting.** Warmth—a simple smile, a gesture, a hug—goes a long way. People remember your warmth!

- **Remember their story.** One of the most remarkable things about Adriana and leaders like her is their ability to remember something about each of their staff members. When you ask about people's children, vacation, or interests, the conversation changes. You communicate that their whole self is valued.

- **Have a natural exit strategy.** What makes conversations with multiple staff members possible is also that Adriana keeps them short. She exits naturally and easily so that the conversation doesn't end too abruptly.

Building relationships builds trust, which lays the groundwork for being able to push your staff in a way that's loving and fair.

Appreciate Your Staff

If building relationships is an area of growth for you, it can be helpful to keep track of it. Adriana creates a "personality profile" for each staff member built on Chapman and White's *The 5 Languages of Appreciation in the Workplace.* You can use any template like the one in the box here to help you leverage even brief interactions with your staff to build strong relationships with them.

Stop and Jot

How would you facilitate powerful small talk with four different members of your staff? Select four staff members, including a balance of new teachers, returners, instructional leaders, and operational staff. In particular, consider staff members with whom your relationships aren't as strong as they could be. Plan what you would do and say to them to make them feel valued, known, and loved.

Staff member	What are the things that matter most to them outside of school?
Ex.: Josh	*Hey Josh, how was camp? It was so great to see all the pictures! What was the best part? How was year 2 different from year 1? It seemed like your staff was awesome . . .*
Ex.: Tasha	*How's your daughter doing? Is she sleeping through the night yet? I'm rooting for that . . .*

If you follow the guidance of this chapter, think about what you will have accomplished: you've hired the right people, you've set clear roles, you lead by example, you build a culture of practice, and you build relationships. How do you maintain that momentum throughout the school year?

PROTECT IT

Jon Saphier is one of the leading authors in education, and he shared with me the idea that staff culture is something you must *protect*. I was struck by that word. Once you've set a clear vision for your staff to follow, the ongoing work of fostering and protecting that culture begins. Protecting a staff culture means three things:

- Create peak moments
- Narrate the positive
- Identify and correct the gaps

Create Peak Moments

In their best-selling book *The Power of Moments*, Chip and Dan Heath identify a fascinating pattern among most leaders and organizations. They state that we are often trained to fix problems but not to build great experiences, or as they call them, *peak moments*. Translated to the school context, we can fix the copy machine more quickly and deal with a challenging student, but neither of those will mean as much to a teacher as having a powerful positive experience. If we can create great peak experiences for our teachers, those peaks can carry them through to regular day-to-day work, and they will make it easier to deal with the frustration of the broken-down copy machine.

The Heath brothers point to four key characteristics for creating peak moments:

- Elevation: lifts us above the every day
- Insight: makes us think differently about the world; stretches us to become even better
- Pride: showcases us at our best and makes us feel recognized
- Connection: draws us close to a group of people

We often spend lots of effort designing moments like this for our students (e.g., a college signing day, rites of passage, etc.), but we often don't think about doing the same for adults! A peak experience is more than a faculty holiday party—that would only meet some of the above criteria. Consider the case in which you encourage a small group of teachers to apply for a summer fellowship/graduate course that they take together. It would meet all four criteria—lifts them above their everyday experience, stretches them to become better at their craft, gives them a sense of pride in knowing that you nominated and recommended them, and allows them to become even more connected with their peers. A year later, if you ask them to recall the highlights of their school year, this could likely rise to the top of the list. Even more, the Heath brothers state, such a strong experience can make you feel better about the rest of the year as well!

Take a little time to contemplate the peak experiences you could make for your staff:

- **First day of teacher orientation before the start of the year.** Make a top-notch welcoming experience like some colleges do for their first-year students.

- **Get Better Faster affirmations/celebrations.** Create a small celebration or affirmation each time a teacher masters the action steps in one of the Phases of the Get Better Faster Scope and Sequence (could be a simple card: "Congrats on mastering Phase 1!"). Think about how that could motivate a new teacher to continue to improve at a time when learning to teach can be so overwhelming!

- **Praise the teachers' loved ones.** Mike Mann has made it a ritual to write to the parents of new staff members right before the winter holidays of their first year at the school. He tells the parents what an amazing impact their child/loved one is having as a teacher and thanks them for what they did to create such an outstanding, mission-driven son or daughter. Think for a moment about the impact. When would a teacher expect that you might write a note to their parents? Once we are adults, rarely do our parents receive notes about what we are doing. You create an elevated experience that builds more pride and connection to the work. At the same time, you plant a seed of pride in the teacher's larger family as well. You could do the same with any loved ones in a teacher's life.

The power of these sample peak moments is not their particular quality but the way they embody the Heath brothers' key characteristics. With little effort, they can transform our teachers' experience of school and give them fuel to deal with the more challenging parts of our work.

Narrate the Positive

If you want a strong staff culture, you have to name it when it happens. Shouting out a teacher who was open to feedback or who put in extra practice sends a clear message about what we value. Acknowledging a staff member who goes above and beyond to help her colleague shows that you notice—and you care. What we praise is what we value. Let them hear about how important staff culture is—day in and day out.

Identify and Correct the Gaps

No matter how well we work to establish a strong staff culture, moments will occur that weaken the culture. Any action where a staff member doesn't follow the norms set by the school—not submitting a lesson plan by the stipulated time, not arriving on time to cover a lunch duty, speaking poorly about colleagues in the faculty room—allows others to believe that those norms are not real. Too often leaders see accountability as the antithesis to positive staff culture, but in fact it's the complement. You cannot have consistency if you don't hold people to it! By doing so, you send a powerful message: we live by what we preach. Remember: culture is what you see, not what you hope for. If you don't follow up when culture is not happening correctly, you allow that to be the staff culture in your school.

The most successful leaders in the field make sure to uphold expectations not just consistently but also swiftly. Principal Mike Mann sends his teachers a note right away if he enters their room to discover that they haven't posted their lesson plans. Antonio Burt provides his leadership team a form to fill out when they deliver feedback to teachers, and sets a weekly deadline by which they'll turn it in to him for review. Adriana will pull aside a staff member to address a negative interaction with his peer. Wait to hold people accountable—or turn a blind eye to what they're doing—and the moments when they don't meet expectations will become their habits. Support them continually, and the steps you take to hold them accountable take on a more meaningful message: "This is who we are as a community."

Core Idea

Turn a blind eye to negative actions, and those will become habits.
Address them immediately, and you solidify the culture.

Sometimes, of course, the negative action taken by a staff member will be such that you'll need to initiate a sit-down conversation—in other words, an "accountability conversation." Leaders who excel at accountability conversations use a pretty simple framework that they adjust to the severity of the situation.

Lead Accountability Conversations

As the common maxim says, if you want to stop a potential problem from growing, nip it in the bud. This is so true with staff. When the first minor issue arises with a staff member, effective school leaders like Adriana avoid two common mistakes: ignoring it or coming on too strongly.

If a staff member arrives late to a faculty meeting or doesn't turn something in on time, it can be tempting to let it go. But doing so communicates the message that this action is OK. Alternatively, if a leader aggressively chastises a teacher the first time there is an issue, she can quickly alienate and antagonize that teacher.

Leaders like Adriana maintain strong staff culture by addressing these relatively minor issues early but also warmly and briefly:

- **State the issue and ask what happened.** Directly let the teacher know why you are having this conversation, and ask him what happened. This enables you to let him explain, and it communicates to him that you want to assume the best.

- **State the impact.** Share with the teacher the impact of what he did. This is less about what the teacher intended and more about the result. "I know you probably didn't mean this, but by arriving late you communicated to your peers that their time is not as valuable as yours and that the PD was not important." This sort of language assumes the best of the teacher: you are not telling him that he meant this, but you are explaining how that action could be perceived. This enables the teacher to share how he doesn't want to communicate that sort of message. It makes the conversation easier and grounds it in what matters most: running an effective school.

- **Identify next steps and remove roadblocks.** Finally, set a plan to ensure that the teacher knows how to address the issue, and provide everything he needs to do so. Asking a question like "What's getting in the way of you being able to do this?" enables a leader to show that she wants to remove any unneeded roadblocks.

Although is it difficult to film conversations like this, I've had a chance to observe them. Here is a sample script of a conversation that is addressing a small issue.

Accountability Conversation Case Study

Addressing a Small Issue

Leader: Thanks so much for taking a few minutes to check in today. I'm concerned because I've noticed there have been a couple times over the past two weeks that your attendance report hasn't gone out on time, and more than once it hasn't gone out at all. So I wanted to check in with you and ask: How are things going?

Teacher: I'm surprised to hear this because I actually thought they'd been going much better. I don't think there's been a single day that I haven't sent one, and I'm pretty sure every time has been before the deadline.

Leader: OK. I'm glad that you think they're going better; that's important. But I have my notes here because I know we've been working on this, and I have two days that I didn't receive it until after the deadline and two times that I didn't receive it. I checked with a few other staff members, and they didn't receive it that day either. Is there anything you can think of that might be going on here?

Teacher: Wow, well, if you checked it, that must be right. I really thought I had sent it out every day on time.

Leader: OK. Well, I know this is something you're working on improving, so today, let's talk about how we can really move the needle so you can get it out every day. It's really important that we send that report out on time, because that's how we hold each other accountable for making sure we know where our students are over the course of the day.

Teacher: I one hundred percent agree. That sounds great.

In the beginning, when they address a single issue, these conversations are genial and brief—a gentle reminder that expresses your belief in your staff that they will improve.

Core Idea

Start by assuming the best: until there is a pattern of behavior,
a simple conversation can reset the course.

A Word on . . . Avoiding Email for Accountability Conversations

Email—the lifeblood of so much of our communication in the workplace—has some major drawbacks for accountability conversations: your words can be misinterpreted, and you have no control over when or where the emails you send are read. Further, by its very nature, email conveys stress and hostility in a particularly clear way because you cannot see the tone or person behind the text. Therefore, strong leaders of staff culture recommend that, whenever possible, you avoid sending emails and instead seek out the individual you need to speak with in person. This way, you gain the opportunity to learn more about your staff, yourself, and the effectiveness of your communication, because you are there to see how the information is received.

On the rare occasion that you need to use email, follow Julie Kennedy's simple advice: always wait a few minutes, or even hours, before sending an email. Sometimes, after twenty-four hours have passed, Julie may not send it at all.

If a single issue devolves into a pattern of behavior, or you have to address a more serious problem, you can use the same framework, but add urgency. Your follow-up actions become more concrete, and you will be a more active leader in setting them. The steps remain the same: state the issue and ask what happened, state the impact, and identify next steps. What is different is the urgency.

Respond to Pushback

The power of the framework we've described here is that it minimizes the antagonism that can be created when having a difficult conversation. In a perfect world, accountability conversations would always go as smoothly as the one modeled. However, as we've all experienced, the reality is that when being held accountable, some teachers will push back—either against the actions we demand or our message as a whole. The framework still works; you will just need to be more intentional on naming the actions you expect to change.

Nikki Bowen is the principal of Excellence Girls, a Blue Ribbon School in Brooklyn. She suggests the following moves when dealing with pushback:

- Acknowledge the concerns and feelings of the individual.
- Pivot back from his or her response to return to the original conversation.

A Word on . . . Resistant Staff in Turnaround

In the vast majority of situations, keeping your "ear to the rail" and openly addressing challenges early will resolve staff culture problems. Teachers genuinely want to do what is best for students, and most will respond to the less confrontational approaches outlined in this chapter. Sometimes, however, teachers will behave in ways that are entirely out of bounds, or will repeatedly resist meeting basic expectations in ways that stem not from misunderstandings but from deeper disrespect or a lack of commitment to the mission. This is particularly likely to happen in "turnaround" situations where teachers may have developed a very different set of habits, attitudes, and expectations for approaching school and the principal's role. In many situations, it is very difficult to dismiss such a teacher.

In the long term, the best way to deal with this sort of challenge is often to change the culture *around* the resistant teacher rather than to confront him or her head on. As Brian Sims notes, " the more unified a culture is around core ideas and values, the more likely it is that 'holdouts' will begin to feel that the culture is simply not for them, leading them to look elsewhere." Indeed, the more consistent a culture is, the more isolated such negativity becomes, ultimately leading the negative person to move on.

Follow Up: Keep Building Relationships

When two people leave an accountability conversation, they can both be uncomfortable talking about other topics. The key for a school leader, however, is to bridge that discomfort gap. Adriana's strategy? Find an opportunity to see the staff member at his best. That way, Adriana can show the staff member that her view of his work is balanced: she sees it when he stumbles and supports him, but she sees it when he shines and celebrates him, too. "If you allow teachers to show you their best," shares Adriana, "they will try much harder to improve on their shortcomings."

Core Idea

Let teachers show you their best,
and they will try much harder to improve on the rest.

Building relationships after accountability conversations maintains a virtuous cycle: build relationships, maintain them through accountability, keep building relationships, repeat. That's how holding your staff accountable ultimately functions to make your culture stronger.

TURNAROUND—COMING TOGETHER

Even the most successful schools can face serious challenges when it comes to building a rich and supportive staff culture. At schools where negativity has prevailed and where teachers have become factionalized, politicized, repeatedly chastised, or otherwise disengaged, the challenge of fixing "adult culture" seems very daunting. Brian Sims, formerly the director of high schools for the Academy for Urban School Leadership (AUSL) and of education for Ark in London, has seen this firsthand. Improving staff culture was one of the critical components to AUSL's success in transforming fourteen of Chicago's least successful schools into solid community bedrocks. To transform staff culture during turnaround, Brian rolls out the vision just as described at the beginning of the chapter—he just takes more time doing so.

The core principle of a staff culture turnaround is that teachers need to know the school's core mission . . . and be unified in putting it into practice. "What most undermines failing schools is that everyone on the staff is doing his or her own thing," Brian explains. "Turning a failing school around demands a culture where everyone is on the same page, supports the school's mission, and accepts what is needed to get back on track." To set this expectation, each of Brian's turnaround schools holds a three-week training before school starts to set the new culture's expectations and to teach the common language that students will be responsible for during the year. Perhaps the most important part of these weeks comes during role-play exercises, during which staff practice the responses they will give to students and to each other. "Getting teachers used to a culture of positivity, of high expectations for students, and of respectful interaction with peers is the most important work we do over the summer," Brian notes. "If we don't build a strong expectation and shared culture early in the turnaround, it's extremely difficult to build it later."[9]

CONCLUSION

Of all the powerful moments Teresa Khirallah has experienced as a leader, she says that one of the most magical has been watching other educators seek out the Teaching Trust over time. Once people see what a staff culture based on achievement growth looks like, she says, "They're hungry for it." By holding her family of school leaders to a high standard and sharing their successes publicly, Teresa has created a community that other leaders and teachers are eager to learn from.

In short, Teresa's family has grown into a movement. That's the power of a great staff culture: it makes it possible to sow the seeds of change both in and beyond our own schools. As another great leader named Teresa once said, the most important step anyone can take to make the whole world more loving is to build a loving home.[10]

Keys to Successful Staff Culture

- **Set the vision**
  - Name the behaviors you want to see
  - Set clear roles
  - Set clear schedules
- **Roll it out**
  - Lead by example
  - Create a culture of practice
  - Build relationships
- **Protect it**
  - Create peak moments
  - Narrate the positive
  - Identify and correct the gaps

Action Steps for Principals
Staff Culture

LEVER	KEY ACTIONS IN SEQUENCE
	PLAN
	1. **Set the vision for staff culture:** • Name the behaviors you wish to see (connected to belief in the mission and hunger to learn). • Set clear roles for staff, and weekly schedules. • Design the meeting/PD where you will roll out your vision. • Create and use a tracker to track regular positive staff interactions.
	ROLL OUT
STAFF CULTURE	2. **Lead PD of your vision:** • Develop a concise and compelling story about why you do this work. • See It and Name It: give exemplar of the routines and habits that will support positive staff culture. • Do It: practice implementing that culture.
	EXECUTE
	3. **Lead by example:** • Faithfully implement all the norms of the staff culture. • Always state the why: use regular communication to remind everyone of the mission and the important role they play in achieving it. 4. **Build relationships and be present:** • Conduct quarterly/monthly check-ins with staff members you do not regularly coach. • Be present and have "small talk" in staff work spaces, at social events, and at other less structured times.

Lever	Key Actions in Sequence

- ID bellwether staff members and seek their input on staff culture on a regular basis.
- Respond to harsh feedback/poor staff culture moments with emotional constancy.

Monitor

5. **Assess the quality of staff culture (keep your ear to the rail):**

   - Name key staff members as leaders of that vision and establish regular touchpoints with them focused on staff culture.
   - Administer staff surveys and develop questions based on focus areas identified in data.
   - ID trends in staff survey data and establish 1–2 focus areas to improve.

6. **ID and close the gap—create a plan to realign the school to your staff culture vision:**

   - ID gap between current staff culture and ideal staff culture.
   - Develop 3–4 high-leverage, specific action steps to respond to poor culture.
   - Communicate your actions to staff with reference to their feedback.

7. **Lead accountability conversations with staff members who are not implementing the vision:**

   - State what happened: ask if this assessment is accurate or what they would add/change.
   - State what was communicated by these actions (e.g., "When you arrived late to PD, you sent a message—even if you didn't intend to do so—that PD doesn't matter or that you don't need it.")
   - Let the staff member react and state what she was intending/feeling.
   - State or ID the gap between her intent and what was communicated.
   - Jointly name the actions to improve for next time.

Lever column (vertical): Staff Culture

Pulling the Lever

Action Planning Worksheet for STAFF CULTURE

Self-Assessment

- Review the key action steps for successful staff culture. What are three steps you'd like to take right away?

_____

_____

_____

_____

Planning for Action

- What are your next steps for improving your staff culture?

Action	Date

Chapter 7

Managing School Leadership Teams

It's said that a picture is worth a thousand words. The same is true of a school leadership team meeting. It's not what they say but what they do. Let's take a journey through a series of vignettes of successful leadership team meetings to understand their power.

School Leadership Teams: A Painting, Part 1

At Ford Road Elementary School, principal Antonio Burt and his leadership team are sitting around a table with their notes from the week's classroom observations in front of them. The notes are familiar to Antonio, because he has his leaders share them with him throughout the week. This meeting, however, is the team's chance to look over them together and reach a shared understanding about where they are as a school—and where they want to go next.

"Where are we this week?" Antonio asks, kicking things off. "What are the patterns that you saw?"

Assistant principal Laquita Tate peruses the notes from her observations and begins by praising the third-grade teachers she observes for having students annotate the texts they're reading in class. Then she expresses concern that students seem to be reading more for summary than for well-backed analysis.

"I saw that as well in fourth and fifth grade," says coach Chavon Van Hooks. "Students aren't backing up their arguments with the best evidence. I noticed that during discussion as well as with written assignments," she adds.

Antonio nods. "I had the same impression when I observed this week," he says. "So if this is the pattern, what should we do to address it?"

Antonio Burt's success at school leadership is no secret. Following his first year as principal of Ford Road Elementary School in Memphis, Tennessee, the *Memphis Daily News* reported that Ford Road had already seen 20.2 percent gains in the number of students who were proficient or advanced in math, and 26 percent increases in the number of students who were proficient or advanced in science (see Figure 7.1).

Figure 7.1   Tennessee State Test Results: Ford Road Elementary, Percentage at or Above Proficiency

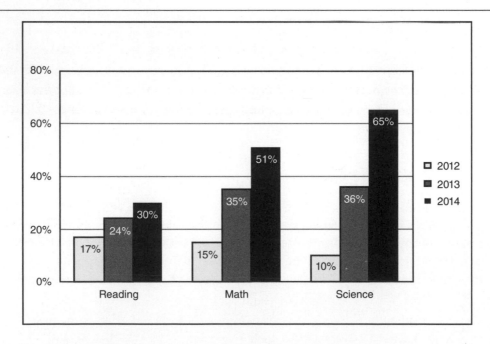

Prior to Antonio's leadership, no more than 17 percent of Ford Road's students had been proficient or advanced in any subject. It was no wonder that Ford Road was in the top 5 percent for growth for all schools in the state of Tennessee.[1]

This data makes it clear that Antonio implemented data-driven instruction extraordinarily effectively at Ford Road. But he didn't do it alone. Look no further than his school leadership team meeting.

If you follow Antonio's entire meeting, a few things jump out at you. This isn't a meeting with a bunch of announcements. And it's not focused on administrative tasks and compliance. The bulk of Antonio's meetings are spent on what matters most: student learning and teacher development. How did he get there? He was relentless about the way he used his time and the way his team used theirs.

Core Idea

Exceptional school leaders succeed because of how they use their time. And they get their leadership teams to use their time just as effectively.

"My leadership team and I went in with one united mission: to get our school from the bottom 5 percent to the top 25 percent in the state," Antonio says. "We knew the true measure of improvement would depend on data-driven instruction, but the power of the personal leadership of a school leader—how you spend your time and how that ripples out to the other people around you—can't be overstated."[2]

The previous chapters in this book have been about moving the key leadership levers for your own work. This one is about tripling your impact by getting your team to do the same. Let's find out how.

CHOOSE YOUR TEAM

We all know the power of a "dream team": the joy of working with colleagues toward a common goal, and the heights we scale together when we build on each other's strengths. Antonio's leadership team is one of those dream teams—but it didn't become so by chance.

The first thing Antonio had to do to set up an effective leadership team was to identify who his instructional leaders would be. The structure of your leadership team will vary depending on the resources available to you at your school. Some principals, like Antonio, have designated leaders such as assistant principals and reading coaches that are built into their staffing model. Others find instructional leadership from among their teachers. Regardless of the precise role each instructional leader holds, following these core guidelines as you choose your leaders will go a long way toward making your leadership team strong.

Look for Reliability and Receptiveness

Just as there is no one "principal personality," there is no one "instructional leader personality." More than anything, these leaders need to be reliable: their dependability will help facilitate that of everyone else in the school, yourself included.

"Our teachers were impacted by seeing on the first day of school that our leaders were ready to go," Antonio recalls, "and every day, getting materials from my leaders pushes me into my next tasks." Antonio needs to be able to trust that his leaders will implement the actions they decide on, so reliability is a must.

Just as essential is openness to feedback. If an instructional leader is going to develop teachers with lots of coaching, they need to be models of being open to being coached themselves. And they need to be receptive to the leadership practices mentioned throughout *Leverage Leadership 2.0*. "They don't need to know how to do it," notes Antonio. "They just need to be willing to learn." Teachers or administrators who cannot make this leap will not be good choices for this role.

Remember 12:1—The Golden Ratio

As noted in Chapter 3 on observation and feedback, even the most diligent school principal usually cannot serve as a weekly instructional leader for more than twelve teachers. Fortunately, principals need not (and indeed should not) be the sole instructional leaders. Members of the administrative team, such as vice principals or deans of instruction, also take on this instructional role. External coaches are also aligned to the same instructional leadership model. Through the creative use of such personnel, virtually any school can meet this 12:1 threshold to ensure that every teacher is observed and receives key feedback. (If you can only get to 24:1, don't worry: that just means you'll have biweekly rather than weekly feedback for teachers.)

Still struggling to get to the 12:1 ratio? Leverage teachers as additional leaders—without having them leave the classroom. Highly successful principals identify strong teachers in their building to coach one or two teachers each.

In order to plan how much time instructional leadership will take, we like to refer to a three-hour rule. For a new instructional leader who will also be teaching, we assume it is a three-hour weekly time commitment for each teacher he or she will lead. Although the fifteen-minute weekly observation and thirty-minute check-in take up less than an hour, we build in two additional hours for the preparation work and lesson plan support that occur. Based on these calculations, as a lead teacher takes on a teacher for instructional leadership, the principal reduces the lead teacher's other responsibilities (for example, by cutting back that teacher's lunch duties) or provides a stipend that is similar to what others would receive for a three-hour weekly commitment. When that teacher takes on more than two teachers, his or her course load may need to be reduced or modified.

TRAIN YOUR TEAM—ROLL OUT THE VISION

School Leadership Teams: A Painting, Part 2

"Let's review your schedules for the upcoming week," says Antonio. Each leader pulls out his or her observation schedule. "Given the patterns we just identified, what changes would you make to it?"

All of the leaders quietly look over the weekly schedule of observations that they had from the previous week. "Given that most of the problems are occurring during guided reading, I think we need to double down on our observations during the reading block."

"That sounds right," shares Laquita. "I will change my observation block from Tuesday afternoon to Tuesday morning so I can observe an extra third-grade reading block and second grade as well."

"Sounds good," replies Antonio. "And I can observe [the other third-grade reading teacher] at 9:30 on Tuesday so that we can compare notes."

When people talk about creating a vision for their team, they focus most on the aspirational dream the team aspires to achieve. Antonio certainly did that: "In those summer meetings, we agreed on five pillars of school improvement we'd focus on that year," Antonio recalls. "We made observation and feedback a big focus, because we knew so much more growth would come from building a culture of coaching with our teachers."

But that opening meeting is not what set Antonio apart from other leaders—it was how he turned that vision into something concrete and actionable.

Antonio treated his leadership team like a football team: he trained them before the season started.

Core Idea

Treat your leadership team like a football team:
train them before the season starts.

Build the Team's Schedule

A vision is meaningless unless we spend our time pursuing it.

Core Idea

A vision is meaningless unless we spend our time pursuing it.

That means that a leadership team's work must be not only envisioned but also scheduled. The success of Antonio's leadership team every week starts at the team meeting, when Antonio sits down with the team to finalize each leader's observation schedule for the following week. Antonio sets a rotating observation and feedback cycle that gives teachers the opportunity to receive coaching from different instructional leaders over the course of the year. Other leaders prefer to assign set teachers to each instructional leader and leave those assignments in place. What matters most is that at any given time, each instructional leader has locked in observation time and weekly standing check-ins on his or her schedule. As we discussed in Observation and Feedback (Chapter 3), locking in your observations is the fastest way to make sure your teachers develop more quickly.

What might this look like in practice? For a full-time instructional leader, it can look very similar to the principal's schedule—which we'll show in more detail in Chapter 8, Finding the Time. For someone who also teaches, it will look slightly different. Consider the schedule of Julia Goldenheim, a middle school instructional leader at Eric Diamon's Vailsburg Middle School.

Managing Leadership Teams

An Instructional Leader's Schedule

	Monday	Tuesday	Wednesday	Thursday	Friday
6:00 AM					
:30		Morning Greeter Duty			
7:00 AM					
:30					
8:00 AM	Teach Ganas English	Teach Ganas English	Teach Ganas English	Teach Ganas English	Teach Ganas English
:30					
9:00 AM					
:30					
10:00 AM					
:30	7th-Grade Planning Meeting				
11:00 AM		Observe Tabrikah	Meet Tabrikah		
:30				Monitor Lunch	English Dept. Meeting
12:00 PM	Teach 12th-Grade English	Observe Jazmin			
:30					

	Monday	Tuesday	Wednesday	Thursday	Friday
1:00 PM	Observe Juan	Meet Juan			
:30					
2:00 PM	Lesson Planning/ Grading Time		Lesson Planning/ Grading Time	Meet Jazmin	
:30					
3:00 PM					
:30					
4:00 PM		Tutoring			
:30					
5:00 PM					
:30					

As you can see from this sample, the instructional leader's role is, in important ways, a microcosm of the school leader's. By delegating these responsibilities, leaders of large schools can ensure that every teacher in the building is observed, receives feedback, and conducts data analysis with an instructional leader.

In Chapter 8, we'll give you even more strategies for locking in this sort of calendar. Once it's locked in, you can focus on how to use that time effectively.

Train Your Team

Leadership team meetings don't only work at the elementary school level, as in the case with Antonio's. They are also highly effective—and even more necessary—for high schools. Let's look at a sample of the leadership team meeting of Mike Mann at North Star Washington Park High School.

School Leadership Teams: A Painting, Part 3

"Let's pull out the videos you each took of the Do It part of your feedback meetings," comments Mike. "Today, we're going to put Syrena on the hot seat."

Syrena smiles as they project her video on the wall in Mike's office. All the other instructional leaders had already showed their own video at previous meetings, so she knew she was next.

"As you watch," Mike instructs, "identify the actions Syrena took that were most effective, and the one to two highest-leverage actions she could take to improve."

Mike plays the video, and each leader takes notes. After it concludes, Mike opens the floor: "What is your feedback for Syrena?"

"I thought her See It was particularly effective," comments Kate. "Her prompt, 'What is the purpose of What to Do directions?' set up her teacher to see her own gap." Others concur. "My highest-leverage action step for Syrena would be to perfect the plan before the practice. I noticed that the teacher made a number of errors during the practice part of the meeting that could have been fixed ahead of time. Take the time to revise the teacher's script before the practice begins."

Heads nod, and a few others add on praise and recommendations. Syrena takes notes.

"OK," Mike says. "Time to let Syrena try it again. Syrena, take out your plan for your upcoming feedback meeting. Why don't you take a few minutes to incorporate the feedback you received so you can practice it?" Syrena nods and pulls out her laptop.

"Kate, you can also get out your plan for the next meeting so that you can plan as well."

Mike Mann is no stranger to leadership team meetings. Yet early on, his leadership team meetings were not every effective. "We spent more time talking about the events of the week than improving our own leadership."

As Mike worked to improve his leadership, he came to realize a key idea about school leadership teams that was the same as Antonio Burt's: teachers don't get better faster without good coaching—and neither do instructional leaders. Planning for your teachers' training is as important as the actual training.

> ### Core Idea
> Teachers don't get better faster without good coaching—
> and neither do instructional leaders.

Carrying out such training would normally be a daunting task. The purpose of this book, however, is to reduce that burden. Parts 1 and 2 of this text are devoted to making each necessary principle clear to you. The DVD offers all the materials, scripts, videos, and PowerPoint presentations you will need to train your instructional leaders in those same principles.

Guide to Training Materials

All the Resources for Training Leaders (DVD Appendix)

Leadership Lever	Training Materials (Found in DVD)
Data-Driven Instruction	Videos of leaders in action (training materials can be found in the book *Driven by Data*)
Planning	Exemplar lesson plans and curriculum plans that can be used as the foundation for a PD
Observation and Feedback	7 hours of training materials and videos of leaders in action
Professional Development	7 hours of training materials and videos of leaders in action
Student Culture	7 hours of training materials and videos of leaders in action

This is far more material than you'll likely have time to use! Accordingly, prioritize the training that matches the immediate needs of your school and instructional leadership team. Remember: data-driven instruction and student culture are the super-levers. However, if you have instructional leaders who don't have to lead student culture, then you can choose data-driven instruction and observation and feedback as a starting place.

Equip Your Team

The power of each leadership lever is that you can equip your leadership team with the tools to make this work easier. The quickest way to do so is to create a spiral-bound Leverage Leadership Quick Reference Guide. This guide has all of the key one-pagers and guides from the entire book and can be found on the DVD in the folder by the same name:

- Leverage Leadership Quick Reference Guide:
    o Weekly Data Meeting one-pager (Chapter 1)
    o Planning Meeting one-pager (Chapter 2)
    o Giving Effective Feedback one-pager (Chapter 3)
    o Get Better Faster Scope and Sequence (Chapter 3)
    o Get Better Faster Coach's Guide (Chapter 3)
    o Leading Professional Development one-pager (Chapter 4)
    o Student Culture one-pager (Chapter 5)

With the tools in this book, the initial training and equipping become the easy parts, letting you focus on what matters: monitoring and following up.

MONITOR THE SCHOOL

Like Antonio Burt and Mike Mann, Hannah Lofthus leaves nothing to chance, which is why Ewing Marion Kauffman School in Kansas City is one of the highest-performing schools in all of Missouri.[3] With one thousand students, Hannah knows that the only pathway to success involves all instructional leaders, not just herself. (You can read more about her results in *The Principal Manager's Guide to Leverage Leadership*.) This is why her leadership team meetings continue even after she and her team have left the office.

School Leadership Teams: A Painting, Part 4

"So what should we expect to see?" Hannah asks Ben, her instructional leader, as they stand outside the classroom they are about to enter to observe.

"Well," replies Ben, "we've been working on monitoring during independent practice, so I hope to see the teacher name her lap [what she will be looking for], follow her pathway around the class to monitor all students' work, and mark up the work with either a check mark, correct, or circle, incorrect. I also want to see her collecting data on the right and wrong answers on her clipboard."

"Great," Hannah says. "If that isn't happening, what real-time feedback are you going to give her?"

Ben replies, "I will simply walk alongside her and whisper to her to follow her pathway, or name or help, or collect the data—whatever is missing."

"Excellent," Hannah says. "Let's walk in and observe."

The interaction narrated here is commonplace in Hannah's school: leaders walk the school, observe, and coach—together. "You have to walk the talk: until you do it together, you don't really know if it will work."

Think about the power of what Hannah is doing: her school leaders don't just get instructions on how to coach—they have a partner helping them get better while leading. That is the ultimate definition of a culture of practice: getting better is the norm.

Core Idea

Build a culture of practice for your leaders where getting better is the norm, not the exception.

Think back to each of the leadership team meeting vignettes you have seen in this chapter. They all connect together: build your schedule, monitor the school, and meet to discuss it.

No matter how often Hannah, Mike, or Antonio observe classrooms and walk around their schools, they cannot see everything. The power of uniting a leadership team in this way is that you've exponentially increased what you can see—and what you can do. Leaders like these three set a process for the leadership team for observing the school that enables them to find the gaps and quickly address them. Here are the steps they take when monitoring the school.

See It—Start from the Exemplar

You cannot solve a problem until you know what you're looking for. Before Antonio rushes to observe the "hotspots" of his school, he makes sure to know what the bar is.

He starts by looking at his top teachers: their culture routines, their student work, and everything in between. This lets him know what to look for. Where he doesn't have an exemplar in-house, he uses the resources in this book and elsewhere to help him: exemplars, videos of great teaching or leadership from *Get Better Faster* or *Teach Like a Champion*, rubrics, the 30-Day Playbook, the Get Better Faster Scope and Sequence, and so on.

Before visiting any classroom, you want each member of your leadership team to be able to answer the question, What do you want to see? What is the exemplar we are aspiring toward? You cannot find a gap until you know that answer.

See the Gap and Name the Pattern

With the right observation schedule and exemplar in hand, leaders can look for the patterns and the gaps. Here is where the resources from every previous chapter can come alive. Depending on the needs of the school or time of year, the leadership team can observe and look for patterns in any of the following:

- **Data-driven instruction:** the quality of student work and weekly data meetings
- **Planning:** the quality of lesson plans—from the objective to the Exit Ticket to the execution of the lesson
- **Feedback:** the quality of instructional leader coaching sessions
- **Culture:** the quality of student culture in each classroom or in whole-school routines
- **PD:** the quality of grade-level meetings or school-wide PD

Do It—Take Action

The power of a set schedule is that Antonio is able not only to identify the gaps but also he can immediately start coaching and fixing them in subsequent weeks! During their next team meeting they can name the next actions and build a continuous cycle of school improvement.

LEAD EFFECTIVE LEADERSHIP MEETINGS

School Leadership Teams: Completing the Painting, Part 5

"OK," affirms Antonio, "let's review. We've identified our gap and changed our observation schedule to monitor those teachers more closely. What should we do at our next faculty PD to help close this gap?"

"I think we can split up the staff. With the newer teachers, we can do a 101 PD on citing evidence in class discussion, and for the more developed teachers, we can look at student work to identify the gaps in students' citing of evidence. That group could follow the protocol of a weekly data meeting to build an action plan to increase the use of evidence in student writing."

"Got it," says Antonio. "Will you lead the first group, and I'll take the second one?"

"Sounds good," she replies. "Do we have an exemplar video clip of a teacher citing evidence? Or should I just model for them?"

When I first met Antonio and interviewed him for this book, I was struck by his answer to my simple question, "How often were you able to stick to your observation schedule?"

Every other time I have asked that question of a school leader, I have gotten a variety of answers, mostly ranging from 10 percent to 70 percent of the time. But Antonio answered me directly, "What do you mean? Every week. I mean, that's what makes the leadership team so effective: we adjust the schedule right at the meeting, and our team depends on each other to get our observations done. We can't let each other down."

How do they do it? It's simple: they don't leave a leadership team meeting without an observation schedule in place. Here's a sample of what that looks like.

Fort Road Walkthrough Schedule

Schedule for All Instructional Leaders

Morning Meeting				
Mon	Tues	Wed	Thur	Fri
Burt–Gordon	Burt–Jones	Burt–Martin	Burt–McGhee	Burt–Thompson
Tate–Jackson	Tate–Thompson	Tate–Cosby	Tate–Barham	Tate–A. Hunt
Van Hooks–T. Jones	Van Hooks–McCoy	Van Hooks–Batson	Van Hooks–Buntyn	Van Hooks–Wilson

Calendar Math				
Mon	**Tues**	**Wed**	**Thurs**	**Fri**
Burt–Gordon	Burt–Mathews	Burt–Veale	Burt-Haile	Burt–Thompson
Tate–Jackson	Tate–Thompson	Tate–A. Hunt	Tate–Jackson	Tate–Gordon
Van Hooks–Mathews	Van Hooks–Wright	Van Hooks–Batson	Van Hooks–Haile	Van Hooks–Mathews

Content Blocks				
Mon	**Tues**	**Wed**	**Thurs**	**Fri**
Burt–all of 2nd and 3rd grade	Burt–all of 2nd grade	Burt–all of 3rd grade	Burt–all of 2nd grade	Burt–2nd and 3rd grade
Tate–all of K and 1st grade	Tate–all of 1st grade	Tate–all of K; formal	Tate–all of 1st grade; formal	Tate–K and 1st grade
Van Hooks–all of 4th and 5th grade	Van Hooks–all of 4th grade	Van Hooks–all of 5th grade; formal	Van Hooks–all of 4th grade; formal	Van Hooks–4th and 5th grade

For Antonio, the weekly leadership team meeting is the glue that keeps everything in place: observations, coaching, data, and culture.

Core Idea

Weekly leadership team meetings can be the glue that keeps everything in place.

Avoid Common Errors of Leadership Team Meetings

Of course, not every leadership team meeting is as successful as Antonio's, Hannah's, or Mike's. The following actions do *not* meet the goal of enhancing the quality of instruction. Ask yourself if any of these errors are present in your own leadership team meetings:

- **More announcements than instruction.** Peruse the agenda for your leadership team meeting. How many items on the list are directly connected to student learning and teacher development? More important, how much time do those announcements and logistics take up of the actual meeting? Honing instructional leadership takes time, and it requires prioritizing.

- **More reading about leadership than doing.** Another trend in leadership team meetings is holding a book club or reading articles about leadership. If all you do is read this book, I can pretty much guarantee it will have little impact. What changes practice is actually practicing: putting ideas into action. This is beyond leaders sharing their big takeaways from reading: it means role playing or acting on the spot.

- **More opinion than evidence.** Now look more closely at the agenda items that are centered around teachers. How often are leaders sharing opinions about teachers' development without evidence? There is a real danger to a principal simply listening to an instructional leader talk about a teacher's development. First, you are assuming that the leader has been observing regularly (if not, he or she could hold an opinion based on one observation of the teacher from over a month ago). Second, you assume that the leader is correct in assessing what the teacher is struggling with (but we know how hard it is to select the right action step, as seen in Chapter 3!). Third, you are assuming that the leader's feedback to the teacher is fine and that the issue is simply the teacher's lack of following the leader's advice. You cannot have a real conversation without an observation tracker that lists the frequency of observations and nature of action steps, and without having evidence of the nature of their feedback meetings. None of those are addressed by simply listening to leaders share unbacked opinions.

- **Walkthroughs or observations without feedback.** Consistent walkthroughs or observations are a step better than simply sharing opinions about teachers: at least you can observe together and discuss what would be the best action step to focus on for the teacher's immediate development. But if we use these as our only tools for developing leadership, we are still missing two of the four key components of observation and feedback: giving effective feedback and holding teachers accountable to that feedback. Walkthroughs can have their place in leadership team development, but that should be a much smaller place than it currently holds for many teams.

Core Idea

If you want to develop high-quality instructional leadership, talking about teachers is not enough. You need to take action to support them.

Stop and Jot

What are the most common errors you make in your own leadership team meetings that you want to eliminate to become more effective?

_____

_____

_____

_____

_____

_____

_____

Redefine the Agenda

What makes a leadership team the glue for a school is the content—and the protocol. "The agenda drives the day," Antonio underscores. "If the agenda is focused on great instructional leadership, great instructional leadership will be the outcome." What's critical during your leadership meeting isn't just *what* you spend time focusing on but *how* you cover it. You've already learned the protocol in all the other chapters:

- **See the exemplar.** Start by establishing the exemplar: What do you want to see?
- **See the gap.** Look at the patterns across teachers and student work: Where are the biggest gaps to close?
- **Name It.** Select the actions to close the gaps.
- **Do It.** Plan the schedule and plan and practice the actions that will close those gaps.

Core Idea

What makes your meeting powerful isn't just *what* you cover but *how* you cover it. See It. Name It. Do It.

Depending on your lever or area of need, this protocol can take different forms. Here are examples of how to implement the protocol with each leadership lever.

See It and Do It for Every Lever

Agenda Frameworks for Leadership Team Meetings

Lever	See It	Do It
Data-Driven Instruction	• Look at student work from weekly data meetings. • Analyze data from the last round of interim assessments. • Observe the data analysis meeting (in person or by watching video of it).	• Plan and practice the analysis meeting the leader will have with each grade-level team. • Set the schedule to observe reteach lessons and upcoming weekly data meetings.
Planning	• Stack audit: review a stack of teacher lesson plans from that day: What are the patterns of strengths and areas of growth? • Observe with lesson plans in hand: What are the patterns in execution of the lesson plans? • Review a leader's feedback to a teacher's curriculum or lesson plan. Is it the right feedback? Do teachers seem to be implementing the feedback?	• Plan and practice leading a planning meeting.
Observation and Feedback	• Review the observation tracker. What are the patterns across the staff? Which teachers need extra support? Where are leader observations falling short? • Observe teachers: Do the action steps in the tracker match the teaching?	• Plan and practice leading a feedback meeting. • Plan and practice real-time feedback. • Identify the best action steps for teachers across the school.

Lever	See It	Do It
	• Observe the feedback (in meetings or in real time): How well is the leader implementing feedback?	
PD	• Identify the gaps via any of the other levers. • Observe a leader's PD session (in person or by watching video of it): Where can she improve in her planning and delivery?	• Plan and practice delivering PD that closes a gap.
Student Culture	• Observe student culture in action (in classrooms or whole-class moments): What are the patterns or gaps in teacher actions?	• Plan and practice a whole-school rollout or reset. • Plan and practice a rehearsal/practice clinic with teachers.

Here is an example of what a leadership team meeting agenda could look like. This is adapted from St. Louis Public Schools' network superintendent Jeanine Zitta. (You can read more about her leadership in *The Principal Manager's Guide to Leverage Leadership*.)

Weekly Instructional Leadership Team Meeting

Sample Agenda—60 minutes

Agenda

- **Review of Action Steps from Prior Week (3–4 minutes)**
- **Celebrations (2–3 minutes)**
  - Each leader will share out one thing he or she is most proud of from the week.
    - Exemplary action: link the celebration to the school's mission, vision, and values

- **Action Step Audit and Coaching Cycle Review (~30 minutes)**
  - Pull up Get Better Faster tracker: review quality of action steps and teacher implementation.
    - Exemplary action: instructional leader will review this data in advance of the meeting to focus the conversation on the gaps in action steps, quality of teaching and learning, frequency and timing of walkthroughs, etc.
  - Each team member will name the patterns he or she sees and the highest-leverage gaps to close.
  - Name the key lever to use: feedback meetings, real-time feedback, practice clinic, faculty PD, and/or intervention plan.
- **Plan and Practice (~20 minutes)**
  - Plan the action that each leader will take (from previous list).
  - Practice: either hot seat (one person practices and all others give feedback) or in pairs.
- **Follow-up (~5 minutes)**
  - Determine a focus "look-for," as applicable.
  - Team members will adjust individual schedules to focus on these action steps.
  - Determine owners, deliverables, and deadlines for all group tasks (PD planning, practice clinic leadership, etc.).

Take a look back on each leader we've highlighted in this book. Nearly all of them utilized their leadership team to accelerate the implementation of the levers of leadership. For example, Laura Garza has used the leadership team meeting system to raise the bar on data-driven instruction so that each week, she and her team work together to determine what teachers will reteach. Each week at their team meeting, Laura makes plans to come by each classroom when the reteach is occurring. "I always ask: 'When are you going to work on it, and when can I come see it?'" Laura says.

CONCLUSION

When Antonio and his leadership team meet together, their ultimate destination is never far from Antonio's mind. "Our goal is to change outcomes for children," he says. "Everything we do is designed to build the habits to get us closer to that goal. It's all about structures, expectations, and consistency." Keeping his leadership team's time focused on that goal paid off—and continues to do so. You can see it in the results, both in achievement and with the children. Kailah Valencia, a fifth grader at the time of the writing of this book, shares, "Dr. Burt always wanted everyone to do their best. He always came into the classroom to make sure everyone was on task. He also challenged us to do more than we thought possible."

A school like Ford Road cannot fly if the whole leadership team is not in formation. Get everyone in the right place at the right time, and together you can scale incredible distances in even the most challenging conditions. It's a lot easier to fly with a team than on your own.

Keys to Leadership Team Development

- **Choose your team.** Identify instructional leaders.
- **Train your team—roll out the vision.** Build your team's schedule, train them in Leverage Leadership, and equip them with the right tools.
- **Monitor the school.** Start from the exemplar, see the gap, and take action.
- **Lead effective leadership team meetings.** Find the patterns and take the actions to address them.

Sample Instructional Leadership Rubric—Advanced Column

Category	Advanced Score
Data-Driven Instruction	• Leader always effectively uses data outside the IA cycle (WDM) to adapt grade-level/content area and class-level instruction. • Leader holds all teachers accountable to all parts of the postassessment action plans. • Teacher(s) "strongly agree" on mid-year survey that leader "helps me to use data to drive instruction."
Lesson Plans	• Leader always ensures that all teachers have posted up-to-date lesson plans and utilize exemplars/monitoring tools. • All of the instructional leader's teachers show evidence of effective implementation of internalization protocols;

Category	Advanced Score
	leader always meets with teachers who are not proficient with internalization. • Leader always observes with lesson plan and current action plan in hand.
Observation and Feedback	• All of the IL's teachers effectively implement weekly action steps. • Teachers meet at least two of three personal PD goals. • All of the IL's teachers agree (score of 4 or 5) on mid-year survey question "provides helpful instructional feedback." • Leader always adapts frequency of observations/meetings based on teacher needs.
Professional Development (When Applicable)	• Objective/outcome of the workshop is directly tied to the practice and the needs of the school. • Agenda includes See It activities that are tightly planned and 100% relevant to the core objective. • High-quality prompts are scripted. • Highly effective balance of time for See It, Name It, Do It. • Reflection time is well used to capture big takeaways and help participants write their action steps.

Action Steps for Principals

Managing School Leadership Teams

LEVER	KEY ACTIONS IN SEQUENCE
MANAGING LEADERHSIP TEAMS	1. **Apply all actions steps for principals to other instructional leaders (ILs) in the school.** 2. **Evaluate IL performance using observations of their coaching and student data.** 3. **Build and leverage your leadership team:** • Hold a weekly leadership team meeting with a good ratio of speaking to listening. • Develop norms and hold team accountable for strong teamwork. • Develop agendas to enable principals to share data, share initiatives, and get feedback. • Motivate and inspire your team to lead the rest of the school.

Pulling the Lever

Action Planning Worksheet for MANAGING LEADERSHIP TEAMS

Self-Assessment

- Evaluate each of the members of your leadership team on the Instructional Leadership Rubric: What is the average percent proficient for your team?_____%

- What are the biggest gaps for your leadership team based on the rubric? Of those gaps, which are the highest leverage to address first? (Remember: start with the super-levers of data-driven instruction and student culture, then move to observation and feedback, then all the rest.)

_____

_____

_____

_____

Planning for Action

- What tools from this book will you use to improve leadership teams at your school? Check all that you will use (you can find all on the DVD):

  ☐ Observation Tracker

  ☐ Instructional Leadership Rubric

  ☐ Leverage Leadership Quick Reference Guide

  ☐ Videos of leadership (all videos could apply)

- What are your next steps for developing your leadership team?

Action	Date

Part 3

Making It Happen

Chapter 8

Finding the Time

One-on-One: Getting Ready for the School Day

It's 6:15 a.m., and Eric Diamon sits at his desk in what will likely be his final quiet moment of the school day. On his bookshelf are framed pictures of past students, along with one of Serena Savarirayan leading morning circle. She opened Eric's school as founding principal and now coaches him in her new role of assistant superintendent. Just off to the side, Eric's roots as an English teacher are visible in the selection of books he keeps nearby, which include *Esperanza Rising, The Watsons Go to Birmingham – 1963,* and *The Autobiography of Malcolm X.*

He quickly peruses his email and text messages to see if any teachers are delayed or sick. One teacher has emailed him to say that she is ill, so he scans his coverage chart to see who can cover for each class period. Then he scans his upcoming meetings for the day and selects the one that will be most challenging. He pulls out his notes he has prepared from the day before and rehearses them in his head. Satisfied, he closes his laptop, grabs his binder and rainbow guide (his spiral-bound copy of all the *Leverage Leadership* one-pagers and the Get Better Faster sequence) and heads out of his office to the gym for breakfast and student arrival.

The rest of the day will be filled with activity: observations, feedback and data meetings, whole-school walkthroughs, and monitoring lunch and dismissal. Most striking, though, is what it *doesn't* contain: Eric will be spending no time on building management, technology, or state reports. His eyes are on the learning, and the instruction that drives it.

Figure 8.1 New Jersey PARRC Assessment: Vailsburg Middle School, Percentage at or Above Proficiency Fifth to Eighth Grades

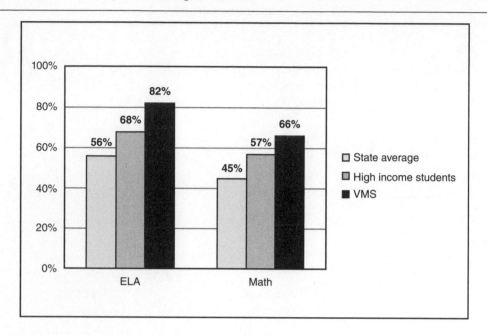

Eric Diamon, principal of Vailsburg Middle School in Newark, New Jersey, is no stranger to the pressures of time management for a principal. "You are constantly bombarded by people and tasks that you can only survive if you can take control of your time." His results show it—he uses his time on the leadership levers, and results follow (see Figure 8.1).

In 1996, Kim Marshall wrote a powerfully accurate critique of the lives of most principals, in which he diagnosed the overwhelming majority of school leaders—including, formerly, himself—with "Hyperactive Superficial Principal Syndrome."[1] Unfortunately, not much has changed since Marshall coined the term. The job of a principal is arguably one of the most interrupted jobs anywhere. You are continually bombarded by students, parents, staff, and the mini crises that occur each day. Because of this, a principal can invest a tremendous number of hours—and heart and soul—into the work of the school without even stepping foot into a classroom. Are the intensity and nature of the job too difficult to overcome?

Eric Diamon offers an emphatic *No!* to that question, and so does every other leader you've met in this book, from Memphis to Dallas to Denver to Newark. And they have the systems to back it up. So many principals believe they don't have control over their time, but in reality, your own time is the one thing you, and any principal, *can* control. School leadership is not easy; it is very, very hard. But the leaders in this book show us one thing: they were relentless about how they used their time—and that made all the difference.

Core Idea

So many principals believe that they don't have control over their time. In reality, your own time is the one thing you *can* control.

Controlling your own time doesn't mean that you can stop your district from adding meetings you must attend or that you can avoid the fight that will occasionally break out in the cafeteria (even though your good work on student culture will certainly limit the frequency of these occurrences!). Principals who control their time don't pretend these things won't happen; rather, they build a schedule that *anticipates* them, and find a way to stay in control anyway.

Although many have written about school leadership, few have offered a concrete path for how to put all the pieces together on a daily, weekly, and monthly basis. This is a serious mistake. Even the best solutions are meaningless if you cannot feasibly put them into place.

So how does this apply to you? Your school, like any other, is unique: you have your own strengths and challenges, be it the size of your staff, the number of additional instructional leaders, or the particular needs of your students. This chapter will help you adapt the lessons learned to meet the context of your own school. If you make a serious commitment to using the tools and strategies in this chapter, you will be able to lock in instructional and cultural leadership—and lock out almost everything else. Results will follow.

Core Idea

By intentionally planning the use of your time, you can lock in instructional and cultural leadership—and lock out almost everything else.

In the pages that follow, you'll see that excellent time management isn't about being so rigid that you can't meet the ever-shifting needs of your teachers, your students, their families, or any of the other dynamic elements of your school's community. On the contrary, it's about putting systems in place that enable you to meet the most urgent of those needs first. "I'm not telling you this so you'll be shackled to your schedule," my colleague Michael Ambriz likes to remind participants during his workshop on time and task management. "I'm telling you this to make you more flexible."

To make this kind of time management feasible, this chapter offers three key tools for putting the vision we've outlined into practice:

- Build your weekly schedule.
- Defend your time from distractions.
- Manage your daily and monthly tasks.

BUILD YOUR WEEKLY SCHEDULE

Whether the leaders highlighted in this book were rolling out routines, giving feedback to a new teacher, monitoring a reteach lesson, or coaching their instructional leaders, one key action made the difference in whether those plans happened or not: scheduling a time to implement them. Without a schedule that makes time for the most important actions you can take to fuel your school's growth, you're not building skyscrapers—you're fighting fires. Exceptional leaders don't let that happen.

Core Idea

Without a schedule that makes time for the most important actions that fuel your school's growth, you're not building skyscrapers—you're fighting fires.

It's your turn to build a schedule that can transform your school. Not every leader will allocate his or her time in the exact same way, but as long as your schedule adheres to the core tenets listed here, it will work.

How can you find time? Let's look at Eric Diamon and watch how he builds his schedule step-by-step. Here is the order for building the schedule:

1. Prework—distribute your teachers across your leadership team.
2. Block out student culture times (Chapter 5).
3. Lock in professional development and other group meetings (Chapters 4 and 6).
4. Lock in time for standing weekly individual or team teacher/leader meetings (Chapters 1–3).
5. Lock in time for classroom observations (Chapter 2).
6. Lock in staff culture.
7. Lock in work time.

What does this process look like? Let's walk through it piece by piece.

(You can print out the provided weekly scheduling template and fill it in as you read!)

Weekly Schedule Template

Time	Monday	Tuesday	Wednesday	Thursday	Friday
6:00 AM					
:30					
7:00 AM					
:30					
8:00 AM					
:30					
9:00 AM					
:30					
10:00 AM					
:30					
11:00 AM					
:30					
12:00 PM					
:30					
1:00 PM					
:30					
2:00 PM					
:30					
3:00 PM					
:30					
4:00 PM					
:30					
5:00 PM					
:30					

Step 1: Prework—Distribute Your Teachers Across the Leadership Team

The number one variable that will influence your schedule is how many teachers you will manage directly and the number of other instructional leaders whom you will supervise in the management of the rest of the teachers. Here are the two core questions to get this started:

- How many teachers are in your school?_____ teachers

- How many in your school are or could be instructional leaders? _____ leaders
    - Formal instructional leaders: assistant principals, coaches, department chairs, and so on
    - Others who could be leveraged this way: SPED coordinators, lead teachers, and so on
- Ratio of teachers to leader (divide the number of teachers by the total number of leaders—full-time equivalent)_____:1

If you are like most schools, you will have a ratio of 12:1 or less. That is the golden ratio: you can make the principles in this book work as is.

A Word on . . . When You Don't Have 12:1

Some of you might be in that small minority of schools that have larger than a 12:1 leader-to-teacher ratio. What then?

First, make sure there isn't anyone else who can assist you in instructional leadership. This could include some of your strongest teachers whom you can give one or two teachers in exchange for a stipend or reduced responsibilities (see Chapter 7, Managing School Leadership Teams, for a sample schedule for a teacher with instructional leadership responsibilities).

If you do that and you still have a larger ratio, then convert your whole schedule to biweekly. Rather than observe and meet with each teacher each week, you can double the ratio to 25:1 and observe and meet with twelve teachers one week and the remaining thirteen teachers the next week. This still allows for a dramatic increase in teacher development and regular contact with each teacher.

Your next step is to distribute the teachers across your leadership team: Which teachers will you manage directly, and which will you delegate to others? In most cases, you should distribute teachers according to each instructional leader's strengths: content expertise, the ability to work with novice teachers or teachers with management problems, and so on. If you are leading a very large school and you have a large number of instructional leaders to lead yourself, you might decide to distribute all your teachers among them and focus on managing the leaders only.

Once you have made this choice, every other decision flows naturally. We're off!

Step 2: Block Out Student Culture Times

Because student culture is one of the super-levers, management of student culture is the most important thing to put on your schedule first. As mentioned in Chapter 5, there are a few critical moments when you have the biggest impact on student culture, and when crises and challenges are most likely to happen. These times are slightly different for every school, but almost everyone would identify breakfast/arrival, lunch, and dismissal as key moments. Because these events occur at set times, they are the least flexible of the scheduling constraints and so should go first. Let's look at Eric's schedule as a guide.

Note that here Eric has left Monday afternoon and Tuesday morning free, as well as Thursday lunch. This means that he will designate another leader to cover those moments. Remember that for a school that needs a student culture turnaround, your calendar will need to be filled with a lot more time to manage the challenge of making significant improvements to a struggling culture.

Step 3: Lock In Group Meetings

The next step to planning your schedule is to lock in group meetings, such as PD, staff meetings, and leadership team meetings. Be careful about scheduling too many meetings. Planning to attend all grade-level meetings every week—on top of your feedback meetings—won't work. Here's what Eric's schedule looks like.

Note that he has kept his group meetings to a minimum: a monthly principal PD, a leadership team meeting, and his weekly staff PD session.

Step 4: Lock In Teacher-Leader Meetings

Now it is time to add the highest-leverage drivers of your work: your standing weekly meeting with teachers to give observational feedback, review lesson plans, and do data analysis. The reason Eric holds these meetings so dear is that they are opportunities to dedicate focused time to whatever his teachers most need. The observation feedback you

Eric Diamon's Schedule: Just Culture

Time	Monday	Tuesday	Wednesday	Thursday	Friday
6:00 AM					
:30					
7:00 AM	Breakfast and Morning Circle		Breakfast and Morning Circle	Breakfast and Morning Circle	Greeting and Breakfast
:30					
8:00 AM					
:30					
9:00 AM					
:30					
10:00 AM					
:30					
11:00 AM					
:30	Lunch	Lunch	Lunch		
12:00 PM					
:30					Early Dismissal
1:00 PM					
:30					
2:00 PM					
:30					
3:00 PM					
:30		Dismissal	Dismissal	Dismissal	
4:00 PM					
:30					
5:00 PM					
:30					

Eric Diamon's Schedule: Student Culture and Group Meetings

Time	Monday	Tuesday	Wednesday	Thursday	Friday
6 AM					
:30					
7 AM	Breakfast and Morning Circle		Breakfast and Morning Circle	Breakfast and Morning Circle	Greeting and Breakfast
:30					
8 AM					
:30					
9 AM			Leadership Team Meeting		
:30					
10 AM					
:30					
11 AM					
:30	Lunch	Lunch	Lunch		
12 PM					
:30					Early Dismissal
1 PM		Principal PD (1/mo) or All-School Walkthrough			
:30					Faculty PD Session
2 PM					
:30					
3 PM					
:30		Dismissal	Dismissal	Dismissal	
4 PM					
:30					
5 PM					
:30					

Eric Diamon's Schedule: Student Culture and All Meetings

Time	Monday	Tuesday	Wednesday	Thursday	Friday
6 AM					
:30					
7 AM	Breakfast and Morning Circle		Breakfast and Morning Circle	Breakfast and Morning Circle	Greeting and Breakfast
:30					
8 AM					
:30					
9 AM	Meet Marcellus		Leadership Team Meeting	Meet Tomas	
:30					
10 AM		Meet Kathryn			
:30		Meet Julia		Meet Becky	
11 AM				Meet Angela	
:30	Lunch	Lunch	Lunch		
12 PM					
:30	Meet Amanda				Early Dismissal
1 PM	Meeting with Principal Manager	Principal PD (1/mo) or All-School Walkthrough			
:30			Meet Jessica		Faculty PD Session
2 PM			Meet Mary		
:30					
3 PM					
:30	Meet Leonard	Dismissal	Dismissal	Dismissal	
4 PM					
:30					
5 PM					
:30					

deliver to your teachers could guide them in lesson planning, reteaching what the data tells you must be retaught, following up about techniques taught in PD, or perfecting student culture. In short, you can leverage one-on-one time with teachers to coach them on any lever you need to.

Here you should take out your school schedule and look for the prep periods of each of the teachers you will manage. Pick a standing thirty-minute window when they are not teaching. Eric has ten teachers to manage, so he locks in ten thirty-minute check-ins.

Some leaders prefer scheduling their meetings with teachers back-to-back whenever possible, because that gives them larger open chunks of time to spend on other tasks. However, you may also schedule breaks between each check-in, if that suits your schedule better. Remember the power of scheduling these meetings: you lock the time into the teacher's weekly plan as well, and then there is no need to chase down the teacher to find time to give him or her feedback! You also hold yourself accountable for observing each teacher, because you need to have observed before the feedback meeting in order to be able to discuss highest-leverage action steps when you get there.

Step 5: Lock In Observations

Now it is time to lock in your observations. Remember our core principle: weekly fifteen-minute observations are far more valuable than twice-yearly full-length observations, and they are also more substantive than five-minute walkthroughs. Assuming you plan your observations back-to-back, we wouldn't recommend planning more than three observations in each one-hour time period: this way you budget for time to get from one classroom to the next and complete your observation tracker on the spot.

Remember to schedule these observations strategically before your weekly meeting with each teacher so that you have relevant observation data in hand going into the meeting. If you need more time to prepare for your feedback meeting, then you might leave a larger gap between the observation and meeting.

Step 6: Add Time for Staff Culture

You have almost finished your schedule—just a few more things remain to be added. The next will be a periodic check on staff culture. This is time to simply walk the building and check in informally with staff: see how they're doing, sense the vibe in the faculty room, and be present for the staff. Nothing instructional occurs during this time—just building a stronger connection with your staff.

Eric Diamon's Schedule: Student Culture, All Meetings, and Observations

Time	Monday	Tuesday	Wednesday	Thursday	Friday
6 AM					
:30					
7 AM	Breakfast and Morning Circle		Breakfast and Morning Circle	Breakfast and Morning Circle	Greeting and Breakfast
:30					
8 AM	Observe Marcellus, Amanda, Leonard				
:30				Observe Angela	
9 AM	Meet Marcellus		Leadership Team Meeting	Meet Tomas	
:30					
10 AM	Observe Kathryn, Julia, Jessica	Meet Kathryn			
:30		Meet Julia	Observe Mary, Tomas, Becky	Meet Becky	
11 AM				Meet Angela	
:30	Lunch	Lunch	Lunch		
12 PM					
:30	Meet Amanda				Early Dismissal
1 PM	Meeting with Principal Manager	Principal PD (1/mo) or All-School Walkthrough			
:30			Meet Jessica		Faculty PD Session
2 PM			Meet Mary		
:30					
3 PM					
:30	Meet Leonard	Dismissal	Dismissal	Dismissal	
4 PM					
:30					
5 PM					
:30					

Eric Diamon's Schedule: Student Culture, All Meetings, Observations, and Staff Culture Checks

Time	Monday	Tuesday	Wednesday	Thursday	Friday
6 AM					
:30					
7 AM	Breakfast and Morning Circle	Staff Culture Check	Breakfast and Morning Circle	Breakfast and Morning Circle	Greeting and Breakfast
:30					
8 AM	Observe Marcellus, Amanda, Leonard				
:30				Observe Angela	
9 AM	Meet Marcellus		Leadership Team Meeting	Meet Tomas	
:30					
10 AM	Observe Kathryn, Julia, Jessica	Meet Kathryn			
:30		Meet Julia	Observe Mary, Tomas, Becky	Meet Becky	
11 AM				Meet Angela	
:30	Lunch	Lunch	Lunch		
12 PM	Staff Culture Check		Staff Culture Check		
:30	Meet Amanda				Early Dismissal
1 PM	Meeting with Principal Manager	Principal PD (1/mo) or All-School Walkthrough			
:30			Meet Jessica		Faculty PD Session
2 PM			Meet Mary		
:30					
3 PM				Staff Culture Check	
:30	Meet Leonard	Dismissal	Dismissal	Dismissal	
4 PM					
:30					
5 PM					
:30					

Over time, checking in on staff culture will become automatic and won't need to be scheduled. But if this is something that doesn't come naturally to you, putting it on your schedule is a great way to start making it a habitual part of your day as a leader.

Step 7: Add Work Time for Big Projects

Your final task is to pick a block of time when you'll work on larger, nondaily projects. In reality, for most principals, this time will occur outside of the school day. Eric gets some help on Friday to free up an additional block. When we polled the exceptional leaders in this book, they were very realistic about the fact that they normally have only about three to five hours of weekly time for big-picture work—the day-to-day work of their jobs consumes everything else! We'll see how you keep that big-project work focused on the right things in the next section of the chapter. For the time being, lock in the planning time, as this final iteration of a sample weekly schedule shows.

Take a Moment and Reflect on What You've Accomplished

Take a moment to consider what this schedule accomplishes. First, half of your schedule is still open, allowing for daily issues and unforeseen challenges to arise. Thus if a student issue occurs during your observation window on Monday, you can reschedule your observations to Tuesday. This is what makes the schedule feasible. If when you build your schedule you don't leave at least 30 percent unscheduled, the weekly schedule won't work. You'll need to cut down on some of your group meetings. (That's the one variable that will make your schedule untenable if you've limited yourself to managing twelve teachers directly on a weekly basis.)

Look at what you've accomplished:

- **Every teacher in the building is observed every week.** For schools that used to observe once a year, this is a twentyfold increase!

- **Every teacher is getting feedback every week.** You've moved from one or two pieces of feedback in a year to forty—more feedback in one year than most teachers get in twenty.

- **Staff are regularly receiving high-quality professional development.** If they're done right, faculty meetings are now PD and not announcements.

- **Interim assessments are substantively and deeply analyzed.** Once every eight weeks, observation feedback gets replaced by data analysis. With locked-in teacher meetings, you don't need to reschedule anything to make this happen.

- **Culture is monitored constantly.** You or another leader is present to drive student culture at each key moment of the day.

Eric Diamon's Schedule: Everything

Time	Monday	Tuesday	Wednesday	Thursday	Friday
6 AM					
:30					
7 AM	Breakfast and Morning Circle	Staff Culture Check	Breakfast and Morning Circle	Breakfast and Morning Circle	Greeting and Breakfast
:30					
8 AM	Observe Marcellus, Amanda, Leonard				Big-Project Work Time
:30				Observe Angela	
9 AM	Meet Marcellus		Leadership Team Meeting	Meet Tomas	
:30					
10 AM	Observe Kathryn, Julia, Jessica	Meet Kathryn			
:30		Meet Julia	Observe Mary, Tomas, Becky	Meet Becky	
11 AM				Meet Angela	
:30	Lunch	Lunch	Lunch		
12 PM	Staff Culture Check		Staff Culture Check		
:30	Meet Amanda				Early Dismissal
1 PM	Meeting with Principal Manager	Principal PD (1/mo) or All-School Walkthrough			
:30			Meet Jessica		Faculty PD Session
2 PM			Meet Mary		
:30					
3 PM				Staff Culture Check	
:30	Meet Leonard	Dismissal	Dismissal	Dismissal	
4 PM					
:30					
5 PM					
:30					

Most important, you have made the same critical step as each top-tier leader in this book: you have taken control over your time. The seven previous chapters have outlined the investments that make a school extraordinary. With this schedule, we've given you the tools to make that school yours.

Core Idea

In the previous seven chapters, we have offered the investments that make a school extraordinary. With this schedule, we've given you the tools to make that school yours.

Make Your Own!

Use your blank template provided earlier in this section to do the same exercise you have seen presented here. Alternatively, the DVD has a simple Excel document that you can use to build your schedule. Other leaders make their schedule directly in Outlook. Whatever your choice, take the time and rebuild your schedule right now.

Exceptional school leaders thrive not by working more hours than other school leaders but by making their hours count. So what is next? Defending your schedule so you can actually follow it.

DEFEND YOUR TIME

If time is a leader's most precious resource, then it is not enough to know how it should be spent; leaders also need to know how to protect it. In this section, we give you the tools to show how you might pursue this. First, though, let's look to the pitfalls: How might a principal lose control of his or her calendar? Read over the following case study of a well-intentioned principal.

Defending Time Case Study

The Well-Intentioned Firefighter

Mr. Reynolds wants to transform his school: to conduct weekly observations, analyze data, and forge a strong student culture. Today he hopes to conduct a school-wide culture walkthrough, observe three teachers, and finish analyzing the first math interim assessment. His day starts out well enough. After getting to school early and working in his office until 7:30 a.m., he walks downstairs to the cafeteria to monitor breakfast and deliver morning announcements.

When he returns to his office, he sees twenty-five emails in his inbox and immediately starts to respond. As he works, a secretary shares the four phone calls he's received: two vendor requests, a call from a prospective visitor, and a parent asking directions for the school field trip. After calling each party back, Reynolds returns to his inbox, continuing to write. After two hours, he still has not watched a single teacher, analyzed a single data point, or observed classroom culture.

By the day's end, things are only marginally better. Reynolds' inbox is empty, he was able to monitor lunch and dismissal, and all phone requests have been dealt with. Yet Reynolds never stepped into the classrooms to observe or support his teachers.

If a school leader's main role is to drive student learning, then Reynolds did not do his job today. Despite his best intentions, he was only fighting fires.

Core Idea

A well-intentioned firefighter is still not an instructional leader.

Mr. Reynolds means well: he knows what a school-wide transformation requires, and he's willing to work hard to achieve it. Yet without a serious change in the way he spends his time, he will not be able to bring his vision to fruition. Without careful planning and scheduling, the tide of distraction will wash away any of the systems in this book. Fortunately, the leaders profiled here built systems to overcome these challenges and to give themselves the time they needed to transform their schools.

This book argues that a school leader's main role is in two areas: instruction and culture. Every minute that a leader is outside of these is a minute when the core levers of school success are not being advanced. Of course, this is easier to say than to put into practice. In the moment, firefighting can seem incredibly compelling and urgent. Yet even if you are able to help put out these fires, your attention is likely needed elsewhere. Minimizing the time that leaders spend on "everything else" is a vital priority.

Defeating Distractions—Build Your Offensive Line Against "Everything Else"

Schools, as principals know all too well, are about far more than learning. Communications, technology, compliance, food service, transportation, safety inspections—the list goes on and on. There are a number of strategies you can pursue to deal with operational work areas like these, regardless of the type of school you are in or the constraints you face. Here are some of the strategies most used by successful instructional leaders that have allowed them to focus on culture and instruction.

Designate an Operations Leader—or a Team

An ideal solution to operations is the designation of one leader position solely to address these tasks. Whether the person is an assistant principal, a dean, or even a secretary, this leader is in charge of managing each of the operation systems. Beyond saving time, there is a more subtle advantage to creating an operations leader: specialization. The skills of operations are far different than those of instructional leadership. Splitting the roles allows a principal to specialize in what matters most—culture and instruction—and someone else can get good at the rest.

If a separate operations leader cannot be assigned, an alternative solution is an operations team made up of teachers, office managers, assistant principals, or others. Each member of the operations team would be assigned a set area of operations; for example, a veteran teacher might be responsible for all field trip logistics, and a head custodian might be responsible for building logistics. To facilitate this process, school leaders must meet with the operations team at the start of the year to record every major operations event (for example, closing down the school for winter break) and then assigning an "owner" to it.

Shutting the School Down for the Holidays

Sample Operations Plan

Task	Who Owns It	Complete By
Turn off boiler	Maria Valdez	12/15
Monitor dismissal	Cassandra Jensen	12/15
Call lunch delivery to cancel	Jeff Liu	12/16
"Deep clean" all desks and hallways	Mike Warner	12/17
Create flyer to send home with students	Carl McManus	12/17

Designate Whom to Go to for What

Whatever system is chosen for operations, it will only save time if it is clear and readily understood. At the start of the year, several of the schools studied distributed a document to each staff member on "whom to go to for what." This document contains clear contact information and instructions for whom to contact. For example, if Jon, a science teacher, is in charge of after-school programs, then the chart would list him as the contact. If the guidelines are unclear, people will email you. We've included a brief example here.

Whom to Go to for What

Sample Guidance for Staff on Operations Support

Questions and Requests	Examples and Notes	Contact
Attendance (students)	Each morning, teachers should enter student absences into the computer database.	• Office manager
Transportation/Dismissal	Notify office manager and copy director of operations of any messages received regarding student transportation or dismissal changes.	• Office manager and director of operations
Certification	Letters, questions, requirements, etc.	• Director of operations
Extracurricular Programs	After-school, sports, summer internships, etc.	• Community engagement coordinator
Facilities and Maintenance	Maintenance requests, cleaning requests, etc.	• Custodian for immediate and low-cost maintenance requests • Director of operations for larger requests

Pick Your First Responder

A first responder is a person with specialized training who is among the first to arrive and provide assistance at the scene of an emergency, such as an accident or natural disaster. In the case of a real emergency, you the principal will always be the first responder. Yet in the daily life of a school, small emergencies or distractions happen all the time. You need a first responder for these situations.

The National SAM™ Innovation Project works with over nine hundred schools in twenty-two states to increase the time school staff spend on instruction. (Researchers have shown that SAM principals, on average, increase their instructional time from 30 percent to 65 percent of the day within one year.[2]) One key factor in their success has been to develop First Responders™: staff members who should be the first to try to deal with minor emergencies and management or operations issues instead of immediately pulling the principal from instructional work.[3] This person is often the secretary or someone in the front office. Deploying a first responder along with implementing the steps outlined in *Leverage Leadership* can make a real impact!

School leaders are continually bombarded with nonroutine events, whether teacher questions, technology issues, or visitor requests. On its own, each of these events is innocuous; three minutes here, two minutes there. Unfortunately, they add up. Imagine if each day, a combination of thirty staff members and parents approach the principal with one question each. If it takes only two minutes to answer every question, this is an hour a day. In "investment" terms, the cost is enormous: three observations, two data conferences, or a lunch and a morning assembly spent supervising. Throw in five hundred students, hundreds of parents and guardians, support staff, and visitors—leaders may soon be entirely overwhelmed, sprinting from one fire to another, but never moving forward.

Your first responder can help you do the following:

- **Maintain locked-in time to check in with teachers.** The quickest way to reduce the number of questions teachers have is to make sure teachers know there's a time when they'll be able to ask those questions. The beauty of the weekly check-in is you've scheduled a moment to answer questions that doesn't fit elsewhere in the schedule. You can do the same for parents by just locking in certain times when parents can come to you with questions. Weekly check-ins are sacred for teachers. If they know they'll have time to ask you any questions they have, then they'll hold their questions until that time. This applies to email, too. Use weekly check-ins to reduce "pop-in" distractions: set an expectation that teachers should hold nonemergency questions (for example, field trip ideas, project proposals) until their scheduled weekly check-ins. Doing so will enable you to address questions much more efficiently.

- **Block and tackle.** Almost anyone with a question about a school—parent, teacher, or guest—will want to talk to the principal. At the schools we've seen in this book, leaders trained their first responder (office staff) to "block and tackle," working to ensure that nonessential requests did not eat into the leader's time. There will, of course, be some meetings with school leaders that can't wait, but 95 percent of the meetings principals need to have do not need to happen in the moment, so you've reduced the 5 percent here.

- **Pull yourself away from pet projects.** Often, school leaders will be drawn to particular aspects of school management that are unrelated to the core priorities of instruction. For example, a principal may be personally interested in student fundraisers and may spend a great deal of time micromanaging. A first responder can help avoid this trap by taking this project away to protect your time for what matters most.

- **Plan blocks of time for communication.** Answering emails or calls as they come in is terribly disruptive; it breaks the flow of a sustained task and can naturally pull leaders away from their core tasks. Setting aside a solid block of time to address all emails is a much better approach, and having a first responder on hand will help you stick to that system. Even if email takes up an hour a day, it's vital that your schedule determines when you deal with your email and that your emails don't determine your schedule.

- **Say it once.** Giving announcements to individual teachers multiple times quickly adds up. Leverage your time more effectively by saying it once in a staff meeting or weekly memo.[4] When your staff have questions you've already answered, your first responder can field them.

THE FINAL STEP: MANAGING TASKS

You're in the home stretch. You've scheduled your weekly routines and protected your time. The last piece is to manage your tasks: your daily tasks and your monthly tasks. To keep track of these tasks, leaders need to "map" their actions and to build a plan beyond the daily and weekly level.

Build Your Monthly Map

Many of the leaders in this book use a tool called the monthly map. The monthly map is in effect a list of the most important things that you should be doing, with each task separated by month. Maia Heyck-Merlin, author of *The Together Teacher* and *The Together Leader*, call this the Priority Plan. She notes that setting up a three-month Priority Plan is essential to mapping out a long-term view of your most important work—and a Later List will help you track the detailed long-term tasks.[5] You don't want your data-driven analysis meetings to sneak up on you, nor do you want to forget to schedule the dates of your interim assessments. (An important note: data-driven instruction is much more a set of monthly tasks than weekly tasks. Thus it is the lever that most needs a monthly map.)

Here's a sample of what two months of a leader's monthly map might look like. Full-length samples of monthly maps are available on the DVD that accompanies this book.

Principal Monthly Map

On My Radar

Month	Task
September	1—Launch reading intervention/guided reading. **(Data-Driven Instruction)** 1—Assess curriculum plans for rigor and alignment, and return to teachers. **(Planning)** 2—Hold quarterly leadership team meeting (principal, dean, instructional leaders). **(Leadership Team)** 3—Videotape planning meetings of all instructional leaders. **(Leadership Team)** 3—Conduct a student and staff culture walkthrough. **(Student Culture, Staff Culture)** 4—Co-observe teachers with instructional leaders. **(Feedback and Observation, Leadership Team)** 4—Set yearly PD goals for all new teachers in observation tracker. **(Feedback and Observation)**
October	1—Design PD session on classroom pacing. **(PD, Student Culture)** 1—Give teachers curriculum planning update and revision time. **(Planning)**

Month	Task
	2—Ensure instructional leaders are reviewing video clips with novice teachers. **(Leadership Team)** 3—Administer interim assessment 1. **(Data)** 4—Evaluate school on data-driven instruction rubric. **(Data)** 4—Coordinate grade-level culture walkthroughs. **(Student Culture, Staff Culture)**

You'll notice that each task is labeled 1–4: the numbers represent which week of the month that task should be done. This not only helps you see your tasks clearly but also makes monthly maps easier to carry over from year to year.

Here's how a school leader builds a document like this.

- **Work on fewer leadership levers well rather than on all of them poorly.** Every leader in this book knew which one or two levers he or she would primarily focus on first. This doesn't mean they ignored the other levers altogether—simply that they chose an order in which to prioritize them. Generally, the clearest route to success is to start with the super-levers: data and student culture. Only add levers when you are confident that those two are solidly in place.

- **Be aware of busy times.** Make sure you pick weeks for completing each monthly driver that are feasible for your particular school during this particular year. For example, when it comes to choosing dates for interim assessments, don't schedule them at the same time that report cards are due. Doing so will mean that teachers will be overwhelmed trying to finish reports *and* analyze their results. Planning drivers for times when they are truly doable will protect your calendar from breaking down later in the year.

- **Pick a week, not a day.** Choose a week of every month from one to four to assign to each driver, as opposed to assigning it a specific date. In addition to adding flexibility and clarity to your plan, this will make your monthly map transferrable to next year, significantly reducing your planning workload when the time comes.

- **Distribute actions as evenly as possible.** Better to strategically delegate a few drivers to later weeks or months than to cram so many into such a short period of time that they aren't accomplishable.

A Word on . . . Turnaround—Focus on Data and Culture

The most important turnaround you can make, and the one over which you have the most control, is changing your own use of time. Your schedule is the key to finding the time you need to put the other systems into place and begin changing your school. Yet as we have noted throughout this book, the first core steps to change must address student culture and data-driven instruction. As Brian Sims observed, "It doesn't matter if it takes a month, three months, or a year: without a safe and stable student culture, nothing else will matter." As a result, during a turnaround, the ways in which a principal uses his or her time will carry a different emphasis. What might this look like? Placing more time on student culture and less on other components.

Be careful, however, about skipping observation and feedback altogether. When leaders do not do observation and feedback from the beginning, they find it very difficult to incorporate later. Without a cycle of data-driven instruction supported by observation and feedback, turning around student culture will not be sufficient to increase student achievement.

With all of this in mind, we've provided a monthly map template for you to fill out yourself. You can also find a copy of this blank template on the DVD that accompanies this book. If you get stuck on your way to planning the perfect calendar, look to the two exemplar monthly maps we've included on the DVD for reference: one for implementing the super-lever of data-driven instruction and a second map that integrates the implementation of both student culture and data-driven instruction.

Monthly Map Template

Month	Task
June	☐
July	☐
August	☐
September	☐
October	☐
November	☐
December	☐
January	☐
February	☐
March	☐
April	☐
May	☐

The Daily Action Plan

A daily action plan gives you a way to organize tasks and hold yourself accountable for getting them done. The action plan coupled with a weekly schedule gives you everything you need to ensure that time and task management never get in the way of your school's success.

Whereas the typical to-do list groups together all of your various tasks, the action plan organizes entries into separate buckets. You can customize these buckets to fit your needs, but the general model should work for any school leader. On the first page of the action plan, there are six buckets: Today, This Week, This Month, Next Month, Leadership Team Agenda Topics, and Faculty Memo Topics. The first four buckets explain themselves. Use the Leadership Team Agenda Topics bucket to jot down ideas for your group meetings with instructional leaders. The Faculty Memo Topics section gives you some brainstorming space as you think of important messages to send out to the staff during the week.

Findings from the Field

James Verrilli

Being a principal means having a thousand little things to do at any moment of the day. Whenever you sit down to deal with one conflict, you're likely to be distracted by another one popping up. It's like having a thousand fires to put out, all at the same time.

When I first became a principal, one of the hardest lessons I had to learn was how to prioritize those fires. Trying to extinguish them as they came at me wasn't always effective. Worse, it left me with very little time for instructional leadership. I needed to observe teachers and give them feedback in order to make sure instruction was happening in their classrooms, and that wasn't really happening. I usually knew which teachers I wanted to see, but I would give myself an impractically flexible schedule for doing so, and I would let it slide altogether if other tasks came up.

I knew I had to develop a better time management system; instructional leadership was too important to be this sporadic. I needed to hold it sacred, and in order to do that, I needed to schedule it firmly, every single week.

I began marking out the time I would spend observing teachers, giving them feedback, and helping them plan lessons and curriculum. It helped to do it visually—with colored Post-it notes on a calendar, or on Microsoft Outlook. Whichever calendar I used, though, I didn't just stick observation time blocks on it—I also put the names of each teacher I needed to observe into each block. Scheduling weekly feedback meetings with those specific teachers helped me stay accountable to my new observation schedule, since I couldn't very well lead a feedback meeting with a teacher whose classes I hadn't observed. My new system put all the pieces of instructional leadership together at the beginning.

As I adjusted to the new system, I still had fires to put out. There were still days when I didn't get through all my observations. In that sense, my job didn't change. But I became much more effective at *doing* my job. Planning every week with this level of detail made it easier for me to keep instructional leadership a priority, even if a parent or another colleague came to me with a problem during that time. Saying, "I can't help you right now, I need to see the teachers," is always hard, but it's a lot harder when you haven't scheduled the time you need to spend observing teachers.

With these changes, when instructional leadership tasks slipped by me, I knew what they were, and I knew to reschedule them. I also always knew what each teacher at my school was teaching and which instructional teams were successful in which ways. I was better at avoiding double booking, because I had an agenda that told me when I was really available to make a new appointment. I interacted with my fellow staff on a more personal level. Best of all, I got to put my classroom expertise, as well as my leadership expertise, into practice.

Admittedly, I also had to be more strategic on completing larger projects than I was before I committed to my instructional leadership schedule. When I had a special project to work on, I'd often end up needing to complete it before or after school, or on a weekend. To me, though, it was clear that the benefits of my new system outweighed the costs. After all, shouldn't we be doing instructional leadership during the day, when instruction is happening?

CONCLUSION

If this book offers a single message, it is that the central question school leaders must confront is how they use their time. Answering this question requires focus, determination, and hard work. Yet as this chapter shows, it does not demand the impossible. To the contrary, the leaders we studied succeeded because they constantly worked to have the greatest impact in the *least* amount of time: the fifteen-minute observation that can change a teacher's career, the thirty-minute data conference that changes a month's worth of achievement, the hour-long PD session that changes your school. The result of that effort is a commitment to ongoing growth that is significant, but manageable.

Yet there is even more than the time you map out in your schedule at stake. The same measures that are outlined here will save you time in the long run: a stronger school culture means less firefighting; stronger instruction means less time spent on emergency remediation; effective and well-aligned planning means fewer chaotic midyear turnarounds. Ultimately, then, the question is not whether it is feasible for leaders to pursue these systems but whether they can afford not to.

Core Idea

Ultimately, the question is not whether it is feasible for leaders to pursue these systems but whether they can afford not to.

Keys to Finding the Time

- **Build your weekly schedule.** Lock in instructional and cultural leadership and lock out nearly everything else.

- **Defend your time.** Build your operations support team to "block and tackle" for you.

- **Manage your tasks.** Utilize a monthly map and daily action plan to stay on top of the most important actions to be taken each week.

Weekly Schedule Building for School Leaders

Summary How-To Guide

Prework

- Determine the number of instructional leaders you will need to manage directly (assistant principals, coaches, etc.).

- Determine the standing meetings you want to convene at least once per month (leadership team meeting, faculty PD).

- Determine the total number of teachers in your school and which people will lead which teachers directly. Determine the number of teachers you will manage directly (ranging from zero if you lead a large school to potentially all teachers if you lead a small school). *Note: Between leaders and teachers, you should have **no more than 10–15 people** you will lead personally.*

- Get out your school's weekly schedule that shows when teachers are teaching and when they have prep periods.

Weekly Schedule

- Create a simple grid for the week in half-hour or hourly segments, 7 a.m.–6 p.m. (modify the grid to match your school class schedule).
- Create the grid so that each hourly block is the size of the Post-its you will use.

Green Post-its—Student Culture:

- Place green Post-its wherever you are likely to be focused on student culture and parental issues (likely breakfast/start of day, lunchtime, and at dismissal)

Yellow Post-its—Meetings:

- Make a decision: Do you work best with back-to-back-to-back meetings, or do you need breaks between meetings to stay focused? Use this criterion to complete the following tasks
- Each yellow Post-it represents a one-hour meeting.
- Label Post-its for each of your team and large-group meetings: leadership team, faculty PD, etc. Place them on the schedule. If they happen only every other week, note that on the Post-its.
- On yellow Post-its, write the names of the 1–3 teachers you will lead, and place them on the schedule where the teachers have a prep period.
  - Two teachers per Post-it for 30-minute planning and feedback meetings
  - Three teachers per Post-it for 20-minute feedback check-ins
- Place on the schedule your check-ins with any other individuals.
- Depending on your preferences, place these meetings as close together as possible, or spread out.

Orange Post-its—Observations:

- Calculate 3–4 observations for every hour (15-minute observations).
- Place one orange Post-it for every 3–4 teachers you will be observing.
  - If you have 16 teachers to observe, you need 4–5 Post-its

Blue Post-its—Uninterrupted Work Time:

- Select three blocks of 2–3 hours of *uninterrupted* time and place blue Post-its on those areas.
  - Unless you can get out of the building and have someone cover for you, these times have to be in the very early morning, very late afternoon, evenings, or weekends.
- Designate one of those planning times for *no email—just large tasks from your monthly map.*

Pulling the Lever

Action Planning Worksheet for FINDING THE TIME

Self-Assessment

- What percentage of your teachers currently get feedback more than twice a month? _____%

- What percentage of your time is currently devoted to instructional or cultural leadership? _____%

- What are the biggest improvements you could make to your weekly schedule in order to increase the time you spend on instructional and cultural leadership?

_____

_____

_____

_____

_____

Planning for Action

- What tools from this book will you use to manage your time? Check all that you will use (you can find all on the DVD):
    - ☐ Weekly Schedule Template
    - ☐ Monthly Map Template
    - ☐ How to Create a Monthly Map one-pager
    - ☐ Sample monthly maps
    - ☐ Daily Action Plan Template

- What are your next steps for finding the time for instructional and cultural leadership?

Action	Date

Conclusion

A Brighter Future

Throughout this book, our focus has been on the use of time and on the strategies that drive learning. In each chapter, we've offered a system to drive school growth and the ways to put that system into place. Taken together, these chapters serve as a comprehensive blueprint for building an exceptional school.

Yet at the end of the day, this book's ultimate purpose is not time management; it's not even great school leadership. This book is about the children—students like Deryk Vences and Derrel Fisher, whose futures are being shaped right now.

Deryk and Derrel were attending Blanton Elementary School before Laura Garza began her leadership there, and both remember fights in the hallways and teachers who struggled to mediate these conflicts. Now, everything has changed for Deryk and Derrel. "I know my teachers care for me," says Deryk confidently. "The principal and the teachers care about us going to college, so they give us more difficult questions so we'll be ready for the next level. When I finish twelfth grade, I want to go to Southern Methodist University so I can get my bachelor's degree—and my master's." Derrel, who is more soft-spoken, also talked about the impact Blanton's improved student culture has had on him and on his classmates. "Here everybody comes and says, 'Do you want to come play with us?' When you come to this school, people actually get to know you, instead of you just sitting in the shadows by yourself."

This book is also for young men like Jay Martinez. Jay jumped at the opportunity to attend North Star Middle School and Washington Park High School, and the academic and cultural values there did more than get Jay through middle school and high school successfully: they also prepared him for his college education at the University of Chicago. "My first college semester was met with failure and I struggled to keep up with my peers," Jay remembers. "I nearly transferred at one point, thinking I might be more successful elsewhere. However, with the grit I developed through North Star, I fought my way back."

He was not alone. Kamani Cook-Christian remembers Washington Park High School as the first place she felt at home as a student. "At my old school, I felt unfulfilled, bored, stuck, and often like I stood out for all the wrong reasons," Kamani says. "But here, my talents were celebrated." Kamani became a hungry learner who embraced challenge joyfully—and continues to do so today. After graduating from Lafayette College, she came back to Newark to teach kindergarten. "My teachers saw things in me that I didn't see. They pushed me and challenged me. Now I'm helping guide future scholars of Newark through the beginning of their journeys."

The reason Jay, Kamani, Deryk, Derrel, and thousands like them are on a path toward college and beyond is not just hard work, but the *right* work. They were a part of schools where adults focused all their efforts on what students needed most—and built the culture and instruction to match. Every day, leaders like Mary Ann Stinson, Wade Bell, Mike Mann, Ashley Anderson, Kelly Dowling, Laura Garza, Adriana Gonzalez, and Antonio Burt are changing destinies and changing lives. In building great schools, they are building great futures.

Ultimately, the goal of the systems we've outlined in this book is to give all students the education they need and deserve. When leaders combine unwavering conviction with the right concrete strategies, greatness is possible. It is our hope to carry that excellence to every child across the globe.

Appendix A:
A Sneak Peek: *A Principal Manager's Guide to Leverage Leadership*

As inspiring as the single success of any single leader at any single school may be, *Leverage Leadership 2.0* isn't a book about individual leaders beating the odds. On the contrary, it's about the way leaders can change the odds altogether, at scale, when enough of them engage the right strategies. Principals accomplish this every day—but just like teachers, they accomplish much more and do so much more quickly when an instructional leader is there to make sure that no instructor is an island. It's with this in mind that we wrote a supplementary guide to *Leverage Leadership 2.0,* one aimed at principal managers.

A Principal Manager's Guide to Leverage Leadership shows how to coach and develop principals around all the levers of leadership, with a particularly deep dive into the two super-levers of school leadership: data-driven instruction and student culture. This guide is meant for anyone in a position to impact multiple school leaders:

- Principal managers/supervisors
- Superintendents and central office leaders
- Principal training organizations
- School boards
- State departments of education
- School turnaround programs

If your role is in any way to make principals better, this book applies to you. Read on for a preview!

PREVIEW OPENING OF CHAPTER 2: IDENTIFYING THE RIGHT ACTION STEP

What Do I Coach?

Walk around with network superintendent Jeanine Zitta from St. Louis Public Schools, and you won't step inside the central office very often. Instead, you'll find yourself in schools, working alongside a principal.

On this day, Jeanine and her principal Angela Glass are seated at the round table in Angela's office. On the bulletin board behind them you can see the school's values written on colorful construction paper, putting words to the qualities that make the school so vibrant.

Jeanine has just finished praising Angela for the improvements in her feedback meetings, and now they are beginning work on her next stage of development.

"Today I want to dive into the Do It of your feedback meeting," shares Jeanine, "specifically the part 'plan before you practice.' What are the main components of that segment?"

"So, making sure the teacher has any lesson material that they need," Angela comments (Jeanine nods), "and also making sure that they think through and script out what they are going to do in the lesson."

"Yes. So what is the purpose of giving the teacher time to plan before taking it live?" asks Jeanine.

"I find that in the past if I did not give the teacher time to plan," responds Angela, "they'll start practicing and you'll have to stop them, versus getting it right first and then starting the practice."

"Agreed," affirms Jeanine. "I'm going to model the 'plan before practice' segment for you. I'll be you, and you'll be Mr. Mitchell [one of her teachers], and I want you to notice the key leader moves that I make." "OK!" Angela says.

Then Jeanine launches fully into role play, playing the role of Angela. "Mr. Mitchell, so your action step is to redirect students using the least invasive strategy. Using nonverbal cues is the new part of this strategy for you. Let's plan our practice . . ."

Over the course of the next five minutes, Jeanine models how to get the teacher to plan effectively during a feedback meeting, and Angela immediately notices the gap between her own feedback and Jeanine's model. "This change will take me to the next level of rigor and help the teaching get better. I can see if they understand and make the practice tighter."

"Exactly," concurs Jeanine. "Let's plan your next meeting . . ."

 WATCH Clip 1: Zitta—See It and Name It

St. Louis Public Schools is Jeanine Zitta's home. She's worked there for eighteen years, beginning as a teacher before coming into her own as a school leader. Today, Jeanine manages a network of her city's elementary schools—and those schools are taking off. For schools that had been mired in mediocrity, student learning is changing. Of the ten schools that Jeanine has managed for three years, every single one of them has improved in both ELA and math (see Figure 2.1). These scores represent the highest growth in the district.

For anyone who has been a principal manager, you know that batting ten for ten in improved scores is nearly unheard of. The secret to Jeanine's success? Following the leader—not herself, but the strongest of the principals she coaches.

"If you manage it correctly, someone else's success can make everyone ask, 'How can I be like that person?'" Jeanine notes wisely. "The highest performers always get the question: 'How did you do that?' but we don't always pay attention to the answer."

That was the hard part for Jeanine in improving her schools: not determining what the challenges were, but naming what action the principals should take that would most effectively address those challenges. The "what to do" was harder than the "what to fix."

> ### Core Idea
> The key to improving school leaders is not only finding what to fix
> but also naming how to do so.

Determining how to fix something becomes more complicated for a principal manager, as the number of things that can go wrong in a school becomes so large!

Figure 2.1 Missouri State Assessment: Network 3 Schools, Percentage at or Above Proficiency in Math (top) and ELA (bottom)

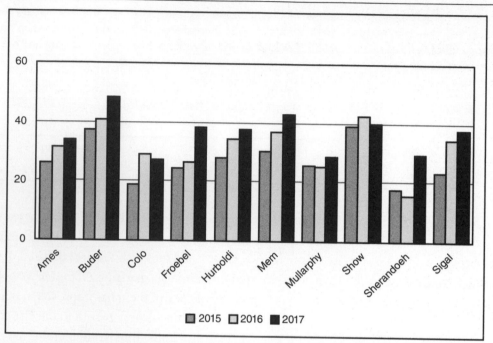

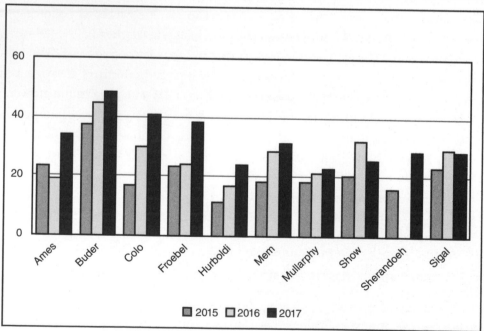

Yet Jeanine remains undeterred. She doesn't rest with seeing the problem: she finds a pathway to focus on what matters most, narrowing in on the specific principal action step that can change the outcome. This chapter will show how.

CRITERIA FOR PRINCIPAL ACTION STEPS

Any guide to home repair will start by telling you to keep a toolbox on hand. But not just any toolbox will suffice. The guide will also give you a list of the most important tools to include in your toolbox so that you can solve the largest and most common issues that could arise.

Working with principals is no different: if you build the right toolbox, you can fix more problems. Take a moment to review a sample of action steps a manager like Jeanine might deliver to her principals. What do they all have in common?

Sample Action Steps for Principals

Data-Driven Instruction

8. **See It:**
   - Start with the standard(s): unpack the key parts of the standard that align to the student error to ID the most essential conceptual understandings that students must master.
   - Unpack the teacher and student exemplars (or rubrics) to ID how the work demonstrates mastery of the standard.

9. **Name It:**
   - Punch it: succinctly restate the key procedural errors and conceptual misunderstandings, then have the teacher repeat them and write them down.

10. **Do It:**
    - Perfect the plan before you practice.
      - Plan the structure of the reteach: modeling or guided discourse.
      - ID the steps, student materials, and students to monitor.
      - Predict the gap: anticipate likely errors in execution, and practice that part of the meeting.
    - Practice the gap.
      - ID the most essential elements of the reteach for the teacher to practice, especially the parts that will be hardest to master.
      - Prompt the teacher to "go live" and practice the prompts that will be used during the reteach.

- Build an effective follow-up plan.
  - ○ ID when to teach, when to reassess, and when to revisit this data.
  - ○ Embed the action plan into upcoming lessons and unit plans.
  - ○ ID when observations will take place to see plan in action and how it will be assessed.

Stop and Jot

Sample Action Steps for Principals

What characteristics do these action steps have in common?
Write your response here.

_____

_____

_____

_____

_____

These sorts of action steps are the pinnacle of simplicity: they are focused, targeted, and self-explanatory. And if you notice a striking similarity in the characteristics of these action steps to the characteristics of action steps we recommend for teachers in *Leverage Leadership 2.0*, you are right. They are not book-size but bite-size. Just like teachers, leaders grow most quickly when their managers narrow their focus to the highest-leverage action step.

Core Idea

The smaller and more precise the action step, the quicker the growth.
Be bite-size, not book-size.

The power of bite-size action steps is well chronicled by Daniel Coyle in *The Talent Code* and by *Leverage Leadership 2.0*:[1] when you focus only on what matters most, you build the right foundation, which accelerates sustainable growth of a person's expertise. If it works for students, athletes, musicians, and teachers, it certainly works for principals as well!

The criteria for an excellent principal action step are the same as those for a teacher action step:

- **Highest leverage.** Will this help the leader develop most quickly and effectively? Is it connected to a larger PD goal?

- **Measurable.** The action step is what the leader can practice: it names the "what" (e.g., See It—start with the standard) and the "how" (e.g., fully unpack the standard to identify what a student must know and do to be able to master the standard).

- **Bite-size.** If your principal can't make the change in a week, the action step isn't small enough!

Keys to Great Action Steps

Great action steps are

- **Highest leverage.** Will this help the leader develop most quickly and effectively? Is it connected to a larger PD goal?
- **Measurable.** The action step is what the leader can practice: it names the "what" and the "how."
- **Bite-size.** If your leader can't make the change in a week, the action step isn't small enough!

Although the criteria for effective principal action steps are universally applicable, what makes action steps for principals more challenging is the number of layers. Let's consider why that's the case.

When Jeanine walks around a school with a principal to observe, she will notice the strengths and areas of growth for each teacher. Her first actions will be to determine what the teachers need to do to improve—a teacher-facing action step. At the same time, though, she needs to determine where the gap is in the principal's leadership that is keeping the teachers from getting better faster. As a result, she often ends up generating both a teacher action step *and* a principal action step. That's complex—and it's one reason why, before we train our eyes, we often forget to identify action steps for our principals as well as our teachers.

To make it easier to see the right principal action steps clearly, we have studied the action steps that top principal managers give to their principals, and we've consolidated them into one document, organized by leadership lever. The full document, Action Steps for Principals, can be found at the end of this chapter. Here is one lever—observation and feedback—as an example. What do you notice about how the action steps are organized?

Action Steps for Principals
Observation and Feedback

LEVER	KEY ACTIONS IN SEQUENCE
	PLAN
OBSERVATION AND FEEDBACK	1. **Build weekly observation schedule for yourself and other instructional leaders/coaches:** • Establish and maintain own observation schedule and Observation Tracker. • Establish observation schedules and trackers for leadership team to effectively distribute observation of all teachers. • Adjust the schedule as needed to address trends and/or support struggling teachers. 2. **Prepare:** Stick to an exemplar script (See It, Name It, Do It feedback protocol) to ensure that your prompts are clear, economical, and aimed at the highest-leverage action step.
	EXECUTE

	Action Steps
	
	3. **ID highest-leverage school-wide and individual teacher action steps:**
	
	• Use your tools (Get Better Faster Scope and Sequence, student data) to create action steps that are
	
	    o Highest leverage (Will student achievement improve tomorrow as a result of this action step?)
	
	    o Measurable and bite-size

LEVER	KEY ACTIONS IN SEQUENCE
	EXECUTE

Effective Feedback Meetings

4. **See It—see the success:**
   - Prepare and deliver precise, authentic praise rooted in previous action step(s).
   - Ask teacher to describe the impact: "What has been the impact of this on your classroom?"

5. **See It—show a model and see the gap:**
   - Show a model—video, live model, script, lesson plan—that highlights key actions for the teacher.
   - Fully unpack the model: start with the end in mind and ask precise questions to ID all key actions (e.g., "What is the purpose of . . . ?" "What did she do next?").
   - Ask "What is the gap between what you just saw and what you did?"

6. **Do It—perfect the plan before you practice:**
   - Give your teacher time to script out her actions before you start the practice and between rounds of practice.
   - Revise the script until it is perfect.
   - Use an exemplar to perfect the plan.

7. **Do It—practice the gap:**
   - Practice at the point of error: anticipate what teachers or students could do/say incorrectly during the practice and plan for those mistakes.
   - Practice the gap: set up practice so that the teacher practices the actions that are most critical for the action step.

8. **Do It—practice. Go from simple to more complex:**
   - Practice with upcoming lessons/meetings to apply the skill to multiple scenarios.
   - Start with simple practice; when teacher masters it, add complexity (student wrong answers or noncompliance).

(Lever label, vertical: OBSERVATION AND FEEDBACK)

LEVER	KEY ACTIONS IN SEQUENCE

	EXECUTE

OBSERVATION AND FEEDBACK

EXECUTE

- Narrow the practice to repeat it more times and get more at-bats.
- Stop the practice, provide real-time feedback, and redo.

9. **Name It—punch it:**
   - Punch the action step by naming the "what" and the "how" clearly and concisely.
   - Be bite-size, not book-size: limit the action steps to what the teacher can master in a week.
   - Have teacher write it down and check for understanding to make sure she has it.

MONITOR AND FOLLOW UP

10. **Do It—follow up. Articulate clear next steps:**
    - Set dates: all deliverables have clear timelines and are written into both the leader's and teacher's calendar.
    - Establish follow-up and (when applicable) real-time feedback cues to be used during the observation.

11. **Provide real-time feedback:**
    - Choose highest-leverage moments for real-time classroom feedback.
    - Use least invasive method for real-time feedback that is appropriate for the teacher.
      - Silent signal
      - Whisper prompt:
        - Name what to do
        - State the rationale
        - State what you'll look for/how you will support
        - (All in 45 seconds max)
      - Verbal prompt/model
      - Extended model

Right from the beginning, you probably noticed an overall structure: plan, execute, monitor. This same organization exists for all the leadership levers. (Some, such as student culture, will add an additional section for rollout, where what you do in the first weeks at the start of school will be distinct from the rest of the year.)

Why use this structure? Imagine you are working with a principal on improving her observation and feedback. You ask her to film one of her feedback meetings, and you note that it is mediocre across the board. Where would you start guiding the principal to improve? You could start by trying to fix the quality of her prompts: getting the teacher to do more of the thinking. But even better would be to start from the first section: plan. If the leader doesn't have a schedule of regular observations and feedback, then fixing the issues of the feedback meeting won't help, because few teachers will be getting feedback in the first place! Here we see the power of the organization of the action steps: always get the plan right before you focus on the execution. Once the plan is in place, you can see where the breakdown occurred in the execution or monitoring.

> ## Core Idea
> To get the execution right, you need to get your plan right.
> Plan. Roll out. Execute. Monitor.

These principal action steps were not created in a vacuum or a think tank: they were developed by observing thousands of hours of footage of principals in action as well as managers meeting with their principals. We noticed that the highest-achieving managers—the ones who got the largest number of their schools to succeed—had much more precise action steps, and they followed a sequence. What we've done here is put them all in one place for you to use.

Appendix B: The DVD: PD Workshop Materials and Key Documents

All key supporting documents can be found on the DVD: rubrics, one-page guides (one-pagers), PD materials, and videos of leaders in action.

HOW TO USE ONE-PAGERS

Every one-pager mentioned in the text can be found on the DVD in printer-friendly format in the folder Leverage Leadership Quick Reference Guide.

The power of the one-pagers that you've seen presented in each chapter is that they can be easily printed for daily use. A number of schools and school districts have created what we call a Leverage Leadership Rainbow Guide: a small spiral-bound resource that includes all of the following documents printed double-sided in the following order:

- Weekly Data Meeting one-pager
- Planning Meeting one-pager

- Giving Effective Feedback one-pager
- Real-Time Feedback one-pager
- Student Culture one-pager
- Leading Professional Development one-pager
- Get Better Faster Scope and Sequence
- Get Better Faster Coach's Guide

Every one-pager in the guide is printed on differently colored paper (thus Rainbow Guide), making it easy for leaders to quickly reach the guide they need without any additional tabs. Leaders can carry this around with them and put it to daily use—so many of the leaders highlighted in this book have been doing so for years!

HOW TO USE SUPPORTING DOCUMENTS

In addition to the one-pagers, the DVD includes key supporting documents for the leadership levers. These include reproducible copies of every document referred to in the text, making it easier to implement each lever in your own school. Included among those documents are the Leverage Leadership Evaluation Rubrics for principals and non-principal instructional leaders that can be used to assess the effectiveness of instructional leadership in your school.

HOW TO USE THE WORKSHOP MATERIALS

On the DVD we also include all the materials you need to lead workshops on three of the key leadership levers. These help you train your leadership teams and bring these chapters alive with lots of practice.

Workshops Included on the DVD

- Observation and Feedback (Chapter 3)
- Professional Development (Chapter 4)
- Student Culture (Chapter 5)

For the workshop on data-driven instruction (Chapter 1), see the book *Driven by Data*.

What Workshop Materials Will You Find on The DVD?

- A cover page that highlights the workshop's goals and intended audience

- A workshop preparation sheet that shows what materials you need for the workshop, how long the workshop runs, and how to assess the workshop's success

- A workshop overview that outlines the subtopics covered in the workshop

- The full-length presenter's notes to be used while presenting the workshop

- The PowerPoint presentation that accompanies each workshop

- The handouts you'll need to provide for each workshop

Read on for a quick preview of what the workshop materials look like!

PREVIEW: OBSERVATION AND FEEDBACK WORKSHOP

An Excerpt from the Full-Length Presenter's Notes

To give you a taste of what it's like to lead this workshop, here's a small excerpt from the full-length presenter's notes you'll find on the DVD.

Context

At this point in the observation and feedback workshop, participants have already identified the four keys to observation and feedback: regular observation, choosing the right action steps, effective feedback, and accountability. Now, at the beginning of section 1.5 of the workshop, they are diving into how to give effective feedback. This segment includes an overview of the See It, Name It, Do It framework and an in-depth look at one See It section of the workshop.

How Do We Coach? Part I: See It. Name It.	
15	**Master Clip, Part 1: See It (S, N)**
	• Context (Slide 38, 1 min):
	o "Now that we've looked at picking the right action step, it's time to consider how to deliver that feedback effectively. We'll watch a complete feedback meeting with a focus around aggressive monitoring."
	o "The star of the next several videos we'll watch is Ashley Anderson, a principal at Uncommon Collegiate High School in Brooklyn, New York. She's meeting with a second-year teacher who has had success in the past and is now working on developing her skill in aggressive monitoring: gathering data during independent practice to respond to student error."

	• Key questions (Slide 39, Handout Page 7):
	   o "How does Ashley launch her feedback meeting?"
	   o "What are all the steps she takes in guiding her teacher?"
	• **Watch Leverage Leadership 2.0 Clip 16**
	• Pair share (1 min):
	   o Partners answer the questions.
	   o Circulate the room to listen to their responses.
	• Large group share out (3 min)
	• Core Idea (Slide 40):
	   o "If you want a teacher to get it, get them to see it. To see it is to believe it."
	• Share the Name It (Slide 41, 3 min)

10	**Master Clip, Part 2: Name It (S, N)**
	• Context (Slide 42):
	   o "Now let's watch the second part of Ashley's feedback meeting."
	• Key question (Slide 43):
	   o "What does Ashley say and do to ensure her teacher knows the action step?"
	• **Watch Leverage Leadership 2.0 Clip 17**
	• Pair share (1 min):
	   o Partners answer the questions
	   o Circulate the room to listen to their responses.
	• Large group share out (2 min)
	• Core Idea (Slide 44):
	   o You don't lock in the learning until you stamp it.
	   o Transformative action steps name the what and the how.
	• Share the Name It (Slide 45).

QUICK REFERENCE SHEET

The following box lists highlights of the key concepts in *Leverage Leadership 2.0.*

The Seven Levers

INSTRUCTIONAL LEVERS

1. **Data-driven instruction.** Define the road map for rigor and adapt teaching to meet students' needs.
2. **Instructional planning.** Plan backwards to guarantee strong lessons.
3. **Observation and feedback.** Coach teachers to improve the learning.
4. **Professional development.** Strengthen culture and instruction with hands-on training that sticks.

CULTURAL LEVERS

5. **Student culture.** Create a strong culture where learning can thrive.
6. **Staff culture.** Build and support the right team.
7. **Managing school leadership teams.** Train instructional leaders to expand your impact across the school.

*   *   *

1. **Data-driven instruction**
   - **Assessment.** Set the road map for rigor.
   - **Analysis.** Identify the gaps in student understanding.
   - **Action.** Reteach key content to get students on track.
   - **Systems.** Create systems and procedures to ensure constant data-driven improvement.
2. **Planning**
   - **Unit plans.** Craft data-driven unit plans that are aligned to the level of rigor you wish your students to reach.
   - **Lesson plans.** Build effective day-to-day lesson plans that will drive student learning.
   - **Coaching planning.** Guide your teachers to master the skills that will make them outstanding lesson planners in their own right.
   - **Monitoring planning.** Observe lessons in action to find out which parts of your plans are working well in practice.
3. **Observation and feedback**
   - **Observe frequently and consistently.** Lock in frequent and regular observations.
   - **Identify the key action step.** Identify the top areas for growth.
   - **Give effective feedback.** See It. Name It. Do It.

- **Monitor and follow up.** Develop systems to monitor teacher development, and follow up accordingly.

4. **Professional development**

- **What to teach.** Create objectives that are highest leverage, measurable, and bite-size.

- **How to teach.** See It. Name It. Do It. Reflect.

- **Making it stick.** Monitor implementation and coach for results.

5. **Student culture**

- **Set your vision.** What do you want students and adults to be doing in school?

- **Roll it out to your staff.** Give multiple opportunities to practice and rehearse before stepping into the classroom.

- **Roll it out to your students.** Give multiple opportunities to practice to lock in habits across the school.

- **Monitor and maintain.** Lead publicly, manage individually, evaluate progress, and implement whole-school resets.

6. **Staff culture**

- **Set the vision.** Name the behaviors you wish to see, and set clear roles and schedules.

- **Roll it out.** Lead by example, create a culture of practice, and build relationships.

- **Protect it.** Narrate the positive, identify the gaps, lead accountability conversations, and follow up.

7. **Managing school leadership teams**

- **Choose your team.** Look for reliability and receptiveness to reach the 12:1 ratio.

- **Train your team.** Set their schedule, lead PD, and use the one-pagers to guide them.

- **Monitor the school.** See It. Name It. Do It.

- **Lead effective leadership team meetings.** Focus on instructional leadership.

8. **Finding the time**

- **Build your weekly schedule.** Start with student culture, then add group meetings, one-on-one meetings, observations, staff culture, and work time.

- **Defend your time.** Defeat distractions with an operations team and a first responder.

- **Manage your monthly tasks.** Build a monthly map for the nonweekly tasks of instructional leadership.

Notes

Introduction

1. From the Teaching Trust 2017 Impact Report, available at https://static1
    .squarespace.com/static/57ff97e8e4fcb510d48ca31b/t/5a9ea8c871c10b81e4343
    b86/1520347342165/Teaching+Trust+2017+Impact+Report.pdf

2. Ibid.

3. Leithwood, Louis, and Anderson have ranked leadership as "second only to
    classroom instruction" as a determining factor as to what students learn in school;
    Branch, Hanushek, and Rivkin have found that effective principals improve
    student achievement by multiple months per year, whereas less effective principals
    lower achievement by the same amount. Leithwood, Louis, and Anderson and
    Branch, Hanushek and Rivkin are cited in Ben Klompus, *Scaling Instructional
    Improvement: Designing a Strategy to Develop the Leaders of Leaders* (doctoral
    dissertation, 2016; downloadable from https://dash.harvard.edu/handle/1/
    27013352). Further, Hattie has shown that "instructional leadership"—consis-
    tently believing that teacher actions shape student outcomes and delivering
    feedback to teachers, among other things—has a far higher impact on student
    learning than "transformational leadership," in which leaders focus on inspiring
    staff, setting common goals, and giving teachers autonomy. John Hattie, "High-
    Impact Leadership," *Educational Leadership* 72, no. 5 (February 2015): 36–40.

4. Kim Marshall, *Rethinking Teacher Supervision and Evaluation: How to Work
    Smart, Build Collaboration, and Close the Achievement Gap* (San Francisco:
    Jossey-Bass, 2009).

5. Robert J. Marzano, Tony Frontier, and David Livingston, *Effective Supervision: Supporting the Art and Science of Teaching* (Alexandria, VA: ASCD, 2011).

6. Ibid. Further, a variety of scholars have confirmed that although the achievement gap is finally closing in some areas, it remains and is even widening in others—highlighting the continuing need for effective instructional leadership, particularly in our most vulnerable communities. See Jerome D'Agostino and Emily Rodgers, "Literary Achievement Trends at Entry to First Grade," *Educational Researcher* 46, no. 2 (March 2017): 78–89; and Sean F. Reardon, Jane Waldfogel, and Daphna Bassok, "The Good News about Educational Inequality," *New York Times,* August 26, 2016, available at https://www.nytimes.com/2016/08/28/opinion/sunday/the-good-news-about-educational-inequality.html.

7. See, for example, Robert J. Marzano, Timothy Waters, and Brian A. McNulty, *School Leadership That Works: From Research to Results* (Alexandria, VA: ASCD, 2005); Charlotte Danielson, *Enhancing Student Achievement: A Framework for School Improvement* (Alexandria, VA: ASCD, 2002); Terrence E. Deal and Kent D. Peterson, *Shaping School Culture: Pitfalls, Paradoxes, and Promises* (San Francisco: Jossey-Bass, 2009); Alexander D. Platt, Caroline E. Tripp, Wayne R. Ogden, and Robert G. Fraser, *The Skillful Leader: Confronting Mediocre Teaching* (Acton, MA: Ready About Press, 2000).

8. Testing results for the leaders highlighted in this book are reported near the beginning of each chapter.

9. For more on the impact that effective time management can have on student achievement, see Eileen Lai Horng, Daniel Klasik, and Susanna Loeb, "Principal's Time Use and School Effectiveness," *American Journal of Education* 116, no. 4 (August 2010): 491–523. For a description of how some school leaders put this insight into practice, see Jan Walker, "Letting Go: How Principals Can Be Better Instructional Leaders," *Middle Ground* 14 (August 2010): 16–17.

10. See, for example, Marzano et al., *Effective Supervision,* 107.

Chapter 1

1. "Truesdell Education Campus," District of Columbia Public Schools, School Profiles, http://profiles.dcps.dc.gov/Truesdell+Education+Campus.

2. For additional resources that show how assessments that reflect clear standards and normalize error benefit students, see Olusola Adesope, Dominic Trevisan, and

Narayankripa Sundararajan, "Rethinking the Use of Tests: A Meta-Analysis of Practice Testing," *Review of Educational Research* 87, no. 3 (June 2017): 659–701; Richard Curwin, "Can Assessments Motivate?" *Educational Leadership* 72, no. 1 (September 2014): 38–40; and Kathleen Porter-Magee and Jennifer Borgioli, "The Four Biggest Myths of the Anti-Testing Backlash," *Education Gadfly,* February 14, 2013, available at https://edexcellence.net/commentary/education-gadfly-weekly/2013/february-14/the-four-biggest-myths-of-the-anti-testing-backlash.html.

3. To read more about the value of setting a clear standard for rigor—and checking in on learning "early and often"—see Grant Wiggins, "How Good Is Good Enough?" *Educational Leadership* 71, no. 4 (December 2013): 10–16.

4. Read more about the ways incorrect answer choices set rigor in Mark Gierl, Okan Bulut, Qi Guo, and XinXin Zhang, "Developing, Analyzing, and Using Distractors for Multiple-Choice Tests in Education: A Comprehensive Review," *Review of Educational Research* 87, no. 6 (December 2017): 1082–1116.

5. For some of the many definitions of rigor that have been offered, see Nel Noddings, "The New Anti-Intellectualism in America," *Education Week* 26 (March 19, 2007): 29, 32, available at https://www.edweek.org/ew/articles/2007/03/20/28noddings.h26.html; Elliot Washor and Charles Mojkowski, "What Do You Mean by Rigor?" *Educational Leadership* 64, no. 4 (2007), available at http://www.ascd.org/publications/educational-leadership/dec06/vol64/num04/What-Do-You-Mean-by-Rigor%C2%A2.aspx; Daniel Baron, "Using Text-Based Protocols: The Five Rs," *Principal Leadership* 7, no. 6 (2007): 50-51; W. Norton Grubb and Jeannie Oakes, *'Restoring Value' to the High School Diploma: The Rhetoric and Practice of Higher Standards*, Issue brief (Boulder, CO: Arizona State University, 2007); Richard DuFour, Robert E. Eaker, and Rebecca Burnette, *On Common Ground: The Power of Professional Learning Communities* (Bloomington, IN: National Educational Service, 2005); Barbara R. Blackburn, "Rigor and Competency-Based Instruction: Are We Asking the Right Questions?" *EdCircuit* 3 (January 2017), http://www.edcircuit.com/rigor-and-competency-based-instruction/; and "The Essentials for Achieving Rigor," materials based on Marzano's *The Art and Science of Teaching,* by Learning Sciences International, 2017: https://www.learningsciences.com/teach/core-instruction/, https://www.learningsciences.com/wp/wp-content/uploads/2017/06/Essentials-Executive-Summary-06-03-14.pdf, and https://www.learningsciences.com/wp/wp-content/uploads/2017/06/School-Leader-Rigor-Paper-2014.pdf.

6. Barbara R. Blackburn, "The Beginner's Guide to Understanding Rigor," in *Rigor Made Easy* (Eye on Education, 2012).

7. Del Stover, "Up to the Challenge: Are You Doing All You Can to Provide Academic Rigor for Your Students?" *American School Board Journal* 202, no. 5 (October 2015): 42–43.

8. You can find Mike Mann's results in the beginning of Chapter 2.

9. Many districts, in the rush to become data driven, are overassessing their students. Assessments are critical, but once every six to eight weeks in each subject is more than sufficient. See Michael J. Schmoker, *The Results Fieldbook: Practical Strategies from Dramatically Improved Schools* (Alexandria, VA: ASCD, 2001). For approaches to cut down on testing and reduce overassessment, see Paul Bambrick-Santoyo, *Driven by Data: A Practical Guide to Improve Instruction* (San Francisco: Jossey-Bass, 2010), 3–35.

10. Basketball Reference, "Shane Battier," https://www.basketball-reference.com/players/b/battish01.html.

11. Michael Lewis, "The No-Stats All-Star," *New York Times Magazine,* February 13, 2009, available at http://www.nytimes.com/2009/02/15/magazine/15Battier-t.html.

12. ESPN's site FiveThirtyEight is an excellent source for all things related to data analytics, particularly for sports or politics. Check out their 2015 documentary on Justin Zermelo, *By the Numbers: Meet the Personal Stats Analyst Who Helped Kevin Durant Win the MVP,* http://fivethirtyeight.com/features/meet-the-personal-stats-analyst-who-helped-kevin-durant-win-the-mvp/.

13. NJDOE PARCC/State Test Results, available from http://www.nj.gov/education/schools/achievement/.

14. Doug Lemov, "Technique 39: Show-Call," in *Teach Like a Champion 2.0: 62 Techniques That Will Put Students on the Path to College* (San Francisco, CA: Jossey-Bass, 2010), 290–299.

15. For the definitive introduction to the concept of "good to great," see James Collins, *Good to Great: Why Some Companies Make the Leap . . . and Others Don't* (New York: Harper Business, 2001).

Chapter 2

1. Liana Heitin Loewus, "Study: Give Weak Teachers Good Lesson Plans, Not Professional Development," *Education Week,* July 12, 2016, http://blogs.edweek.org/

edweek/curriculum/2016/07/study_give_teachers_lesson_plans_not_professional_
development.html?cmp=SOC-SHR-FB.

2. E. D. Hirsch's work on core knowledge dates to as far back as his 1988 text *Cultural Literacy: What Every American Needs to Know* and as recently as 2012, when he penned the article "How Schools Fail Democracy" for *The Chronicle of Higher Education.*

3. Marilyn Jager Adams, "Advancing Our Students' Language and Literacy: The Challenge of Complex Texts," *American Educator,* Winter 2010–11, available at http://www.literacyconnects.org/img/2013/03/Advancing-Our-Students-Language-and-Literacy.pdf.

4. Diane F. Halpern, *Thought & Knowledge: An Introduction to Critical Thinking,* 5th ed. (New York: Psychology Press, 2013); Robert H. Ennis, *Critical Thinking* (Upper Saddle River, NJ: Pearson, 1995).

5. Grant Wiggins and Jay McTighe, *Understanding by Design* (Alexandria, VA: Association for Supervision & Curriculum Development, 2005).

6. Anthony J. Greene, "Making Connections," *Scientific American,* July 2010, https://www.scientificamerican.com/article/making-connections/. For more on how this relates directly to instructional planning, see Diana Oxley, "Creating Instructional Program Coherence," *Principal's Research Review* 3, no. 5 (September 2008): 1–7.

7. Jal Mehta and Sarah Fine, *The Why, What, Where, and How of Deeper Learning in American Secondary Schools,* Students at the Center: Deeper Learning Research Series (Boston: Jobs for the Future, 2015).

8. Sonja Santelises and Joan Dabrowski make a similar point in *Checking In: Do Classroom Assignments Reflect Today's Higher Standards?* Education Trust report, September 2, 2015, https://edtrust.org/resource/classroomassignments/.

Chapter 3

1. Charlotte Danielson has long been an advocate of teacher development as opposed to teacher evaluation. In a 2014 article for *School Administrator,* she writes that particularly in light of the higher standards brought about by the Common Core State Standards, teacher evaluation is only constructive "within the context of a collaborative observation/evaluation cycle in which the teacher plays an active role in self-assessment, reflection on practice, and professional conversation." Jon

Saphier, also a longtime teacher development advocate, draws a direct line between leaders' ability to develop teachers and student achievement. Charlotte Danielson, "Connecting Common Core to Teacher Evaluation," *School Administrator* 71, no. 3 (March 2014): 30–33; Jon Saphier and Pia Durkin, "Supervising Principals: How Central Office Administrators Can Improve Teaching and Learning in the Classroom," September 21, 2011, available through the Research for Better Teaching website, http://rbteach.com/sites/default/files/supervising_and_coaching_principals_saphier.pdf.

2. Robert J. Marzano, Tony Frontier, and David Livingston, *Effective Supervision: Supporting the Art and Science of Teaching* (Alexandria, VA: ACSD, 2011), 69.

3. Ibid., 97.

4. "Teacher Evaluation and Support," Achieve NJ, available at http://www.state.nj.us/education/AchieveNJ/intro/1PagerTeachers.pdf; Grover J. "Russ" Whitehurst, Matthew M. Chingos, and Katharine M. Lindquist, "Getting Classroom Observations Right," *Education Next,* available at http://educationnext.org/getting-classroom-observations-right/.

5. Daniel Coyle, *The Talent Code* (New York: Random House, 2009), 82–84.

6. The importance of focusing on a relatively small number of concrete changes holds across almost all fields of learning and training. As an example, Washington University advises professors to limit comments on student papers to just one to two areas of improvement. See "Commenting on Student Writing," the Teaching Center, Washington University in St. Louis (n.d.), http://teachingcenter.wustl.edu/resources/writing-assignments-feedback/commenting-on-student-writing/.

7. Kim Marshall, *Rethinking Teacher Supervision and Evaluation: How to Work Smart, Build Collaboration, and Close the Achievement Gap* (San Francisco: Jossey-Bass, 2009).

Chapter 4

1. Thomas Guskey wrote about the power of planning PD with student learning outcomes—and the teacher actions that will drive them—in mind "Where Do You Want to Get To?" *Learning Professional* 38, no. 2 (April 2017): 32–37. Sarah Margeson, Chris Eide, and Alison Fox echo this assessment in "Intentionality: Strategic Preparation and Development to Retain Our Most Effective Teachers," *Teachers United* website, Fall 2014, available at https://static1.squarespace.com/

static/579ad890c534a56d0cd9ae67/t/57accd3d37c581d020453fcc/1470942530378/ Intentionality_-_Strategic_Preparation___Development_to_Retain_Our_Most_ Effective_Teachers-3.pdf.

2. Giada Di Stefano, Francesca Gino, Gary P. Pisano, and Bradley Staats, "Making Experience Count: The Role of Reflection in Individual Learning," Harvard Business School Working Paper, No. 14-093, March 2014 (Revised June 2016), available at http://www.hbs.edu/faculty/Publication%20Files/14-093_defe8327-eeb6-40c3-aafe-26194181cfd2.pdf.

3. Ibid. "Once an individual has accumulated experience with a task, the benefit of accumulating additional experience is inferior to the benefit of deliberately articulating and codifying the previously accumulated experience" (p. 1).

Chapter 5

1. Chris B. Brown, "Bill Walsh: A Method for Game Planning," *Smart Football* website, August 2, 2007, available at http://smartfootball.blogspot.com/2007/08/ bill-walsh-method-for-game-planning.html.

Chapter 6

1. Data from the Texas Department of Education and Dallas Independent School District Climate Survey for Lenore Kirk Elementary School from 2014–15 to 2015–16.

2. Jon Saphier has written extensively on the research supporting the positive impact of a strong staff culture on student learning in "Strong Adult Professional Culture: The Indispensable Ingredient for Sustainable School Improvement." Saphier emphasizes the insights of Judith Warren Little, who found in 1989 that adults' willingness to ask for and offer each other help was a key behavioral pattern that resulted in higher student achievement. Jon Saphier, "Strong Adult Professional Culture: The Indispensable Ingredient for Sustainable School Improvement," from *Future Directions of Educational Change* (New York: Routledge, August 18, 2017), ch. 8.

3. The New Teacher Project, *Greenhouse Schools: How Schools Can Build Cultures Where Students and Teachers Thrive* (2012), https://tntp.org/assets/documents/ TNTP_Greenhouse_Schools_2012.pdf.

4. The notion that high expectations build stronger staff cultures also appears in Robert Kegan, Matthew Miller, Lisa Lahey, and Andy Fleming, "Making Business

Personal," *Harvard Business Review* 92, no. 4 (April 2014): 44–52. Kegan et al. name accountability, transparency, and support as the keys to a culture where error is normalized and professionals have the freedom to grow, rather than expending energy presenting themselves as infallible.

5. Jon Saphier, Matt King, and John D'Auria, "3 Strands Form Strong School Leadership," *Journal of Staff Development* 27, no. 2 (Spring 2006): 51–57.

6. See generally Jack and Suzy Welch, *Winning* (New York: HarperCollins, 2005), 81.

7. Fred Jones, "The Importance of Consistency," from the *Fred Jones: Tools for Teaching* website, May 10, 2016, available at http://www.fredjones.com/single-post/2016/05/10/The-Importance-of-Consistency.

8. Jon Saphier, "Strong Adult Professional Culture," unpublished October 29, 2015, draft. Saphier has published a portion of this article on his blog under the title "12 Observable Features of a Strong Adult Professional Culture," available at http://www.saphier.org/12-observable-features-of-a-strong-adult-professional-culture/.

9. In *The Five Dysfunctions of a Team* (San Francisco: Jossey-Bass, 2002), Patrick Lencioni highlights the key patterns a leader must eliminate in order to build a strong staff culture. I highly recommend this text to anyone seeking to roll out an effective staff culture turnaround.

10. Mother Teresa: "Love begins at home" and "What can you do to promote world peace? Go home and love your family."

Chapter 7

1. Bill Dries, "Ford Road Elementary School Charts Progress," *Daily News*, August 20, 2013, https://www.memphisdailynews.com/news/2013/aug/20/ford-road-elementary-school-charts-progress/.

2. A recent article titled "Gauging Goodness of Fit: Teachers' Responses to Their Instructional Teams in High-Poverty Schools" affirmed the value of leadership team meetings that focus on learning. Having principals act as thought partners, comfortable exchange of feedback between colleagues, and meeting agendas rooted in assessment data were some of the keys to doing this effectively. Megin Charner-Laird, Monica Ng, Susan Moore Johnson, Matthew Kraft, John Papay, and Stefanie Reinhorn, "Gauging Goodness of Fit: Teachers' Responses to Their Instructional Teams in High-Poverty Schools," *American Journal of Education* 123, no. 4 (August 2017): 553–584.

3. The Ewing Marion Kauffman School 2015–16 class of ninth-grade students achieved 98 percent proficiency on the state biology end-of-course tests, outscoring peers across Missouri. Kauffman School students also excelled in math, scoring 96 percent proficiency on the Algebra I end-of-course assessment, the second-highest score of any district in the state. In addition, that same year's eighth-grade class was tops in the state in math and third in the state in science.

Chapter 8

1. Kim Marshall, "How I Confronted HSPS (Hyperactive Superficial Principal Syndrome) and Began to Deal with the Heart of the Matter," *Phi Delta Kappan* 77 (1996): 336–345.

2. Formal research studies by Policy Studies Associates, Vanderbilt, and others can be found at the National SAM Innovation Project website: www.samsconnect.com.

3. You can check out the National SAM Innovation Project website for more details, including its software TimeTrack that allows office staff and leaders to track time spent on instruction: http://www.samsconnect.com/wordpress/wp-content/uploads/2015/08/SAM-Info.pdf.

4. For more on removing obstacles to dedicating your time to instructional leadership, see Ben Johnson, "Administrators: How to Get out of the Office and into Classrooms," *Edutopia,* April 17, 2015, available at https://www.edutopia.org/blog/administrators-how-get-out-office-and-classrooms-ben-johnson; John D'Auria, "Learn to Avoid or Overcome Leadership Obstacles," *Phi Delta Kappan* 96, no. 5 (February 2015): 52–54.

5. Maia Heyck-Merlin, *The Together Teacher: Plan Ahead, Get Organized, and Save Time!* (San Francisco: Jossey-Bass, 2012) and *The Together Leader: Get Organized for Your Success—and Sanity!* (San Francisco: Jossey-Bass, 2016).

Appendix A

1. Daniel Coyle, *The Talent Code* (New York: Random House, 2009), 82–84.

Index

Page references followed by *fig* indicate an illustrated figure; followed by *t* indicate a table.

reasoning for math, 30–33; sample US History unit plan, 100–101; as starting point for instruction, 33; "teaching to the test" issue of, 41; unit planning backwards from, 92–93, 111. *See also* Exit Tickets; Self-assessment; Student work; Testing
Attendance (students), 333

College-ready aligned assessment, 37

Collins, Jim, 250

Common assessments, 35, 40

Communication: accountability conversations, 280–284; building trust among staff by modeling respectful, 263–264; effective feedback delivery, 154–169; narrate the positive in staff culture, 279; plan blocks of time for, 335; relationship building with small talk strategies, 275; sample weekly email used to build staff culture, 271–273. *See also* Observation and feedback

Conceptual thinking, 149–150

Content: Both Content and Skill (key needs in core subjects), 94–95; expertise in, 60–61; making learning stick through, 98; monitoring to match rigor of what students need, 117; Stop and Jot on skills and, 96; unit planning to teach both skill and, 94–96

Content expertise/knowledge: as criteria for hiring high school staff, 269; Eric Diamon's application of, 60–61; for leading data-driven instruction, 60–61

Cook-Christian, Kamani, 348

Corburn, Jesse: using Do It to lead PD, 200; video clip 23 (Do It [Plan]—Leading PD), 200, 201

Core ideas (data-driven instruction): assessments are starting point for instruction, 33; data-instruction meetings shift focus to 80 percent of students, 59; data to harness talent to drive results, 42; description and use in this book of, 13; effective instruction results in student learning, 28; interconnection between action, assessments, and analysis, 50; key to effective data analysis, 45; naming what went wrong to plan how to fix it, 64; plan before you practice, 65; reteaching is a relay and not a sprint, 56; See It. Name It. Do It. to develop a skill, 9; spend instruction time on what students need to learn, 43; teachers will rise to level of expectations, 68; transparency in assessments, 36; use the exemplar to start with the end in mind, 62; on what works in teaching, 30; your analysis becomes exemplary when you start with, 63

Core ideas (managing school leadership teams), time-management skills of exceptional school leaders, 291

Core ideas (observation and feedback): benefits of biweekly observations and feedback, 131; development purpose of observation and feedback, 129; get it through See It, 157; on how to choose an action step for a teacher, 153; important to coach every teacher, 130; lock in the learning and punch it, 159; the more precise the action step the quicker the grown, 139; perfect practice to make perfect, 162; understanding your own resistance to turnaround, 175

Core ideas (planning): assessments help you break through imperfect curriculum, 93; content and skill needed for mastery, 94; make learning stick through content, 98; matching unit planning and needs of subject, 96; monitoring to match rigor with teaching, 117; planning as key to achieving rigor, 92

Core ideas (professional development): ask questions to narrow focus of PD, 192; benefits of feedback to, 198; effective PD responds to real needs, 186; lock in learning by writing down your reflections, 204; make the complicated simple, and the simple, powerful, 199; name what you see to see it more clearly, 199; PD only as powerful as what you practice, 183, 202

of practice using, 274–275; Giving Effective Feedback using, 166–169; how to teach using the, 200–202; introduction to the, 9–10; *Leverage Leadership 2.0* vs. *Leverage Leadership* on feedback, 160; with materials to make it happen, 15–17; tools available on the DVD, 165. *See also* See It. Name It. Do It. framework

Do It videos: clip 9 (Frazier—Do It [Plan]—Weekly Data Meeting), 65; clip 10 (Stinson—Do It [Plan]—Weekly Data Meeting), 65; clip 11 (Stinson—Do It [Practice]—Weekly Data Meeting), 66; clip 12 (Frazier—Do It [Practice]—Weekly Data Meeting), 66; clip 13 (Stinson—Do It [Follow Up]—Weekly Data Meeting), 67; clip 14 (Frazier—Do It [Follow Up]—Weekly Data Meeting), 67; clip 15 (Anderson—Do It [Practice]—Feedback Meeting), 128; clip 18 (Anderson—Do It [Plan]—Feedback Meeting), 160–161; clip 23 (Frazier—Do It [Plan]—Leading PD), 200; clip 24 (Frazier—Do It [Practice]—Leading PD), 201; clip 29 (Carr—Do It—Roll Out to Staff), 238; clip 30 (Do It—Roll Out to Staff), 239–240; clip 31 (Carr—Do It—Rehearsal), 240

Do Nows: ending guided discourse with, 56; Enlightenment and Revolution lesson plan, 106–107; monitoring by adjusting, 57

Dowling, Kelly: helping PD participants to find success, 183; helping to build great schools and student futures, 348; leading a PD session on close reading, 182, 184; teaching with the See It. Name It, Do It framework, 197–202; using assessment data and student work to identify PD objective, 187–188; video clip 20 (Do It [Practice]—Leading PD), 182, 201–202; video clip 21 (See it. Name It—Leading PD), 197–198

Driven by Data (Bambrick-Santoyo), 4, 39, 45, 51

DuFour, Rick, 36

Durant, Kevin, 42

DVD: data-driven instruction materials available on the, 79, 87; elementary and middle school schedule samples on the, 76; examples of unit plans available on the, 99; Excel document to build your own schedule available on the, 330; finding the time tools available on the, 344; Guide to Training Materials available on the, 298; monthly map template available on the, 338–339; monthly maps samples available on the, 336; observation and feedback tools available on the, 180; planning materials available on the, 124; professional development materials available on the, 10, 11, 16, 216–217; sample culture rubric available on the, 231, 236; Sample Minute-by-Minute Student Culture Plan available on the, 233–235; school leadership team management resources available on the, 298–299, 311; See It. Name It, Do It. tools available on the, 165; student culture resources available on the, 260; Student Culture Rubric available on the, 259; symbols in the text indicating video availability on the, 12; The 30-Day Playbook: High School Version available on the, 245–246; video clips on school leaders included in the, 11–12; weekly schedule template available on the, 330; A word on … Preparing Presentations available on the, 204. *See also* Video clips

E

Edmonds, Ron, 265

Effective Supervision: Supporting the Art and Science of Teaching (Marzano, Frontier, and Livingston), 3,131

Meetings, 71–72; what PD look like inside classrooms, 187. *See also* Videos clips

Fine, Sarah, 98

First responder strategy: defending your time with the, 334; what your first responder can do for you, 334–335

Fisher, Derrel, 347–348

The 5 Languages of Appreciation in the Workplace (Chapman and White), 276

Follow up: feedback meeting, 163–165; Giving Effective Feedback, 169; professional development (PD), 208–209; Weekly Data Meeting, 67–68, 71

Ford Road Elementary School, 289–291

Foreign Language content, 95

Frazier, Denarius: on monitoring students, 56–57; using Do It to lead PD, 200; video clip 9 (Do It [Plan]—Weekly Data Meeting), 65; video clip 12 (Do It [Practice]—Weekly Data Meeting), 66; video clip 14 (Do It [Follow Up]—Weekly Data Meeting), 67; video clip 23 (Do It [Plan]—Leading PD), 200; video clip 24 (Do It [Practice]—Leading PD), 201

Frontier, Tony, 3, 131

Fullan, Michael, 265

G

Gaps: building student culture by finding the, 231–232; data analysis step of seeing the, 46–48; effective feedback by seeing the, 157, 159; Giving Effective Feedback to see the, 167; identify and correct staff culture, 279–284; identify gaps in school's curriculum and your assessments, 93; PD purpose to close gap impacting learning, 186; practice the gap, 162–163; video clip 2 (See It, Name It (Gap)—Weekly Data Meeting), 26, 63; Weekly Data Meeting best practices for, 68–69, 70–71

Garza, Laura: helping to build great schools and student futures, 348; her success at Blanton Elementary School, 1–2, 4, 222–224; on importance of data analysis meetings, 43; leading PD of their leadership team meeting, 184–186; setting the vision for student culture change, 224–227; Stop and Jot on her PD team meeting, 185–186; transforming Blanton's student culture, 222–228, 230–231, 236, 239, 246–247, 248, 253; video clip 1 (See It, Name It, Do It—Weekly Data Meeting), 12; video clip 27 (See It [Model]—Morning Routines), 222, 226

Get Better Faster (Bambrick-Santoyo), 56, 137, 151, 198, 228

Get Better Faster Scope and Sequence, 141–150, 153

Gino, Francesca, 203

Giving Effective Feedback, 166–169

GMAT, 34

The golden ratio (12:1), 292–293

Gonzalez, Adriana: on "belief in your mission" staff trait, 267–268; on building trust among the staff by modeling, 263–264; challenges faced at her new school, 264; creating a "personality profile" for each staff member, 276; helping to build great schools and student futures, 348; her success at Lenore Kirk Hall Elementary School, 2; holds people accountable for their behavior, 280; on "hunger to learn" staff trait, 268

Good to Great (Collins), 250

"Good-to-great" mentality trait, 7

Graham, Bill, 199

Great Habits, Great Readers (Bambrick-Santoyo, Settles, Worrell, and Atkins), 198, 203

Guide to Training Materials (DVD), 298

"Making Experience Count: The Role of Reflection in Individual Learning" (Di Stefano, Gno, Pisano, and Staats), 203

Making It Work, 17*t*

Management trajectory action steps: develop essential routines and procedures, 141–142; engage every student, 144–146; no steps necessary to stretch it, 149; roll out and monitor routines, 142–144; set routines for discourse, 146–147

Managing school leadership teams: Action Planning Worksheet for MANAGING LEADERSHIP TEAMS, 311–312; Action Steps for Principals Managing School Leadership Teams, 310–311; description of the lever, 8; distribute observation and feedback across the team, 132; DVD resources available on, 298–299, 311; keys to team development and, 291–308, 309; leading effective meetings, 301–308; leading PD of your team, 184–186; monitor the school component of, 299–301; roll out the vision, 293–299; Sample Instructional Leadership Rubric— Advanced Column, 309–310. *See also* Instructional leaders

Managing your tasks: build your monthly map, 335–339; daily action plan, 340; Finding from the Field on, 340–341; as key to finding the time, 318, 342

Manaugh Elementary (Cortez, CO), 29

Mann, Mike: on assessments with clear targets, 35; on designing interim assessment, 37; helping to build great schools and student futures, 348; on need for teachers to be effective quickly, 7; sample weekly email sent out to staff by, 271–273; sends his teachers reminder notes, 280; setting clear teacher roles and responsibilities, 269–270; testing score improvements due to planning by, 90,

91*fig*; on training his leadership team, 296–297; writes to parents of new staff members before winter holiday, 278

Marshall, Kim: on his experience of briefer observations, 174; on "Hyperactive Superficial Principal Syndrome," 316; *Rethinking Supervision and Evaluation* by, 3, 174

Martinez, Jay, 348

Mary Ann. *See* Stinson, Mary Ann Green

Marzano, Robert J., 3, 131

Mastery: action for teaching and reteaching, 50–57; content and skill needed for, 94; Stop and Jot on feedback, 162

Math: assessments related to, 30–33; Both Content and Skill (key needs in core subjects), 94–95; Teacher PD—Reteaching Math, 194, 196

Math assessment: core idea on math standards, 32; questions used for, 31–33; ratio and rate reasoning standard, 30

Mather School (Dorchester, MA), 174

McTighe, Jay, 97

Meadowmount School of Music (New York), 139

Meetings: data-driven instruction, 57–60; Eric Diamon's Schedule: Student Culture, All Meetings, and Observations, 326; Eric Diamon's Schedule: Student Culture, All Meetings, Observations, and Staff Culture Checks, 327; Eric Diamon's Schedule: Student Culture and All Meetings, 324; Eric Diamon's Schedule: Student Culture and Group Meetings, 323; feedback, 128, 158–165; leading PD of leadership team, 184–186; Observation and Feedback schedule for, 17*t*; planning, 121–122; your weekly schedule for teacher/leader, 318, 321, 325. *See also* Weekly Data Meetings

Mehta, Jal, 98

Memphis Daily News, 290

years, 7; there is a "principal personality," 7, 292. *See also* Leadership models

School leadership team development: choose your team, 291–293, 309; lead effective leadership team meetings, 301–308, 309; monitor the school, 299–301, 309; train your team and roll out the vision, 293–299, 309

School leadership team meetings: leading effective meetings, 301–308; leading PD of, 184–186

School leadership team painting: Antonio Burt (Part 1), 289–290; Antonio Burt (Part 2), 293–294; Mike Mann (Part 3), 297

School leadership team roll out: Antonio Burt on starting the process, 293–294; build the team's schedule, 294–296; equip your team, 298–299; Managing Leadership Teams—An Instructional Leader's Schedule, 295–296; train them like a football team, 294; train your team, 296–298

School leadership teams: Action Planning Worksheet for MANAGING LEADERSHIP TEAMS, 311–312; Action Steps for Principals Managing School Leadership Teams, 310–311; Antonio Burt and Laura Garza leading PD of their, 184–186; choosing your team, 291–293; distribute observation and feedback across your, 132; DVD resources available on managing, 298–299, 311; keys to development of, 291–308, 309; lever of managing your, 8; look for reliability and receptiveness in members of, 292; a picture of the Ford Road Elementary School, 289–290; remember the 12:1 golden ratio, 292–293; Sample Instructional Leadership Rubric—Advanced Column, 309–310. *See also* Instructional leaders

Schools: with curriculum planning autonomy, 119; PD responding to real needs of, 186; sample operations plan for shutting down for holidays, 332; when you have larger than 12:1 leader-to-teacher ratio, 320; without curriculum planning autonomy, 119

Science: Both Content and Skill (key needs in core subjects), 95; content knowledge when hiring for high school, 269

Scope and Sequence for action steps: Findings from the Field on using, 154; Kathleen Sullivan's reflections on using, 153; "think waterfall" mantra for, 153

See It. Name It. Do It. framework: how to teach using the, 197–202; implementing any of the seven levers using, 11; introduction to the, 9–10; tools available on the DVD, 165. *See also* Do It (See It. Name It. Do It.); Name It (See It. Name It. Do It.)

See It (See It. Name It. Do It.): coaching for effective planning using, 112–113; create a staff culture of practice using, 274; for effective feedback delivery, 156–158; Giving Effective Feedback using, 166–169; help teachers to get it by having them, 157; how to teach using the, 197–198; *Leverage Leadership 2.0* vs. *Leverage Leadership* on feedback, 160; Stop and Jot on feedback meeting, 156; tools available on the DVD, 165

See It videos: clip 1 (Garza—See It, Name It, Do It—Weekly Data Meeting), 11–13; clip 6 (Stinson—See [Standard]—Weekly Data Meeting), 61–62; clip 7 (Bridges—See It [Exemplar]—Weekly Data Meeting), 62–63; clip 8 (Worrell—See It [Gap]—Weekly Data Meeting), 64; clip 16 (Anderson—See It [Model, Gap]—Feedback Meeting), 156; clip 21 (Dowling—See it. Name It—Leading PD), 197–198; clip 26 (Burnam—See

Walsh, Bill, 244

Warm greetings, 275

Washington Park High School, 348

Weekly Data Meeting schedules: Data-Driven Instruction Monthly Map on, 73–76, 78; scheduling for teachers and leadership team, 78; Weekly Schedule—Week of Interim Assessments, 76–78

Weekly Data Meeting videos: clip 1 (Garza—See It, Name It, Do It—Weekly Data Meeting), 11–12; clip 2 (Stinson—See It, Name It (Gap)—Weekly Data Meeting), 26, 63; clip 6 (Stinson—See [Standard]—Weekly Data Meeting), 61–62; clip 7 (Bridges—See It [Exemplar]—Weekly Data Meeting), 62–63; clip 8 (Worrell—See It [Gap]—Weekly Data Meeting), 64; clip 9 (Frazier—Do It [Plan]—Weekly Data Meeting), 65; clip 10 (Stinson—Do It [Plan]—Weekly Data Meeting), 65; clip 11 (Stinson—Do It [Practice]—Weekly Data Meeting), 66; clip 12 (Frazier—Do It [Practice]—Weekly Data Meeting), 66; clip 13 (Stinson—Do It [Follow Up]—Weekly Data Meeting), 67; clip 14 (Frazier—Do It [Follow Up]—Weekly Data Meeting), 67

Weekly Data Meetings: content expertise issue of leading, 60–61; example of a, 14–15; Findings from the Field on, 71–72; follow up at the end of the, 67; as highest-leverage thirty minutes for a school leader, 57–59; Instructional Leader PD—Weekly Data Meetings, 194–195, 196; Laura Garza on importance of her, 43; leading the, 57–72; Mary Ann Green Stinson's thirty-minute, 25–27, 29–30; summary of best practices for leading, 68–71. *See also* Data analysis; Data-driven instruction meetings; Meetings; Scheduling

Weekly Data Meetings preparation: content expertise, 60–61; data analysis, 59–60; have the room and materials ready, 60; summary of best practices for, 68

Weekly schedule: making time for important actions instead of crises, 318; now make your own, 330; reflect on what you've accomplished, 328, 330; steps for building your, 318–328; time management by building your, 318–330; Weekly Schedule Template, 319

Weekly schedule steps: 1. prework for building your, 318, 320–321; 2. block out student culture times, 318, 321; 3. lock in PD and other group meetings, 318, 321; 4. lock in teacher-leader meetings, 318, 321, 325; 5. lock in time for classroom observations, 318, 325; 6. lock in staff culture, 318, 325, 330; 7. lock in work time, 328

Welch, Jack, 268

Welch, Suzy, 268

Westwood Elementary (Caddo Parish, LA), 29

Wheelington, Tanya, 249

Whisper prompt feedback strategy, 165

White, Paul, 276

Whole-group understanding, 144

Wiggins, Grant, 97

Winning (Welch and Welch), 268

A word on . . . Preparing Presentations, 204

Work time: add to schedule for big projects, 328; build your weekly schedule, 318–330; defend your time during, 318, 330–335; exceptional school leaders use their time wisely, 291; "Hyperactive Superficial Principal Syndrome" impacting, 316; lock in leadership by planning your, 317; managing tasks to manage your, 318, 335–341; Observation and Feedback schedule during, 17t; time pressures on school leaders, 316–317